Tales from the Road

The Life of an Itinerant Musician as Lived by...

BOB HAWORTH

HELLGATE PRESS 

ASHLAND, OREGON

Tales from the Road

Published by Hellgate Press
(An imprint of L&R Publishing, LLC)

Hellgate Press
72 Dewey St.
Ashland, OR 97520
email: sales@hellgatepress.com

Cover and Interior Design: L. Redding
Cover photo: Meri Haworth

ISBN: 978-1-954163-58-4

Printed and bound in the United States of America
First edition 10 9 8 7 6 5 4 3 2 1

"This is dedicated to the one I love..."
To my beautiful wife, Meri – she's the wind in my sails.

Praise for Bob Haworth's *Tales from the Road*

"Reading Haworth's book is a revealing glimpse in to just what happened to a kid with a dream, who never let that dream die and met with a lot of success. A four-string banjo player getting work in mid-'60's L.A.? Well, he did it and dug his way in to the business that would take him around the world in several different groups, all of which you have heard the names of over the years. It is 'the life he picked' (to paraphrase my book title), and I wish I could have 'borrowed' some of his remembrances for my book! If you want to laugh, and hear about how difficult – and rewarding – the music business can be for someone with the dream and hard work ethic, (without being a 'superstar'), check out Bob Haworth's Tales from the Road, *and you will have a fun ride."*

—John McEuen, musician, author of *The Life I Picked*, member of CMA/AFM/SAG-AFTRA/IBMA/BMI

"I saw The Kingston Trio play their very first college concert on the campus of the University of Oklahoma in '56 or '57 (look it up!). I already loved folk music but I was unptrepared for the explosive performance that blew me away that night. While leaving the field house I told my date I was going to do what the trio did. She laughed. These guys made it impossible for me to do anything else with my life, for which I thank them sincerely."

—Tom Paxton, musician

"Bob Haworth is an incredibly talented performer and a great asset. I always said he saved our ass more than once. He was always there when I needed him."

—Bob Shane, Owner/Leader, The Kingston Trio

"Well, he's done it! Bob Haworth and I made music and travelled together for a fun, amazing decade and a half. He's a magical performer, a tasty arranger and musician, and now brilliant storyteller. I guarantee this joyful book is more than just a tale of motels, sing-alongs and curtain calls! From sound-check to last call, Bob's true stories will make you understand and chuckle as he reveals just how and why performers stay with it, night after endless night on the road. Well done, Bob...Encore!"

—Bob Flick, Founding Member, The Brothers Four

"Bob's life has been a treasure chest with so many stages, so many regal opportunities, and so many stories from behind the curtain. I met him in the '80s when we were both playing the showrooms on the Boardwalk in Atlantic City. You'll enjoy these iconic tales of Bob doing what he was driven to do. In the words I wrote for his pal Bob Shane, Bob Haworth was 'singing every inch of the way!'"

—Jim Ratts, Entertainer, Songwriter and Record Producer

"Bob Haworth and I have been pickin' & grinnin' together for the past six years. He's a cool cat and a good one to ride the river with as this entertaining read will fully attest."

—John Hollis, the "Hollis" in Hollis & Haworth

"I first met Bob Haworth when he performed with The Brothers Four. When my group, The Kingston Trio, lost Roger Gambill to an untimely death, Bob Shane and I asked Bobby if he felt comfortable leaving the Brothers Four and joining The Kingston Trio. We recognized his outstanding musical ability and his dedication to both the music and an audience. Bobby was instrumental (pun intended) in returning the KT to its original instrumental approach of six-string guitar, banjo, and Nick Reynolds' tenor guitar, an instrumental sound that was imbedded in the minds and ears of millions of fans. During my reading of Bobby's book I was transported back to some wonderful times and memories, both personal and professional, and I heartfeltfully (yes, I said that) recommend it to every fan of music in general, folk music specifically, and the music business."

—George Grove, Member of The Kingston Trio

"I have known Bobby Haworth for 30 years and have had the pleasure of working with him for many of those years when he was a member of The Kingston Trio. I have always been amazed at his ability to play just about any known instrument, and play them all well. Bobby is funny, talented and very loyal. He has a long rich history in folk music – many years in The Brothers Four, three times in The Kingston Trio, and now on his own. I hope he continues to write and entertain us for years to come."

—Bobbie Childress, Wife of Bob Shane of The Kingston Trio

"There is no more captivating storyteller than a folk singer. This candid memoir is informed by mastery of the entire body of work that is The Kingston Trio. Bob Haworth has captured the singular likeness of that legendary Grammy-winning trio who until now defied intimate portrayal. His entertaining tales are the portal to an era. The breadth of his limitless reminiscence energizes colorful prose moving with spirit and agility."

— Larry Crawford, Longtime Kingston Trio Fan and Good Friend

CONTENTS

Acknowledgments

FIRST AND FOREMOST, I ACKNOWLEDGE my Father in Heaven for giving me this amazing adventure to live and share.

And my wife, Meri, who has stood by me through thick and thin, and shared much of this adventure with me.

My son and best friend, Graham, who still called me "Dad" when I came home from a long tour.

Lynn Sjolund, my musical mentor who helped me hone my talent to the degree required to pursue this adventure.

Bobbie Childress, Bob Shane's widow, who has been a great friend and supporter in this project.

Thanks to John Hollis for his critical proof-reading eye, great musicianship and loyal friendship.

Thanks to Gary Ballard, George Grove, Tom Green, Paul Gabrielson, Bob Flick, Mark Pearson, Jack Mullen, Larry Crawford, Jean Ward and Tomm Rivers, all of whom added their recollections to flesh out many of my Tales.

Thanks to Harley Patrick of Hellgate Press for providing the means to tell my Tales.

And thanks to music fans world-wide who have begged me for years to share a glimpse of my life on the road. Naming you all individually here would require another book, but without you – well, what's the sound of "one hand clapping"?

Tales from the Road

Preface

WHO WOULD WANT TO READ a book about my life? That's the question that's been haunting me since it was first suggested that I write such a documentary. Oh, sure – I've had some interesting adventures and I have some bizarre and hilarious stories to tell, but is it really worth committing hours and hours of time to put all of that into a book that someone might actually find interesting?

My friend and advisor, Mike Kavanagh, finally gave me the reason from the perspective of a wannabe musician who had, himself, fantasized about doing the things I've done. He assured me that there were many like himself who have dreamed of being part of a hit-producing musical ensemble and traveling the world performing in front of huge crowds. The image of bras and panties being hurled at you from teen-aged admirers seems to capture the imagination of just about any guy who has ever picked up a guitar or sung in a karaoke bar. I can't speak to the fantasies of female wannabe performers, but I know I've had my own mental images of being swarmed by adoring fans after a brilliant performance. It's this fascination with stardom that attracts the curious, and I guess there may be something to be gained by vicariously experiencing it through the eyes of one who has been touched by that lifestyle.

To be a rock star is certainly a dream that every budding musician aspires to. I have grade-school-aged guitar students who believe that if they learn a few chords and riffs on their instrument that one day they'll stand and deliver to the cheers and applause of their peers. And more power to them for those dreams! In reality, it takes a lot more than musical proficiency to attain that position. I know hundreds of very capable musicians who have never made it beyond their local Holiday Inn lounge. And, conversely, I know of many mediocre talents who have risen to stardom on the wings of sheer luck.

In my case I wouldn't classify my success in the music business as "stardom." Nor do I consider myself a world-class musician by any means. My success was a function of being in the right place at the right time and knowing the right people. I had enough musical ability and stage presence to capitalize on my connections to get to where I wanted to be, but I know that luck played a huge role in my career. I also credit a technique called creative visualization for moving my life in the direction I needed to go to find the opportunities and open the doors.

True stardom has eluded me throughout my career, but I do count myself fortunate to have made a very good living as a working musician. I've had my ups and downs, and I guess that's part of the story I have to tell. It's not all glory and hoopla in the music business. The reality is that fame and fortune are as elusive as the dreams that produce them and you can never count on them as a foundation for your life. In that regard I've always relied on my Boy Scout motto: "Be prepared." I've learned to carry a Plan B in one hip pocket and a Plan 3 in the other. When those failed I somehow had the ability to fly by the seat of my pants. Life is a constant learning experience – a winding road of adventure and misadventure, and I've had my share of both. I guess since you cracked the cover of this book you want to hear about all that. I really have no plan A, B or 3 for writing this book. I'm taking the approach of flying by the seat of my pants, so, fasten your seatbelt and away we go...

Tales from the Road

CHAPTER ONE

The Beginning

I WAS BORN AT A very early age at Deaconess Hospital in Spokane, Washington. I was the first child of Robert Lyle and Elizabeth Ann Haworth, or Bob and Betty Ann, as they were known to their friends. They met while attending the University of Idaho in Moscow and they married before Dad went off to Europe to fight in World War II. I came into the world on October 9, 1946, after he was discharged from the Army. I was named Robert Larry Haworth to distinguish, I guess from my Dad. Apparently my folks didn't want a Robert Jr. in the family. But, while all my brothers have names honoring other family members and ancestors, my middle name is found nowhere on the family tree. Larry? Who was Larry? Sadly my folks are gone now and I'll never know the answer.

Mom and Dad finished their educations at the U of I. Moscow was Mom's hometown and my first couple of years were spent there with my maternal grandparents, Edith and Raymond Woesner. Mom's brother, my Uncle Ray, lived at home and occupied an upstairs bedroom next to my grandparents, while Mom and Dad and I had the downstairs bedroom. Grandma raised chickens in the back yard and sometimes she'd let me bring in a newly hatched chick to poop all over the house. And being Idaho, she grew potatoes in the parking strip along West A Street.

Mom majored in Art at the University and played violin in the orchestra. Dad majored in Chemical Engineering, ran on the track team and played on the football team. One of my early memories is seeing the crowd tear down the goal posts after the Vandals beat the visiting team one Friday night. My folks had a job cleaning a bar in town after closing and they used to take me with them. They'd play the juke box as they worked and I have another early memory of standing in front of that juke box dancing to the music. I guess I was hooked – music became a focal point of my life.

After graduation, Dad took a job as Parks and Recreation Director for the City of Weiser, Idaho. This little farming town just across the border from Oregon had one swimming pool and one city park, and Dad ran the whole shebang. I think he would have made a great entertainment promoter, because the first year he was there he put on an aquatic show that featured one of his classmates from U. of I., Ken Lyons. Ken was a champion diver and his grand finale was doing a triple tuck off the high dive through a ring of fire on the water. Dad also organized the very first Old-Time Fiddling Contest which later grew to become the National Old-Time Fiddlers Contest, attracting fiddlers from all over the country to vie for the best fiddler in various categories. Years later I returned to Weiser as the agent for ten-year-old Tiffany Paulin, who won Best Fiddler in her age group.

My brother, James Dennis, was born October 19, 1950 and I became a proud big brother. I think the addition of a new family member put a strain on the family budget because Dad took a higher-paying job as Assistant Parks and Recreation Director for Spokane County. Spokane was Dad's hometown and growing up there in the 1950s laid the foundation for the direction my life would take.

Dad had a lot of pools, parks and events to oversee all over the County and summer brought plenty of fun times. I learned to swim in Comstock Pool and I became pretty good at it, even joining the Spokane Swim Team when I was about seven. One Saturday, Dad invited me to tag along with him to a park out east of town where a weekend music festival was happening. There was a small stage set up for entertainment and the performers were none other than Les Paul and Mary Ford. I was fascinated with their music and in later years I came to be a big fan.

The month of May brings Spokane's annual Lilac Festival. One of the events is a big parade downtown and in 1953, Mom decided to enter me in the Junior division. She dressed me up like a hobo and with my dog, Cindy, we won a prize in the pet category. I also got to meet my hero, Hopalong Cassidy and his horse, Topper, who were the parade marshals.

Two more brothers, twins Samuel Ray and Gary William, joined the family on August 10, 1953, once again impacting family finances. Dad took a night job at a local produce company, loading trucks and Mom signed on as a bus driver for the Spokane transit company. There was enough money from their endeavors for me to take piano lessons when I was eight years old, and Mom also enlisted me in the Spokane Boys Choir. Things were taking root.

Our extended family included my paternal grandparents,

Gladys and Raymond Haworth. Grandma's father, Samuel Wimmer ("Gramp" to us kids), lived with the grandparents and he was always fun to be with. He had worked all his life as a carpenter, but had lost his eyesight in his later years. He could still play the old Cable-Nelson upright piano in Grandma's foyer, and he loved to entertain us with "That Old Rugged Cross" and "Onward Christian Soldiers." That was the same piano I practiced my lessons on and it resides in my music room to this day.

Grandpa's brother, Carl and his wife, Grace, lived across town and every holiday was a family get-together. Often Grandpa's other brother, Wayne and his wife, Vera, would drive over from Seattle to join the family reunions. Both Uncle Carl and Uncle Wayne played the banjo and those reunions were filled with hours of listening to my great-uncles play and sing songs from the 1920s and '30s.

Uncle Wayne played tenor banjo and during his youth he had played in several bands. One of his gigs was on a cruise-ship that sailed from Seattle to Hong Kong. He brought back souvenirs from his trips, including an amazing carved ivory art piece that graced the grandparents' mantel. Uncle Carl played plectrum banjo and had also played in several bands, mostly around the Spokane area. One of his groups included a student from Gonzaga College on drums and vocals – a kid named Bing Crosby. And in 1928, Carl landed a recording contract with Columbia Records, releasing four 78 RPM records on that label.

A good friend and sometimes band-mate of Uncle Carl's was a local banjo player named Dutch Groshoff. Dutch taught banjo, guitar and ukulele out of a studio at Blessing and Thue Music. On Uncle Carl's recommendation, Dutch took me on as a student. I didn't own a banjo and my family certainly couldn't afford one, but Uncle Carl was kind enough to loan me his Weymann plectrum which he rarely played. His instrument of choice was a vintage Paramount Style-A.

Dutch took me under his wing and I caught on pretty quickly. Within a year I was invited to join Dutch's banjo band, a group of his students that he loved to show off around town. My first professional gig was with that band at age eleven. We played for a Kiwanis meeting at a swanky hotel downtown and we each made $5.00. There was a revolving membership in our banjo band and one of Dutch's students that I didn't get to know very well until years later was a kid named Mark Pearson. His dad was a well-known doctor in town and they had a nice home in the ritzy part of South Spokane. I think I was probably a little intimidated by him, but as adults we became good friends when I took his place in The Brothers Four, and then he replaced me in that group when I joined The Kingston Trio.

Dutch had us all outfitted in red and white striped jackets that each of our mothers sewed for us. We looked pretty professional and apparently we played quite well. Well enough to be the grand-prize winners one year on KXLY TV's *Starlit Stairway*, a weekly televised talent show that featured all kinds of youthful talent – dancers, singers, acrobats and musicians.

Mom was a bit of a stage mother and she always coached me: "Look up at the audience and smile!" It was sound advice that no-doubt enhanced my career. She had so much enthusiasm for my ability that she would often enter me in local talent contests. I won second place in pretty much every contest only to be beat by an accordion player doing "Lady of Spain." Out of frustration and revenge I finally worked up an arrangement of that song on the banjo, but to no avail. Accordions always won.

In 1958, I was in the sixth grade at Finch Elementary School, the school I'd been attending since kindergarten. One of my classmates was Dutch's daughter, Katy and we were in Mr. White's class. Katy's desk was right next to mine and we often got in trouble for talking when we were supposed to be listening. I don't think girls ever got punished, but I got busted on multiple occasions resulting in the Mr. White shake-down. He would grab my left arm, yank me out my seat and shake me like a rag doll. Once should've been enough, but it took me several shake-downs before I learned to keep my yap shut. The other thing I learned from Mr. White, besides the capitol of Washington, was his firm belief that someday China would dominate the world. As I watch events unfold today I can't help but think how prescient he was.

By the mid-1950s, our family had acquired a television set and we each had our favorite programs. All of us kids loved *The Mickey Mouse Club* and Mom's favorite was Liberace. Dad like to watch the Friday night boxing matches, but my favorite was *Ozzie and Harriet*. I was fascinated when little Ricky Nelson would close the show singing to a room full of giddy girls and I knew that's what I wanted to do someday. After school I'd turn on the radio and hope to hear "Poor Little Fool," which I had memorized and sang along with. But then one day in 1958, I heard this song that featured a banjo. My ears perked up and I listened as The Kingston Trio sang this jaunty little ditty about a guy named Tom Dooley. Every time the station played that record I would grab my banjo and try to play along. I eventually found the key and figured out the chords – there were only two – and soon I was hooked on this new group that featured a banjo. How cool was that? Little did I know...

In 1959, Dad made a major career change and took a job as Parks and Recreation Director for the city of Medford, Oregon. So, in the summer after I graduated from grade school we packed up our 1949 Chevy and headed south. That fall opened the next chapter in my life.

"Little Bobby Banjo," age 11.

Me and my Great Uncles: Carl (*left*) and Wayne (*right*).

'utch and His Two-Beat Banjo Are Part of S

By Joe Baily Jr.

IERE'S a long, lean and lanky
harácter around Spokane who is
bout as well known as anyone in
Over the years his beanpole arms
egs, his sharply pointed chin and
hed-out angular nose, have be-
familiar sights. He's a hatchet-
red fellow who has provided about
uch entertainment, all totaled up,
ay one entertainer hereabouts.
g folks know him, and so do old-
Men and women who are grown
w, and have their own youngsters,
mber him when they were young.
their own youngsters know him
the same way Mom and Pop used
ow him.
is character was christened Law-
J. Groshoff, but it's as Dutch
hoff that he's known. It seems
one time when he was a boy he
fishing at the Moyie river ranch
his father, George B. Groshoff, a
ane contractor, and his father's
man, Fred (Pop) Cooper, and Pop
er called him "Dutch" because
it a stick of dynamite beside a fire
got in "dutch" for it. Anyway,
h stuck with him as a nickname
after.
tch is a banjo plucker. He's been
ng banjos hum and drum and
s and do everything under his
er hand for something like 30
around Spokane. His banjo pluck-
goes back to a class picnic in 1921
e Gonzaga high school. One of his
mates, Jack O'Brien, had been en-
ining the gang with his banjo and
it down to take a swim. Father
h Lynch suggested Dutch take up
e Jack left off. Dutch took up, and
tertained the Gonzaga gang that
soon that he took up from there
Of course, before he could charm
Gonzaga gang he had to have some
of banjo background, and that
from his father, who strummed
njo whenever he wasn't building
ings. Dutch learned his banjo at
ather's knee. He was self-taught.
tch's career with the banjo car-
him through lively years of orches-
playing and solo entertaining in
ane during which he made pals
and often helped on the way up-
many young musicians who later

Groshoff, hat awry, plucks out a rollicking banjo tune.

younger brother,
around 1930, go
join Anson Week
sey brothers an
to form his own
Dutch's scrap
pings about his
them and with
them. They're h
Crosbys and the
on in Spokane,
of everything t
took real pride
There's a clippi
"Spokane Boy,
Torch Song Croc
bar Hindley of T
all about Bing or
a clipping, some
Son Makes Hit."
There's the copy
Hendricks, "Ope
tomorrow night.
a wire from Bo
night as an orch
Dutch's banjo
years from his
scribed with sco
tunes. Dutch got
Eddy Peabody.
for a dance of an
open for "names
When a band be
ered with them,
a new band an
names are the bi
tra world, big-
others. Dutch re
he asked Babe
her autograph o
the Babe procee
and sing in the g
seemed to have
instinct for rhyt
hour or so in w
high heaven bec
us." didn't matt
whether she
moved along wi
That's been th
moved along wi
he found joy an
written his own
by Bob Crosby,
song; he's taug
his own method,
of all it's as a
fondest memori
great moments,
ing couples, may

Dutch Groshoff

Uncle Carl

These Central Lions club members are tuning up for their mid-winter dinner dance at Manito Golf and Country club Saturday, when they will stage a specialty act. In the combo (left to right) are Carl B. Haworth, banjo; Lester M. Peuck, trombone; Mannie C. Sullivan, trumpet; Harvey E. Guertin, clarinet, and Ralph E. Goodhue, piano.

Uncle Carl (*left*) with the Lions Club Band.

Uncle Wayne with The Westerners.
Wayne is second from right with banjo.

1919 — 1923

SPOKANE DAILY CHRONICLE.

PERSONNEL OF SPOKANE'S NEWEST FIFE AND DRUM CORPS

Spokane's newest fife and drum corps, under the leadership of F. S. Tremain, made its first public appearance esterday in the Grand Army parade. Members of the new corps are, left to right, William Hart, Ira W. Terry, . L. Bates (color bearer), F. S. Tremain, Samuel H. Wimmer and L. G. Skinner. Mr. Skinner, the only G. A. R. an in the drum corps, served in Company A, 81st Ohio infantry volunteers, First brigade, Third division, 14th rmy corps, Army of the Cumberland. He has been an active member of Sedgwick post of the G. A. R. in Spokane or 18 years. Mr. Bates, who resides at 8807 Sherman street, is a member of the United States Marine corps, home n furlough. The others are members of the Sons of Veterans.

Gramp's band, ca. 1919-1923.
Gramp is second from right.

Banjo Band on the *Starlit Stairway*. Larry Groshoff, Dutch's son, far right – I'm the chubby kid 2nd from left.

Tales from the Road

CHAPTER TWO

Medford, OR

MEDFORD, OREGON, WAS A MUCH SMALLER town than Spokane, and southern Oregon was a much different place. The trees were different, the climate was different and I was different. Puberty was upon me and I was excited to see what this new environment had to offer.

In September I enrolled at Hedrick Junior High, seventh grade. I was a decent student, getting nearly straight A's. I enjoyed all my classes and teachers, but I always especially looked forward to choir period. Carroll Graber was our choir director and he really seemed to take delight in working with us. He chose fun music for us and our daily rehearsals were casual yet productive. One day as we were getting ready to run through a piece we were learning, Mr. Graber called for the girl with the pitch pipe to blow the starting pitch. At that very moment I had to blow my nose. A resonant "honk" rang out and by chance, it happened to be the exact pitch he'd called for. The class erupted in uproarious laughter and Mr. Graber credited me with having perfect nasal pitch.

In addition to occasional concerts throughout the year, our choir produced an annual spring musical - a full-blown stage show with costumes, choreography, dialog and music. In 1962 we produced a show called *Oh Susanna*, a minstrel show based on the music of Stephen Foster. I played the part of Clem, as well as Possum in the minstrel band, and I played the banjo. This was well before the dawn of political correctness, so we were unaware that going on-stage in black face would disqualify us from ever running for public office in the future.

Uncle Carl had allowed me to take his Weymann plectrum banjo when we moved to Oregon, but I knew that was only a temporary loan. One day my dad spotted a classified ad in the Medford paper for a "Vega banjo – $150.00." He called the phone number in the ad and set up an appointment for us to see the banjo. When we arrived at the home of the nice lady who was selling it, she said it had belonged to her brother who was deceased. It had been in her attic for years and she hoped that someone would enjoy playing it again. At my young age I really didn't have a lot of knowledge about vintage instruments, but I knew it played well and I had exactly $150.00 in paper route earnings burning a hole in my pocket, so we closed the deal. As it turned out, I made a pretty good investment. The instrument I bought that day is a 1922 Vegaphone Deluxe plectrum, valued now at over $3,000.00! And I still love to play it!

That following summer, the Jackson County Fair featured Eddie Peabody as one of the headliners. I got a ticket for the show and it was a thrill to see and hear one of my musical heroes up close and in person. After the show I somehow found the nerve to make my way back to his trailer. I knocked on the door and when he opened it, he looked down and said, "Well hi there, kid. What do you want?" And I said, "Well, Mr. Peabody, I'm a banjo player too and I really enjoyed your show and I just wanted to say hi and thank you." He responded, "Well come on in and show me what you know." So I stepped up into his trailer and he pulled his banjo out of the open case on the counter, offered me a seat and handed me his banjo. *Oh my gosh! I'm holding the banjo that I'd heard on dozens of Eddie Peabody recordings that I'd tried to copy.* I was so nervous that I think I wet my pants – just a little. I played a couple chords to make sure his banjo was in tune (as if!) and I immediately noticed that the neck of this banjo was greased up like Elvis Presley's hair. No wonder he could fly around that fingerboard like lightning. Well, I did my best to slide through a rendition of "Bye Bye Blues" prompting him to say, "Well, that was pretty good, kid. Keep practicin'." Then he autographed his picture for me, handed me a Tootsie Roll and showed me out the door. I stood there in awe for a moment thinking, *Wow, I just peed for Eddie Playbody*!

♪ ♪ ♪

I had just started taking guitar lessons from Dutch Groshoff before we left Spokane. My folks had purchased a Gibson ES-125 for me for around $100.00, but for some reason my fourteen-year-old self had decided I really wanted a twelve-string guitar. So Dad took the ES-125 with him on a business trip to Portland and managed to trade it straight across at Portland Music for a Gibson B-12-25, cherry sunburst finish. I loved that guitar and I made good use of if for many years. I wish I still had it, but like many instruments I've owned over the years, it was sold or traded for the next gleam in my eye. Sadly, while I did okay on my Vega banjo investment, I really blew it on these two guitars. A '60's vintage ES-125 now sells for $7,000 – $9,000. The twelve-string isn't quite as valuable, but they can fetch up to $2,500.

♪ ♪ ♪

One of my fellow choir members at Hedrick was a kid named John Eads. John and I shared an interest in the popular folk music that we were hearing on the radio. The Kingston Trio was dominating the charts, but we actually favored the music of The Chad Mitchell Trio. And then one day my dad brought home an album by a group called The Limeliters. It was their live album, "Tonight In Person," and featured some of their stage banter between songs. Lou Gottlieb stole the show with his dry wit and John and I were hooked. We learned several songs from that album, and then we began to explore other folk musicians, most of whom were under the radar. People like Tom Paxton, Pete Seeger, Josh White and Odetta fueled our repertoire and by the time we were sophomores at Medford High, we were performing as The Kinsmen.

I have no idea how the Hedrick Junior High auditorium would have been on the tour schedule for a major national act, but The Limeliters packed that venue one night and John and I had front-row seats. We sang along on every song and after the show we both went back stage and introduced ourselves to Glenn Yarbrough, Alex Hassilev and Lou Gottlieb. Little did any of us know that someday I'd be lucky enough to share a dressing room with those guys.

John's dad was a professional magician and he was very supportive of our effort to break into show business. He bought John a beautiful blond Kaye bass and my dad bought us a PA system with a couple mics and stands. The Kinsmen were in high demand, playing at high school parties and social events around town. Our claim to fame was using our gigs at Rotary and Kiwanis meetings as an excuse to skip school. We did have a few out-of-town appearances, including performing on a flat-bed trailer at the Pendleton Round-Up in 1964. And according to an article in the *Medford Mail Tribune* dated September 1, 1964 entitled "The Kinsmen To Appear at Roundup": "The Kinsmen are seniors at Medford High School and they have also performed in Klamath Falls, Corvallis, Grants Pass, Ashland and Portland." Not exactly a world tour, but we did get a taste of the road.

One day the *Mail Tribune* ran an article announcing that Will Rogers, Jr. was coming to town to host a talent search. The winner of the local competition would be entitled to a REAL Hollywood audition with a REAL Hollywood agent. When you're seventeen you have big dreams, and we did for sure. We were going to win this talent show and go to HOLLYWOOD!

So, Will Rogers Jr. and his crew rolled into town and set up their show in the auditorium at Hedrick Junior High. John and I had played that stage many times, having spent three years at Hedrick, so we were on home turf. The audience that night was heavily weighted in our favor and we got a standing ovation. We won the contest and the chance to audition with a REAL Hollywood agent! And then we read the fine print: "Travel to Hollywood is at Artist's own expense." Well, put that on hold for a moment.

Medford High was a breeding ground for all sorts of talent in the 1960s. Our music programs were highly rated and our sports teams were state champions. One of my classmates was a kid name Dick Fosbury. Dick and I were both in choir and we'd actually sung together in a barber shop quartet back at Hedrick. We were also on the track team at MHS. My event was the mile and Dick's was the high jump. Dick gained notoriety for developing a unique method of clearing the bar with a back-flip maneuver that came to be known as "The Fosbury Flop." Years later he won a gold medal at the 1968 Olympics clearing the bar with a 7'4-1/4" Flop. My time in the mile was less than stellar, so I opted to stick with music.

I took up string bass and played in the school orchestra. I was also choir president (not sure why we needed one) and our choir was one of the best in the state. Lynn Sjolund was our choir director, and I credit him with much of my development as a singer and performer. Besides our seasonal choir concerts, Mr. Sjolund directed some of the best high school musical productions to rival Broadway. *My Fair Lady* was a prime example, receiving rave reviews from parents and even the local newspaper. I played Freddy Hill in that show, providing my rendition of "On The Street Where You Live." I was honored to reprise that performance years later for Doris and Lynn Sjolunds' fiftieth wedding anniversary party.

♪ ♪ ♪

My parents always encouraged me to get a summer job and learn the responsibility of making some money for myself. One summer I picked pears for Harry and David.

Another summer found me getting a nice tan as head lifeguard for the pool at the Rogue Valley Country Club. In the summer of 1963, I landed a job as grounds keeper for the Britt Music Festival in Jacksonville. This was the first year of the festival, featuring a two-weekend schedule of classical music in August under the direction of John Trudeau. The site was (and is) a sloping hillside on the grounds of the Peter Britt Estate. I was tasked with maintaining the lawn prior to and during the festival. I watered, mowed and pulled weeds in exchange for my meager hourly wage.

One afternoon as I was making my rounds on weed patrol, I noticed a man strolling around the grounds, talking into a portable tape recorder. As I approached within earshot I immediately recognized his voice – it was Jim Bailey, a DJ on radio station KSHA. I was a regular listener and I especially enjoyed Bailey's morning show on my way to school. I don't remember what I did to get his attention, but I introduced myself and told him that I was a fan. He asked me about my job and I told him what I knew about the upcoming performance schedule. As he headed off down the hill he hollered back that I should come and visit him at the radio station sometime. Chance encounters with the right people can often change the trajectory of your life, and although I was certainly unaware of it at the time, this was one of those moments for me.

A group of us guys had developed an unofficial club called the BFD Breakfast Boys Club. Once a month about thirty of us would invade one of the local restaurants before school and respectfully raise a little ruckus. Someone was assigned at each meeting to give a speech and there was always plenty of hilarity. After I met Jim Bailey on the Britt grounds, he took to doing a remote broadcast once a month from the basement banquet room at the Medford Hotel. We moved our BFD meetings to that location and became Bailey's live audience for his broadcasts. Occasionally he'd invite me to bring my banjo and play a couple tunes. These encounters solidified my friendship with Bailey and he was destined to play a major role in my career advancement.

I graduated from Medford High School in 1965, boasting a 4.0 grade point and membership in the Honor Society. I was focused on pursuing my music education with the dream of a possible career in show business. The best location on the west coast to find those opportunities was Los Angeles and I thought that would be a great place to go for my higher education. John Eads was off to study law at the University of Oregon in Eugene, but I had other plans. I was accepted as an applicant to the music program at UCLA, and in the fall of 1965, I was off to Hollywood. Remember – I had Will Rogers, Jr.'s guarantee of a REAL audition with a REAL Hollywood agent. And I was paying my own way to get there!

8 A WEDNESDAY, MARCH 4, 1964

Featured on the "Let's Hoot" program to be given Saturday, March 7, at the Holly Theater as a Red Cross benefit will be these two Medford High School students, The Kinsmen. Bob Haworth plays the guitar and banjo and John Eads the string bass. Both also hing. The two have been teamed together since the seventh grade and in recent years have rehearsed and sung together at least twice a week. Both are honor student and in addition to maintaining a heavy study schedule for their high school classes, have other activities such as debate and dramatic appearances. They wrote at least one original number, a "pep" song for "Tolo Tech," a fictitious school, and the song is played from time to time on a local radio station. The students prefer the more serious type of folk music for their programs and are constantly searching for more material and for different adaptations. Young Haworth is a son of Mr. and Mrs. Robert L. Haworth, and his companion's parents are Mr. and Mrs. John W. Eads. The Red Cross Hootenanny will be in three different programs, 1:45 p.m., 6:45 p.m. and 9:45 p.m. and the public is invited to attend all performances. Each will be different, the committee chairman, Gilbert E. Stuart, stresses.

(Knaekstedt photo)

The Kinsmen in the *Mail Tribune*, March 4, 1964.
That's John Eads on the stand-up bass, me on the guitar.

8 A TUESDAY, APRIL 7, 1964

TALENT CONTEST WINNERS — The Kinsmen, who have been featured in many Medford shows, are scheduled to appear with the Will Rogers Jr. Destiny Show here Thursday, April 9 at Hedrick Junior High School. The two local youths, winners of the talent contest last week staged by KMED-TV, are shown with Francine Aiken, chairman of the talent show. John Eads strums the big bass viol and Robert Haworth Jr., the guitar. The Kinsmen, along with four other finalists will be auditioned this week by Loren Nichols, song writer, singer, dancer and artist. Other finalists are: The Hermy Glotz Trio of Larry White, Steve Harper and Joan McFarland, Grants Pass; Sid Yarnell, Phoenix, jazz tap dancer; Sherri Linn Bethel, Medford, comedy jazz ballet performer; and The Crestones, Don Zeleznik and Anthony Morgan, Medford, who imitate The Beatles.

The Kinsmen win the Will Rogers, Jr. contest!
Mail Tribune, April 7, 1964.

Barbershop quartet. *L to R*: Dick (Foz) Fosbury, Bob Haworth, Greg Becken, Allen David.

The autographed photo I got from
Eddie Peabody, the "Banjo King."

Advertisement for radio DJ Jim Bailey at North's Chuck Wagon in Medford, OR.

DJ Jim Bailey.

CHAPTER THREE

College

IN AUGUST OF 1965, DAD drove me to Los Angeles, towing my 1952 MG-TD behind us on a trailer. The Housing Assistance department at UCLA had found me an apartment just off campus on Veteran Avenue, complete with a roommate. Shigeru Inamine was a grad student from Okinawa, and although we shared that apartment for a year I never really got to know him. But he was polite and we stayed out of each others' way.

Dad helped me get settled in and we found a spot in the parking garage for my MG. Then he hit the road back to Medford. I was on my own, and boy was I ready for it! I got registered for all my classes, bought my books and spent some time getting familiar with the campus. Our apartment building was right next to a fraternity, which proved to be entertaining on many occasions. For my meals I joined a co-op where we all shared kitchen duties in exchange for a fairly cheap meal ticket.

One of my first orders of business after I got settled in was to make an appointment for my REAL Hollywood audition with a REAL Hollywood agent. Will Rogers, Jr. had guaranteed that by virtue of The Kinsmen winning his talent search in Medford and I had the certificate to prove it. Even though John wasn't there to audition with me, I felt confident that I could hold my own in a REAL Hollywood audition with a REAL Hollywood agent. UCLA is just about fifteen miles from Hollywood, and one day I got a friend of mine to drive me down to the address we'd been given for the audition. When we arrived at the address we drove around the block a couple times looking for the building – any building. It was a danged vacant lot! It was my first lesson in a class I hadn't even enrolled in at UCLA: Showbiz 101. I wonder if Will Jr. ever got busted for his scam?

My stated major was Music Composition, so in addition to the required language (I took Italian) and math courses, I got to take music theory, music history, composition, keyboard and an elective, for which I chose choir. UCLA was privileged to employ one of the premier choir directors in the world - Roger Wagner. Though he was a hard task-master, he was inspiring to work with and he knew how to break the work up with some levity. And being Roger Wagner, we all wanted to give him our very best. The repertoire he chose was challenging, and one spring he invited us to augment his professional Chorale at a special performance of Handel's *Messiah* up in Ojai. Wow – to be part of a group like that performing music of that caliber was a pretty awesome experience.

I had procured a student loan to cover my out-of-state tuition and some living expenses. But I needed to make some cash for gas and toothpaste and beer. I joined Musicians Local 47 in hopes of getting some gigs through the union, and before long I got a call to play banjo at a

Shakey's Pizza Parlor. Shakey's had restaurants all over the area and the format for live entertainment was to have a piano/banjo duo play songs from the 1920s and '30s. So I showed up for my first night, met the piano player and we just winged it – no rehearsal. He'd shout out a title and a key and away we'd go.

The union had me jumping all over, playing a different Shakey's with a different piano player every weekend. One night driving back from a gig in Sherman Oaks, my poor MG broke down. Dad drove down and rented a trailer to tow it back to Medford, leaving my Honda 50 motor scooter as a replacement. I came up with a way to strap my banjo on my back so I could get to my gigs.

I got a call to play a Shakey's in Pico Rivera, an hour-and-a-half scooter ride from Westwood. When I arrived, a little saddle-sore, I found that the union had double-booked and there was another banjo player there. The manager came out to sort out the mess, knowing he couldn't afford both of us. He took one look at me and told me to go home. The reason? I had long hair. Yes, it was 1966 and I was a hippie, and that didn't fit this manager's image of a banjo player at Shakey's Pizza Parlor. So I got back on the scooter for my hour-and-a-half ride back home. When I called the union on Monday to register my complaint they told me to cut my hair.

Despite the discrimination, I had no choice but to stick with the union if I was going to work in LA. It took several years and many other negative experiences before I was in a position to finally, and with great delight, abandon my union affiliation. For now I was forced to bite my tongue, trim my hair and continue to do the Shakey's gigs. One night I was paired with a piano player named Ben Sands, who was the father of a famous singer and actor named Tommy Sands. He was an older gentleman with a sparkling personality and we hit it off immediately. He put in a request to the union for me to be his regular banjo player and we ended up playing together for several months.

LA was blossoming with new talent in the mid-'60s. I would occasionally buzz over to Santa Monica to visit McCabe's Guitar Shop, where on any given day you might run into a yet-unknown Jackson Browne or one of the soon-to-be-formed Nitty Gritty Dirt Band members. Randy Sparks (father of The New Christie Minstrels) had a club right down the street from us on Westwood Boulevard called Ledbetters. Nightly entertainment usually featured Randy's "farm team" for the Christies, The Back Porch Majority, and I remember one night seeing a kid named John Deutschendorf there. Little did I know at the time that some of these budding entertainers would soon be topping the charts.

My DJ friend from Medford, Jim Bailey, had taken a job in Portland working for an advertising agency. One of his clients was a group of Chrysler Motors dealers in the area. He came up with a scheme to draw customers out by having a local band play at the various car lots. To tie in with Chrysler he required that the groups he hired take on names of Chrysler models. For example, one group became the Imperials, another, The Valiants and another, The New Yorkers.

The New Yorkers were brothers Bill, Mark and Brett Hudson, along with their fourth wheel, Kent Fillmore. After hearing them play on several area car lots, Bailey perceived that he had a gold mine on his hands. He signed the group to a management contract and began an aggressive marketing campaign. Bailey had some connection to the Lawrence Welk Orchestra and he managed to get guitar player, Buddy Merrill, to put together a small group of string players to enhance a couple songs that the Hudsons had written. He planned to bring the band to Los Angeles for the recording session and he called me and asked if I would write the charts for the musicians. I was more than happy to comply, and in a couple of weeks we all gathered for the session. We ran a quick rehearsal with the string players and then I directed the recording. One take per song and we were finished. That's how they do it in LA.

It was great to see Jim Bailey again and I enjoyed meeting the Hudson brothers as well as one of my guitar heroes, Buddy Merrill. We said our goodbyes and promised to keep in touch. Jim was off to sell these fresh recordings to a record company and I was back to the books with finals looming.

♪ ♪ ♪

I was notified by the Admissions Office at school that as of the fall term of 1967 my out-of-state tuition was going to increase substantially. I made the decision to leave UCLA and transfer to University of Oregon. My dad had taken a new position as Parks and Recreation director for the city of Springfield, and the family had moved north. Being an Oregon resident allowed me to pay a much lower tuition at U of O and I could live at home to save money.

That was fine for a while, but having experienced independent living while in LA, I was hankering to get my own place. My friend and fellow banjo player, Terry Warner, was also looking to move out so we found a house in Eugene to rent together. This meant I had a new expense to cover and I started looking for work. There were no Shakey's Pizza Parlors in Springfield or Eugene at that time, but there was a Pietro's Pizza. I was hired to perform on Friday and Saturday evenings as a solo. No longer limited to music of the early 20th century, I started playing mostly guitar and doing more contemporary music.

Restaurants and other venues that provide live music are required to pay a licensing fee to two companies that collect royalties for songwriters for the use of their music. ASCAP (American Society of Composers, Artists and Publishers) and BMI (Broadcast Music, Inc.) represent the publishing companies of most music composers and apparently they do enforce their contracts.

It turns out that Pietro's was paying their annual licensing fee to ASCAP but not to BMI. BMI sent in a spy to see if any of their published music was being performed and they came on a night when I was playing. Of course, I had no knowledge of any of this, and my repertoire contained plenty of BMI material. The next week I got a call from Pietro's manager informing me that they'd been busted for avoiding the licensing fee and they had to pay a big fine. But rather than pay the licensing fee, they were opting out of BMI and I was not allowed to perform any music that fell under their jurisdiction.

I had my work cut out for me if I wanted to save my job. Had I known the extent of the problem I was facing I probably would have considered finding another gig. I took my repertoire list to the library (this was way before the internet) and did my best to find out which songs I had to eliminate from my repertoire. All my Beatles songs were gone as well as most every song written after 1960. I went back to playing stuff like "Let Me Call You Sweetheart" and "You Are My Sunshine." Boring! A couple weeks later the manager called me, rather irritated, and informed me that I had played a BMI song and the spy had busted me again. Who was this person, anyway? How had I missed one? Just one! So Pietro's relented and paid their BMI license and I got my repertoire back.

In addition to my paycheck I got to take home a pizza each night when I played. For a college kid, free cold pizza for breakfast was perfectly edible. That is, until the day I was told that one of the cooks had been fired the previous night and in retaliation he had urinated in a vat of pizza sauce. That sent me out looking for another source of income. I took a job at Eugene Music as a sales person and they also let me use one of their lesson rooms to teach guitar and banjo.

My classes at U of O were not particularly inspiring and I was starting to lose interest in school. I was itching for a change and it came in the spring of 1968 when I got a call from Jim Bailey. Kent Fillmore had left The New Yorkers and they were looking for someone to take his place. Would I be interested? Could I get to Portland by next week to start rehearsing? I packed my car and headed north.

Me giving my MG a bath.

My MG ready for transport.

12-15-65

CHRISTMAS SONGS—The A Capella Choir, under the direction of Roger Wagner, will present selections of Christmas music at 8:30 tonight in Royce Hall. Music by Bach, Kodaly, Petters and Palestrina will be featured. Admission is 75 cents for students, $1.50 for public.

UCLA Choir under the direction of Roger Wagner.
Camera angle missed me in the photo.

Shakey's Pizza big band.
Yours truly with banjo on the far left...

...and Ben Sands at the piano.

Bobby Banjo and Walt Simmons
entertaining pizza diners.

Tales from the Road

CHAPTER FOUR

The New Yorkers

THE HUDSONS LIVED IN A house on Yukon Street in Southeast Portland. It wasn't a very big house, but it managed to provide shelter for Bill, Mark, Brett, their mother Ellie, her brother (Uncle Bill) and her parents, Grandma Theresa and Papa Guiseppe. The grandparents had one bedroom on the ground floor, Uncle Bill had the other and Mom and the boys shared a room upstairs. The basement was set up for band rehearsal.

I was hired on to sing back-up and play rhythm guitar, keyboard and banjo. For that I was to be compensated $5.00 per week plus room and board. Oh, and I was allowed to use the van one day each week. My "room" was the couch in the living room. Hey, what the heck – it beat school and I was in a band.

Mark and Brett were still in high school, so Bill and I spent the first few days getting me up to speed on their repertoire. After school we'd all rehearse for a couple hours and then again after dinner. It all fell together fairly quickly and just in time for the bookings that were already on the calendar. The repertoire was primarily '60's pop bubble-gum songs and the audience was primarily teenage girls.

Jim Bailey had signed the group to Scepter Records, and we were getting considerable airplay regionally. That fueled our audiences at the weekend dance gigs. There was a circuit of teen dance halls around the Northwest operated by local promoters and we played them all. One promoter that we worked with regularly was Ed Dougherty of EJD Productions in Salem. We got a lot of airplay in Salem and the teenage girls came out in droves whenever we played there. One day we got a call from Ed with an offer to play a concert date – not a dance – at the Salem Armory. And there was another act on the bill – The Doors.

The stage in the Salem Armory was along the long wall of the room and probably measured a good sixty feet from stage left to stage right. When we arrived, Ed had us set up on the left side and The Doors had stage right. This double-billing seemed a little odd to us since our music was hardly in the same genre as The Doors. And backstage, Morrison and company had no interest in interacting with us at all. But apparently it was all about packing the house. We were scheduled to open the show and when we walked out on stage we were kind of stunned. There was an aisle right down the middle of the room with about 800 seats on each side. Over to our right, in front of where The Doors were set up we saw half a house full of hippies. On our side of the aisle every seat was filled with a thirteen-year-old girl. We played our set and they all screamed like we were the Beatles, while all the hippies sat impatiently waiting to hear their idols. But despite the disparity, the date was a financial success for both acts as well as the promoter.

♪ ♪ ♪

The Hudson's Aunt Shar was married to the actor Keenan Wynn. Bill wanted to make a recognizance trip to Los Angeles to see about making some connections and he invited me to tag along. He called Aunt Shar and asked if we could stay with her and Uncle Keenan while we were in LA, and they happily rolled out the welcome mat for us. We spent several days there and Uncle Keenan regaled us with hilarious stories about his career. The walls of their house were covered with framed pictures of Keenan and his father, Ed Wynn, along with every major Hollywood star on various movie sets. One night after dinner Bill and I were playing music for the Wynns and I ventured to play "Indian Love Call" on my banjo. Uncle Keenan actually broke into tears as he listened and praised me mightily when I finished the song. I think he'd had a bit too much wine for dinner, but it was a gratifying moment for me.

The next morning Bill and I were sound asleep when, at around 5:30, Uncle Keenan walked into the room where we staying. Simultaneously, without him even saying a word, Bill and I both sat straight up in our beds. I felt a very powerful aura emanating from Uncle Keenan as he told us to get up and come with him. So we hurriedly dressed and met him downstairs. He said we were going out to the Pacific Coast Highway (PCH) to ride his motorcycle and that Lee Marvin was going to meet us there. So we piled into his truck and off we went.

We pulled into a restaurant and offloaded his bike. We took turns riding it up the road a ways and back again, feeling the rush of the morning coastal air in our faces. After we'd each had a turn on the bike we went into the restaurant and he bought us breakfast. Lee Marvin never showed up so we loaded the bike up in his truck and headed back to Beverly Hills. As we packed our car that day to head back to Portland, Keenan gave me a little gift – a Japanese school boy's cap that he'd acquired from one of his movie roles.

♪ ♪ ♪

Back in Portland one of Mark's female classmates from Cleveland High School had caught my eye and we were thinking seriously about sharing our futures together. But marriage was not on my radar yet. The band was chasing fame and fortune and girlfriends were just that – for now.

Scepter wasn't doing much promotion for us on a national basis and Jim Bailey thought it was time to switch labels. Another Portland band, The Kingsmen, had scored big with their recording of "Louie Louie" on the Jerden Record label out of Seattle, and Bailey thought that would be a good label for us. He contacted Jerry Dennon, owner of Jerden Records, negotiated a deal for us and booked us some studio time at Audio Recording in Seattle. Operated by producer/engineer, Kearney Barton, this was where the Fleetwoods had recorded "Mr. Blue" and the Ventures had tracked their big hit, "Walk Don't Run." We were working on sacred ground.

Our two single releases on Jerden got us plenty of regional airplay, but again, nothing nationally. Bailey headed for Hollywood to try to open some doors. He had already invested heavily in our career, and I think he was burning out. He really believed in the band but he felt he'd gone as far as he could for us. After some negotiation he arranged a management deal for us with the Clive Fox Agency. I don't know if any money changed hands on the deal, but we were now a client of Clive Fox.

We had recorded a cover of Harry Nilsson's "I Guess The Lord Must Be In New York City," and Clive set about shopping us to record labels. He landed us a deal with Decca Records and they released that song. As part of their promotional scheme they arranged for us to meet Harry Nilsson at the bank where he worked his day job. That got us a photo op and a write-up in *Billboard* magazine. We were booked on *The Steve Allen Show* and *The Dating Game* and things were looking good. Clive rented us a house in LA and we headed back to Portland to pack up and move to our new digs.

Waiting for me in the mail back in Portland was a letter from the Selective Service Administration instructing me to report for my draft physical. The Vietnam war was raging and President Johnson needed more young bodies. I let my draft board know that I would be out of town on the date they had scheduled me, and amazingly they said they would reschedule. The next date they scheduled was also conflicted and after contacting them again, they rescheduled me a third time. This time I had no excuse and, short of slipping off to Canada in the dead of night, I had no choice but to show up. Sitting in the waiting area after my physical, one of the doctors called me over for an interview. He informed me that my blood sugar level had tested very high and in order to confirm this, I was required to return the next day and retest. The next day my blood sugar was again off the charts and they advised me to see a doctor. "Oh, and by the way, here's your 4-F." Well, that was a relief! But did I have diabetes? A subsequent visit to my doctor revealed a normal blood sugar level, so what was up with my draft physical? I can only assume that God had intervened to keep me on the path He had chosen for me.

Clive Fox had arranged for us to play for the Decca Records people at a club in Times Square on New Year's Eve, 1968. He bought us all new show clothes and put us on a plane to The Big Apple. The Decca reps met us at the airport and got us checked into a one-star hotel in Manhattan. I didn't sleep very well that night due to the occasional sound of gunfire coming from the streets below. We played our promo show the next night for a non-packed house of two record company PR guys and a bartender. Being New Year's Eve. the whole town was gathered below us waiting for the ball to drop. We had a view of just a corner of the ball from the club's third-story window as we played "Auld Lang Syne" for the Decca boys. The next day they dropped us back at the airport for our flight home to LA.

Arriving back at our Los Angeles rental house, we walked in to find all our belongings were gone. In our absence the place had been robbed and all we had were our instruments, the clothes on our backs and the show clothes in our suitcases. I got more bad news the next day when Clive Fox informed us that the group was being rebranded as The Hudson Brothers and all future promo would focus on the three brothers. I was out of a job and had no plan for the future. I headed back to Oregon to open the next chapter in my life.

The Hudson Brothers went on to have a one-year run on Saturday morning TV with their *Razzle-Dazzle Show*. Bill later married the *Laugh In's* Goldie Hawn and fathered an actress named Kate Hudson. Mark established himself as an A-list producer and songwriter, working with Aerosmith, Ringo Starr, Cher, Ozzy Osbourne, Harry Nilsson and others. And Brett made his mark as a motion picture and TV producer, with credits including the Burt Reynolds movie, *Cloud 9* and Bravo TV's *All The Presidents' Movies* starring Martin Sheen.

The New Yorkers autographed photo to a fan named "Pam." I guess she never got it. *L to R*: Bill Hudson, Mark Hudson, Bob Haworth, Brett Hudson.

The New Yorkers at Redmond, Oregon VFW in 1969. *L to R*: Me, Brett (bass), Mark (drums) and Bill (guitar) Hudson.

Me and my Gibson B12-25, Brett and his Rickenbacker bass.

Brett and Mark cut it up while I play banjo.

Mark, me and Bill.

Promotional poster for our gig at the Redmond, OR, VFW Hall.

CHAPTER FIVE

The Brothers Four

WITH MY TAIL BETWEEN MY legs, I headed home to Eugene. I was able to resurrect my sales job at the music store and I signed up a few guitar students. I got a nice discount for being an employee there and, scanning a catalog one day, my eye caught sight of a foot-pedal bass unit made by Kruger. It occurred to me that if I could play bass with my foot while playing the guitar or banjo, I could add a new dimension to my live performances. So I got the store to order one of these units for me and before long I was able to play a simple 1 – 5 pattern while playing my guitar and singing. I was a one-man band!

I played the bass pedals with my right foot and my left foot was feeling left out, so I got a hi-hat cymbal for poor left foot to play. I was a big fan of the Lovin' Spoonful and I'd seen John Sebastian play harmonica on a rack. So I bought a harmonica rack and a few Hohner harmonicas in different keys (all thanks to my special music store discount) and I continued to expand the band. This turned out to be a pretty unique act, and I started getting lounge bookings around town, and before long, even out of town.

♪ ♪ ♪

Thanks to my friend, Jim Bailey, I had gotten to know Jerry Dennon during the Jerden Records phase of my stint with the New Yorkers, and one day out of the blue I got a call from him. He asked if I'd be interested in writing and recording a radio commercial for a client of his. I immediately jumped at the chance and began working for him occasionally producing radio spots.

♪ ♪ ♪

I'd kept in touch with that girl from Cleveland High School in Portland and our relationship had developed into a full-blown love affair. In August of 1970 we were married and we rented our first house in Eugene. My solo career was gaining some momentum and now I was getting bookings as far away as San Francisco and Seattle.

Then in October, I got another call from Jerry Dennon. He asked if I knew of a group called The Brothers Four. I replied that I did, of course, and sang him a few bars of "Greenfields." Jerry went on to tell me that he was a partner with the Brothers Four in the ownership of radio station KSWB in Seaside, Oregon. He explained that he'd been contacted by one of the members of the group to ask if he could recommend someone to take the place of their tenor, who was leaving. Jerry asked if I'd be interested in auditioning for the job.

I'm sure my jaw dropped to the floor and when it finally found its place again I responded, "Of course I would!" Jerry gave me Dick Foley's phone number and told me that Dick was expecting my call. I was invited up to Seattle to meet the guys and audition for this awesome opportunity. I was surprised to learn that the tenor I was replacing was Mark Pearson, that kid from Spokane who also took banjo lessons from Dutch. He had replaced original member Mike Kirkland a couple of years previously, and now Mark was off to Nashville to pursue his song-writing career.

I showed up at Dick Foley's house in Bellevue at the appointed time and met him, John Paine and Bob Flick. They brought out some vocal charts that had been written by their producer, Milt Okun, and I managed to breeze through the arrangements without much hesitation. After a couple hours of singing, the three of them excused themselves for about five minutes, and when they came back into the room they asked me if I'd like to go to Bermuda with them. Apparently I'd passed the audition and was destined to become an honorary "Fiji."

Okay, maybe a little history is in order here. The Brothers Four formed at the *Phi Gamma Delta* (Fiji) fraternity house at the University of Washington in the mid 1950s. There were four of them and they were fraternity brothers, thus the name, Brothers Four. Another fraternity played a prank on them by calling and pretending to be someone from Seattle's Colony Club. The prankster invited them to come down to the club and audition. When they arrived at the club, unannounced and quite unexpected, the manager allowed them to go ahead and sing a few songs. Well lo and behold, they were hired on the spot and ended up performing there for several months.

At the invitation of a fellow frat brother at a California school, they made a trip to San Francisco and managed to get an off-night gig at the hungry i. In the audience was Dave Brubeck's manager, Mort Lewis, who liked the group, signed them to a management contract and procured a record deal for them with Columbia records. Their second single release, "Greenfields," topped the charts at #2 in 1960, and sold over a million copies. By 1970, the group was still riding the wave created by that hit and several that followed.

So off I went to Bermuda as the fourth Brother. We did two weeks in the showroom at the Princess Hotel and I was on cloud nine. I'd made the big time – just like I'd dreamed about as a ten-year-old fledgling banjo player. See? Dreams do come true! I was making some serious money and the next fifteen years were destined to reap immeasurable rewards on many levels.

ROY RADEN TOURS

The Brothers Four toured a couple times for a promoter out of Long Island named Roy Raden. We were pretty sure he was connected to the mob, but he paid well, so we took these extended road trips, playing mostly military NCO and Officers Clubs in the south. I remember doing an afternoon show at this one base and as the MC announced, "The Brothers Four" we walked out on stage to a packed room of black faces. We broke into our opening number, "San Francisco Bay Blues," and the whole crowd got up and walked out. Our road manager told us later that they were all saying, "These guys ain't bruthas!"

And who was that road manager? None other than Mickey Deans, Judy Garland's fifth (and last) husband. He would lull us all to sleep on those long drives between shows with his endless name-dropping stories about his life on the "inside." And Mickey's constant chatter only added to the stress of hours in a van driving from one show to the next. We were all getting a bit road-weary as the tour wound on. Some of us hid our frustrations better than others. After a lunch stop at a just-off-the-highway HoJo's (Howard Johnson's) one afternoon, we came out to find John Paine jumping up and down on top of the van. He just couldn't restrain himself any longer. When we got into the van we found that the headroom had been severely impacted by John's mad dance, so I laid on the back seat and pushed on the bulge with my feet. It wasn't pretty but at least now we wouldn't be scraping our heads on the ceiling. It would have been interesting to hear Mickey's explanation to the rental car company.

On another Roy Raden tour we were doing military bases in Texas – usually two shows a day. We'd do an afternoon show at an NCO club and an evening show for the brass. On this tour, we were being carted around in a van by two former Air Force guys who worked for Roy as combo roadie/sound and lighting techs. (Lighting consisted of one four-can tree that they hauled around with us in the trailer along with the Shure PA system and our instruments.) Behind their backs we dubbed our roadies Frick and Frack. One of these guys – I think it was Frack – used to greet Foley in the morning with a resounding "DICK-EEEEE!!!" Of course we all took to mimicking him.

It was a daily grind to get from place to place, Texas being pretty spread out. One day we pulled into our motel at the end of a long two-show day plus drive. We were all dead tired and cognizant of the fact that after a few hours sleep we'd be facing another six-hour drive to the next matinee show. So Flick (not Frick) called us all into his room and said he had a plan. We were gonna fly to the next gig and we were "leavin' in an hour and we were not tellin' Frick and Frack." He'd called the airport, booked us four seats on the last flight out of town so we'd be able to get a good night's sleep and not have to endure a long drive.

The next day we were lounging by the pool at the hotel when Frick and Frack showed up, remarkably unperturbed after their long drive. I guess they were more worried than pissed, but they had called the hotel, and found out that we were already there. The only bummer was that we did miss out on our morning "DICK-EEEE" that day.

BISMARCK OR BUST?

We accepted an offer to play a county fair in North Dakota and I'm not sure why the decision was made to drive there rather than fly. We rented a van and Dick Foley drove most of the trip. It was a two-day, ten-hour-a-day drive across half the country from Seattle to Bismarck and I spent most of it in one of the back seats reading or writing. Since I was a kid I've been fascinated with "The Man in The Moon." I'd been captivated by a picture in one of my Grandma's story-books of a smiling-faced crescent moon. Somewhere in the middle of Montana I stared drawing a man in the moon on my writing pad. I added arms and legs and gave him a name: Boregard "Bo" Mooney. Then I drew a sidekick for him, a potato with arms, legs, face and striped pants. Of course his name was Spud Tater. Then I dreamed up this cartoon strip based on an old joke and I drew Bo and Spud as the characters in the joke. Thus was born Bo Mooney. More about him later...

Two days after leaving Seattle we arrived in Bismarck and checked into our hotel. Dick called the promoter to let him know we'd arrived and find out about sound-check. All we heard on our end of the conversation was, "WHAT???!!! NO – NOBODY CALLED US. BRING US OUR MONEY NOW!!!" Apparently the show had been cancelled and, no, nobody had called us. All that way and we never even unpacked our instruments. The drive back to Seattle was just as boring as the trip out had been, but I had discovered cartooning, so at least the time wasn't totally wasted.

JAPANESE TOURS

The Brothers Four were big in Japan and I can't remember a year when we didn't tour there. We usually went in late summer for anywhere from three weeks to two months one year. The Japanese audiences loved our music and we were told that Brothers Four recordings were often used to help teach English because our diction was so precise.

My first Japanese tour with the Bros was in 1971. I'd never been out of the U.S. before, except to Canada. I'd never flown first class before and I'd never eaten sushi. This was a whole new experience and I was soaking it all in. Tats Nagashima was the head guy at Kyodo Productions and he always welcomed us to Tokyo with a night on the town.

Our first show was in a 4000-seat hall in the suburbs of Tokyo. This would be the biggest audience I'd ever sung to. Since the group had been visiting Japan for years, Dick, John and Bob all spoke some Japanese. Bob was especially conversant, but I had only learned a few words at that point. One of the first was *benjo* which means "toilet." Of course we couldn't resist the opportunity to play on the obvious similarity to the name of the instrument I play – the "banjo." To assist with our occasional attempts at *gaijin* (foreigner) humor, we were provided with a local comedian who served as our MC.

After a quick sound check we donned our stage clothes, checked our tuning and waited for the MC to introduce us. When I walked out on that stage and saw that huge theater filled with people, I experienced something I had never known before: stage fright. It was a sudden feeling of insecurity and it lasted for a couple songs before I managed to calm down and tell myself, "You got this."

These concerts were precisely structured so that the MC would come out after every three or four numbers and tell the audience about the songs and inject a little humor. As our limited language skills allowed, we would interact with the MC in an attempt to get a laugh. Every night was the same show with no variations, unless the MC said something different, which we never would have known. Town after town we traveled all over the country, often by the high-speed (120 MPH) bullet trains. The production crew would drive the equipment truck overnight to the next venue and have everything set up for us when we arrived for sound check the next day.

SOME FAMILY STUFF

In 1972, we were booked for a one-month tour starting at the end of August. My wife was pregnant and she was due any day as our departure date crept closer. Finally I had no choice but to get on a plane and head west to get to the East. Two days after we arrived in Tokyo our son was born Caesarian. Graham Whitney Haworth came into the world on August 22nd and by the time I met him he was already a month old.

Graham's mother never let me live down the fact that I had deserted her in that moment. Did I have a choice? I did ask my partners if there was any way to rearrange my travel schedule to give me a couple more days. But that would have complicated months of planning and even required the cancelation of our first show in Tokyo. Dick Foley did somewhat console me (but never her) by informing me that he'd been on the road the day his first son was born. That's show biz!

♪ ♪ ♪

Living in Eugene became a bit of a logistics issue since the other Brothers all lived in the Seattle area. We decided to relocate and bought a house in Bellevue. A couple years later we found a vintage house overlooking the beach on Vashon Island, a place accessible only by ferry boat. Vashon was, and is, a hippie enclave and we fit in quite well. We had a nice garden plot where I grew some outrageous twelve-foot tall marijuana plants that kept us and the neighbors in high spirits for months. Life was good. (More about Vashon in Chapter Six.)

YAMAHA GUITARS

Dick Foley and John Paine had a wild idea one year to open a music store in Seattle. Brothers Four Music featured a good selection of quality guitars, banjos, keyboards, amps and accessories. I would occasionally drop in to hang out and test-drive the instruments. One day I pulled a Yamaha FG-150 off the wall and I really liked it. For an inexpensive guitar it was well-made, had decent tone and played in tune all the way up the neck. I decided that on our next Japanese tour I would see about picking up a Yamaha guitar over there. The monetary conversion at the time was 360 yen per dollar, so things were really cheap.

When we arrived in Japan, I mentioned to our road manager, Nakamura-san, that I was interested in buying a Yamaha guitar, and I wondered if he could possibly hook me up with a music store and a good price. A week later he sat us all down and said that Yamaha Guitars was interested in having us endorse their product line. In exchange for our endorsement we would each be given a guitar of our choice. We all loved the idea and a date was set for us to take photos for print ads and shoot a TV spot.

The operative words in this deal for me were "guitar of your choice." Oh boy, I get to pick the one I really want. The FG-150 was what I had been shopping for but now the door was open to options. On a day off I went down to the Yamaha store in the Ginza and when I walked in, the first thing that caught my eye was a beautiful guitar that was slowly turning around inside a glass display case. The words "guitar of your choice" immediately came to mind as I ogled this marvel of craftsmanship. I couldn't get it out of the case that day to play it, but I knew that was the "guitar of my choice." So I told Nakamura-san about my discovery and on the day of our endorsement shoot, I was presented with "the guitar of my choice." The other Brothers each got a very nice lesser model. We later heard from Nakamura-san that there was some egg on the faces of the Yamaha folks over this deal. Apparently something had been lost in the translation and they had not really intended to cough up such a valuable instrument for our services. I believe the retail price on this guitar, even at 360 yen to the dollar, was around $3,000!

♪ ♪ ♪

I consider all the instruments I "own" to be in my temporary care. I hope that they will be played and enjoyed long after I'm gone, so I simply think of myself as their caretaker. This particular guitar has a story of its own that will hopefully go with it to it's next "owner." The label inside the sound hole identifies it as a Folk Custom III, signed by the builder, T. Nakamoto. It's a dreadnaught design with a spruce top, Brazilian rosewood sides and back and abalone inlays on the fingerboard as well as the headstock. I have a photo of the guitar on my website and one day I got a call from someone in Aspen, Colorado, who identified himself as being involved with an effort to establish a John Denver museum. This was after John's untimely death in the crash of his experimental aircraft. Anyway, this person had seen the picture of my guitar on my website and wondered if it had once been owned by John. They were trying to collect as many of his instruments and other memorabilia to populate the museum. I told them that I was the original owner, and that truthful response probably cost me at least $10,000. I had heard that one of John's guitars had sold to a collector for $30,000.

So, hearing that John had owned guitars that resembled

my Folk Custom III, I decided to do some research. I contacted Yamaha and gave them the information I had about my guitar and asked if John Denver had ever owned this model. The response I received really surprised me, because I found out that this is a really rare item. It turns out that my Folk Custom III was the prototype for a model designated L-53. John Denver had owned three L-53s but they were all copies of my prototype model.

♪ ♪ ♪

I had purchased a twelve-string guitar from Brothers Four Music that was built by a fellow named B.C. Rich. It was a nice guitar when I bought it but, despite the fact that I tuned it down a whole step, by the time we left for that tour when I scored the Yamaha guitar, this twelve-string had developed a bulge at the bridge. This caused the strings to be nearly 3/8" off the fingerboard at the twelfth fret. I had called Mr. Rich to ask what I should do about it and he said to live with it, that it would settle back down at some point. Well, it never did, but I only played it below the fifth fret so I continued to live with it.

♪ ♪ ♪

As I mentioned before, our Japanese production crew carried our instruments in the truck from one venue to the next. We would always find our cases neatly placed in the dressing room when we arrived. At one venue we arrived to find that the dressing room had been left unlocked and someone had gone in there with bad intentions. All our new Yamaha guitars were there as well as John Paine's vintage

Martin D-28 that he had played on the original recording of "Greenfields." All our cases had been opened, but one case was missing. Someone had stolen my "very valuable" B.C. Rich 12-string and left all these other worthless instruments behind. Well, the production company was held responsible for the loss since they had neglected to lock the dressing room. After many *gomen nasai's* I was informed that they would replace my loss with "the instrument of my choice." Here we go again. But this time they meant it. I suggested to Nakamura-san that perhaps they could get Yamaha to build me a twelve-string to match the beautiful Folk Custom III model six-string that I'd just acquired.

Arrangements were made for me to travel to Hamamatsu on a day off and meet the guitar builder, T. Nakamoto. When I arrived at the train station that day I was met by one of the Yamaha reps who took me to lunch and then over to the factory. I met Nakamoto-san and we discussed the details of my replacement twelve-string. It was to have the same design features as my six-string, right down to the audience-blinding abalone headstock. I got a full tour of the factory that day and they treated me like a star. Well, after all, I was a Yamaha endorsee. The production of the twelve-string took a year, so it wasn't until our next tour that I was able to play my Bob Haworth Model Yamaha twelve-string guitar. Well, actually the label inside the sound hole reads "Bob Hawarth Model." Close enough. It's a beauty and I can tune it to standard pitch.

OUR NEW MC

When my son, Graham, was five years old we thought it

would be fun to take the whole family on tour to Japan. Somebody hatched the idea to put Graham to work as our MC for this tour. Being a cute little towhead, he was sure to bring smiles to those Japanese faces. So we had him outfitted in a miniature tuxedo and we taught him how to introduce us in Japanese. He learned to say, "*Minasan konbanwa* (Good evening everyone). And now, The Brothers Four." So our Japanese MC gladly relinquished his opening intro to Graham and every show started with Graham behind the curtain, microphone in hand, awaiting his cue. When the curtain went up, the spotlight would hit him and he'd stretch out his left arm towards us and say his line. The audience erupted with delight and after the show everybody wanted to meet Graham.

One evening we were taking our places on stage to start the show. Graham was on his mark, mic in hand ready to deliver his line. Suddenly he turned to me with a panicked look on his face and said, "Dad, I don't want to do it." At that moment the curtain began to rise and Graham realized he was on the spot. He turned back to the audience and delivered his line like a trooper. Apparently showmanship runs in the family.

CHIBA

My Aunt Jewel's brother, Sammy Smith, had been stationed in Japan after World War II. He'd married a lovely Japanese lady named Kozy and they owned a nice home south of Yokohama on the coast. Kozy's brother was a musician and he had a band that played around the area. I had a night off, and Sammy and Kozy invited me down to party and play music with Kozy's brother and his band. We had a great evening and consumed more than one bottle of sake and at least one bottle of Japanese whiskey. There were no doubt a few beers added to the mix as well and the music got louder as the night progressed. Finally about midnight the band stumbled out the door and headed home while I was laid to rest in the guest bedroom.

The Brothers had a concert the next day in Chiba, about an hour drive north of Tokyo and I had to be back to the Tokyo Hilton by 11:00 a.m. for our departure to the gig. The train from Yokohama left at 8:00 in the morning and Sammy woke me from my stupor at 7:00 for breakfast and then a ride to the station. My hangover from the night before was relentless and the train ride back to Tokyo was miserable. I stumbled into the hotel, grabbed my show clothes and met the guys in the lobby for our ride out to Chiba.

I slept for most of the way except for when the guys woke me up to see the Magic Castle of Disneyland-Japan as we drove by. When we arrived at the venue I was wobbly and sick to my stomach. Breakfast was trying to make an exit and I wasn't sure if I was in any condition to go on stage. But Rule #1 in showbiz is "the show must go on." So despite the jeers from my cohorts, they had some compassion and arranged to have a bucket in the wings in case I needed it.

I managed to make it through the opening number before the nausea hit me hard. As our MC came out to talk to the audience I bolted stage right for my bucket. I was wiping my chin as the MC was announcing the next song. I pulled myself together and walked back on stage as if nothing had happened. I made it through the next two songs until MC-san came back out to MC. I escaped to my bucket again and proceeded to deposit a whole bottle of sake before I had to return to the stage. This went on for several songs until I was left to barf air-balls. I'm not sure what the audience thought of my intermittent departures, but on the ride back to Tokyo, the guys assured me that the city of Chiba was going to erect a statue in my honor.

KYODO PRODUCTIONS

Kyodo Productions was a major concert promoter in Japan and they booked artists in every genre. Often when we had a night off we would be invited to sit back stage and meet one of the other acts that they had touring. One night in Kyoto we had a chance to attend a concert by Cat Stevens. His opening act was Ramblin' Jack Elliot, which we thought was an odd pairing. I'd never met Ramblin' Jack before, although we've crossed paths several times since. On this particular night he had just flown into Japan and was still a little jet-lagged. He claimed that for some reason he was unable to unlock his guitar case, so he had to borrow one of Cat Stevens's guitars for his set. This show did not benefit from having a Japanese MC to act as interpreter, so when Ramblin' Jack came on stage he started telling the audience about not being able to open his guitar case. He went on for about five minutes with his story and we finally realized how he got the name "Ramblin' Jack." Apparently there were very few English speakers in the audience because he got no reaction at all from his ramblin' story.

On another occasion we got to hang out back stage for an Elton John concert. What a show, and the audience loved him. My wife was with me on this tour and she made no bones about her lust for Nigel Olsson, Elton's drummer. I have to admit, he was a beautiful boy, but I'll bet he was Elton's property. Still, I could tell I was no longer the apple of my wife's eye.

♪ ♪ ♪

One of my favorite celebrity encounters was the night we went to see Cliff Richard on my birthday. He was not well-known in the States, but he had big hits in England and other parts of the world. On this tour he had a full band and two beautiful female back-up singers. One of them was Olivia Newton-John. Her song, "Have You Ever Been Mellow," was just rising on the charts, but she had obligated herself to this tour with Cliff before the song's release. We were in awe of her as we stood backstage panting rather obviously.

The Japanese have a tradition that at the end of every concert, lovely ladies in geisha attire will bring flowers out to each of the performers. Somehow we convinced the geishas that night to let us be the flower "girls." At the end of the show everyone was surprised to see four *gaijin* guys bringing flowers to the performers. Before anybody else had a chance, I made a bee-line for Olivia and with every geisha move I could muster I presented her with my bouquet. I told her that I had really enjoyed the show and I hoped we'd see her back at the hotel.

The Lipo Bar occupies the basement floor of the Tokyo Hilton. It was our favorite after-show gathering place and we all headed there to celebrate my birthday. Also on tour that week was The Kingston Trio and Bob Shane and Roger

Gambill were already deep into their first cocktail when we arrived. The table began to fill up as The Brothers Four joined Bob and Roger and shortly thereafter, in walked Cliff Richard and Olivia Newton-John. Olivia took an empty seat next to Bob Shane and directly across from me. Dick Foley announced to the gathering that it was my birthday and he offered a toast in my honor. After the toast Olivia softly announced that it was her birthday too. Another round of toasts much more enthusiastic than mine.

All the while Shane was ogling Olivia like a vulture. The air was filled with cigarette smoke and wild road stories and after several more rounds for everyone at the table, Shane leaned over to Olivia and said, “Huh, can I take you upstairs and fuck yer ears off? Huh-huh!” We all sat there kind of stunned, watching to see her reaction. She took a couple more sips from her drink without acknowledging Shane’s comment. Then she very demurely looked around the table and said, “Goodnight, gentlemen. I’m off to my room – alone.” I stood up and wished her happy birthday as she left and she turned and said, “Back at ya.” After she was gone, we all looked at Shane and said, “Thanks a lot, Bob!”

The next day I got a call from Shane inviting me to come up to his room. He said The Trio was flying back to the States that day and he didn’t want to carry any pot with him through customs. So he loaded up his pipe and we smoked a bowl, after which he turned his jacket pocket inside out and dumped a bunch more pot onto the table. So we smoked that, along with some pocket lint, and said “*sayonara.*” That was only the first of many adventures to come with Bob Shane, aka Mr. Bob, aka deBobwan.

♪ ♪ ♪

I had another celebrity encounter at the Tokyo Hilton one morning. I had gone down to the coffee shop for breakfast and as I was studying the menu, a voice across the room suddenly belted out in British-tinged English, "You mother fucker, you better stay outa my way." I looked across the room and saw, of all people, Barry Gibb, one of the Bee Gees. Kyodo Productions had them on a two-week tour of Japan and before I could formulate another thought, a shout rang out from my right, "Don't call me 'mother fucker,' mother fucker!" I looked at the source of that remark and saw Maurice Gibb. As if on cue, from behind me a third voice shouted some equally offensive retort and the fight was on. I turned around and saw Robin Gibb waving his menu at Barry in a very threatening manner. The three brothers were seated as far apart as they could get in this very large restaurant and as the brothers carried on their loud and rather crude argument, the customers, including myself, sat in various states of disgust and amusement. I ordered my breakfast, ate and left as the shouting match continued.

There's something about brother bands that often breeds this kind of antagonism. I had three younger brothers and we occasionally had some brotherly disagreements, but we were never in a band together. And the Brothers Four weren't related. The Hudson Brothers got along fairly well, although I do recall a few shouting matches between them. But the Smothers Brothers have had long periods of disagreement and separation. And the Everly Brothers, like the Brothers Gibb apparently, literally hated each other. I imagine that sibling rivalry combined with the rigors of the road could lead to a serious failure in familial relationships. And the Bee Gees had no qualms about airing their differences in public!

RECORDINGS

Mort Lewis, who managed The Brothers Four, also handled the Dave Brubeck Quartet, and the two groups often shared billing at college campus shows. Joe Morello, Brubeck's drummer, was highly respected in the jazz world and he was often compared to such luminaries as Buddy Rich, Max Roach and Louis Bellson. Being a humble man, Joe would deflect those comparisons by referring to a mythical drummer named Marvin Bonessa. He would tell people that Bonessa was a recluse and hardly ever performed in public, but that he could play rings around Rich, Roach, Bellson and yes, even Morello. Well, the Brothers picked up on this joke and they and others started voting for Marvin Bonessa in the Downbeat polls. When I recorded my first album with The Brothers Four I noticed that Marvin Bonessa was credited on the jacket as a supporting musician. I believe he "appeared" on many of our LPs.

I recorded a dozen albums with The Brothers Four including one in Japanese. Looking back over the repertoire that we chose for some of these, I'm both puzzled and fascinated by many of the choices. "Greenfields" appears on most, acting as a kind of cornerstone. Our 1977 release on Jerry Dennon's First American label, *The Brothers Four Now*, included covers of "Have You Ever Been Mello?" "Tie A Yellow Ribbon 'Round The Old Oak Tree" and "Killing Me

Softly With His Song" – among others of that smooth pop ilk. The following year we released *Some Nice Songs* including such "nice songs" as "Don't It Make Your Brown Eyes Blue?" "How Deep Is Your Love?" and "You Light Up My Life" (with strings arranged by Yours Truly.) I think we were trying to update and re-imagine The Brothers Four.

Most of these albums were recorded at Kaye-Smith Studios in Seattle. Kaye-Smith was a highly regarded state-of-the-art facility that turned out albums by some of the top names in the industry. Among those who recorded there were The Steve Miller Band, Bachman-Turner Overdrive, The Beachboys, Johnny Mathis, Tower of Power, Elton John and Heart, to name a few. The Brothers Four utilized Studio B, which was better suited to our acoustic productions, while Studio A attracted the rockers.

During the recording of our *Some Nice Songs* album, I often encountered Ann Wilson in the hallway attached to her Old English Sheepdog. It was a beautiful dog that she had acquired from her good friend and local breeder, Merilee Rush. Apparently the pooch enjoyed spending several hours a day in the studio with its mistress. Yes, Heart was busy working on an album in studio A as we worked in B. Although the studio had gone to great lengths to baffle any sound bleed between the two studios, when we would break at the end of a take, we could clearly hear what would become iconic Heart riffs coming through the walls from Studio A. I have often thought of listening to that album carefully with headphones to see if I can hear any residual Heart licks on our tracks.

CHANGES

Even earlier than that, we were experimenting with a mix of songs that were pulled directly from the Top 40 charts of the day, abandoning the folk music that established the group in the '60s. I don't know for sure, but perhaps that was a factor in Bob Flick's decision to leave the group in 1972. In desperate need of a bass player and a fourth voice, I took a trip to Reno to audition the bass player for The New Christie Minstrels. That was the first time I met Bill Zorn, who was acting as leader/road manager for the Christies. Their bass player didn't work out and we continued to cast around for a Flick replacement.

After auditioning a few local bass players, we finally enlisted the services of Tom Coe, a Seattle guy, good singer, but he did not play upright bass. That actually fit in with the direction we seemed to be taking the group at the time. On a 1973 CBS-Sony release entitled *The Brothers Four Live in Japan*, I'm pictured playing pedal steel guitar in addition to my 1968-vintage Gibson Johnny Smith guitar. Oh what a painful experience to see that photo! What was I thinking when I sold that guitar? Just like my ES-125, a '60's-era Johnny Smith now fetches anywhere from $9,000 to $14,000!

But that sad memory aside, what was I doing playing an electric guitar and a pedal steel in a Brothers Four show? Well, here's a sample of the repertoire that was in our show in 1973, as documented on that album: "Teach Your Children," "Take It Easy," "One Toke Over The Line" and "The Cover of The Rolling Stone." Not the Brothers Four I grew up with. But it was the '70s and folk music was passé.

Bob Flick decided to return as our bass player in 1975, and

to some extent we returned to the more acoustic approach that was the trademark of the original group. Bob was very well connected in Japan and he managed to land us some very lucrative deals there. We did a national ad campaign for Coca Cola, and in the radio spots we recorded – yup – we sang "Coca Cora." We also recorded several albums for the Japanese market that included some new songs sung in Japanese, and our popularity there continued to sell out large venues on our annual tours.

THE FOLK MUSIC REUNION

In 1982, The Kingston Trio invited us to join them on a production for Showtime called *The Folk Music Reunion.* (It's available on YouTube at https://www.youtube.com/watch?v=Ozo7LoOMMjw&t=13s.)

We flew to Los Angeles to join the other artists for this show, and it truly was a Folk Music Reunion! In addition to The Kingston Trio and The Brothers Four, the program featured The Limeliters, Glenn Yarbrough, Tom Paxton, John Sebastian, Mary Travers, Judy Collins and The Firesign Theatre. (Not quite sure how The Firesign Theatre fit in, but they were there.)

We spent the afternoon rehearsing, doing sound check and setting up camera shots. As we waited in the dressing room for our turn on stage, I was a bit awestruck to be hanging out with these luminaries of the folk music world. All of these artists had played a major role in my musical development and here I was in their midst and being considered an equal. I was spellbound listening to Lou Gottlieb pontificate on various topics with his professorial locution. I had purchased every Lovin' Spoonful album when I was in college and here was John Sebastian sitting right next to me. Over there was Tom Paxton, whose songs had populated the repertoire of The Kinsmen. And it was hard to keep my eyes off of Mary Travers, who was every young folk musician's wet dream.

The taping of the show went smoothly in front of a packed room of folk music fans. Each of the acts performed two or three songs and then the finale brought the whole cast back on stage to sing Harry Chapin's "All My Life's A Circle." The show was very well produced and I still enjoy watching it. But leave it to Bob Shane to cap off the evening with a bang. We were all lodged at the Beverly Gardens Hotel in North Hollywood and after packing up our instruments, we headed back there for a night-cap and a few hours in the sack before our early morning flight back to Seattle. We were standing in the lobby waiting for the elevator when a loud crash stopped everyone in their tracks. We turned and looked toward the front door of the hotel and there, half-way into the lobby was Bob Shane's car. Sure enough – he couldn't wait to get to the bar and he had driven right through the front door!

♪ ♪ ♪

The Brothers Four turned twenty-five in 1983. Jerry Dennon suggested that we celebrate that milestone with a concert at the Seattle Opera House, and it proved to be a huge success. The Brothers Four Silver Anniversary Concert was held on April 2nd in front of a sold-out house. We were tuxedo clad and in great form as we ran through two hours of old and new songs. In honor of the event, King County Executive, Randy Revelle, proclaimed the day "Brothers Four Day."

Office of the County Executive
King County, Washington

PROCLAMATION

WHEREAS, In 1958, four University of Washington fraternity brothers formed a singing group known as The Brothers Four; and

WHEREAS, The Brothers Four have given more than 2,200 college concerts, entertained in more than 20 foreign countries, and performed at the White House for three different Presidents; and

WHEREAS, The Brothers Four have produced more than 35 albums and sold millions of records, including "Greenfields," "The Green Leaves of Summer," "Yellow Bird," and "Try to Remember;" and

WHEREAS, The King County Executive and his wife, Ann, are among the millions of fans who for 25 years have enjoyed the rich blend of voices and humor which distinguish The Brothers Four; and

WHEREAS, The Brothers Four -- Bob Flick, Dick Foley, Bob Haworth, and John Paine -- are not only outstanding entertainers and professional musicians, they are outstanding human beings; and

WHEREAS, The Brothers Four are celebrating their 25th Anniversary by performing a Silver Anniversary Concert benefitting the Bob Hope International Heart Research Institute;

NOW THEREFORE, I, Randy Revelle, King County Executive, officially proclaim Saturday, April 2, 1983 as

BROTHERS FOUR DAY

in King County and urge all 1.3 million residents to honor the special talents of these four musical "ambassadors" and support the worthy cause for which they have so generously given their time and talent.

Randy Revelle
King County Executive

Despite these occasional high-profile events and our annual Japanese tours, The Brothers Four worked sporadically. We had long periods of time when we were idle, so to occupy the downtime and bring in some extra income, I took on a few side-projects.

Our son, Graham, age five, on stage introducing the Brothers Four in Japan.

Brothers Four promo photo from 1975. Standing, *L to R*: me, John Paine. Seated, *L to R*: Dick Foley, Bob Flick.

Brothers Four promo photo: *T to B*: John Paine, Bob Flick, Dick Foley and me. Year unknown – probably mid- late-’70s.

Party at Sam & Kozy's: Me in the striped shirt with Sammy (*L*) and Kozy (*R*). Band member names all unpronounceable.

Shyakujii Park concert, Japan, 1979.

Dick Foley with a couple of fans.

Poster in Kobe, Japan.

The Brothers Four on Japanese TV.

Graham on Japanese TV.

Jammin' at Romy's Bar in Tokyo (1978?). *L to R*: Me; Dick Foley; the house entertainer, Mr. Kangaroo; and Jack Stamm. Romy's was one of our off-night destinations in Tokyo and Jack Stamm was a regular there. He was a reporter for an English-language Japanese newspaper and he and I wrote a song together.

The Crew at Lipo Bar.

Bob Flick and John Paine
preparing for sound check.

On stage in Japan.

After the show, backstage with fans.

An original Bob Haworth cartoon.

CHAPTER SIX

Side Projects

AFTER MOVING TO BELLEVUE IN 1973, I began to fill gaps in the Brothers Four schedule with solo gigs around the Seattle area. My one-man band act was unique and being a member of The Brothers Four helped open some doors.

I remember one less-than-memorable six-night-a-week gig I had at the Bellevue Holiday Inn. I was particularly beat one Monday evening as I headed to work and I arrived to find the usual Monday night "crowd" – the bartender and one lonely businessman far from home. There really wasn't any point in my being there, but I was under contract, so I played that night to a hearty non-response. At one point I suddenly realized that I'd been unconscious for who knows how long. When I "awoke" I was in the middle of a song and I couldn't remember playing that last couple of verses. After I finished the tune I turned to the bartender and asked if he had noticed anything odd about that song and he said, "No, not really." So apparently, I had fallen asleep in the middle of this song but my feet, hands and voice were on auto pilot. I wish I'd had a recording of that!

♪ ♪ ♪

Through some mutual friends I met a local musician named Gary Ballard, and we hit it off immediately. Gary plays banjo and guitar better than I do, and our voices blended well together. We worked up a duo act, me and my one-man band and Gary with his hot licks. We went through the band-naming process, you know, where you brainstorm all these fabulous band names, make a giant list of the best ones and then start whittling it down to THE one. Somehow my cartoon guy, Bo Mooney, ended up on the list and when we finished whittling, that was the name we chose. Not The Bo Mooney Duo, just...Bo Mooney. I did a real nice rendering of Bo Mooney holding a top hat and a cane and I blew that up on a sheet of plywood with an overhead projector. After tracing the four-foot by three foot image onto the plywood, I cut it out, painted it up and we would hang that thing on the wall behind us wherever we played.

One of our regular haunts was the lounge in the basement of the University Towers Hotel in Seattle's U-District. We drew a mixed crowd of college-types and businessmen and our repertoire was an appealing mix of folk, rock, country, bluegrass and...smut. Smut, you say? That's right, we put together a set of songs like "The Rodeo Song," "Dolly Parton's Tits," "Asshole From El Paso," etc., and dubbed it "The Hour of Smut." It was some pretty hilarious stuff and the crowd really got into it. We would save it until later in the evening to allow the audience to get well-oiled.

At closing time we would always get a visit from the Seattle police on beat patrol. Frank the cop was one of the regular beat cops and he was full of jokes. He would hang around the bar after all the patrons had cleared out telling hilarious stories and we would often joke-joust with him. He was a fun guy and we considered him a friend, which is why I still feel some guilt about the caper we pulled on him one night.

Gary and I had packed up for the evening and we were walking to our cars in the parking lot. Frank and his partner were still in the lounge and we spotted their patrol car. Up in the space behind the rear window we could see Frank's cop hat. I tried the door – it was unlocked! I reached in, grabbed the hat and headed for my car. Frank – I'm sorry. I don't know what they do to a cop if he loses his hat, but I hope your punishment wasn't too severe. I still have that hat – in case you want it back.

♪ ♪ ♪

There was a local band that had a loyal following and I became one of the loyal. It was a nine-piece swing band called "The New Deal Rhythm Band." They played jumpin' jive music from the '30s and '40s, and they were hot. At some point in the mid- '70s the group went through a major personnel change and they asked me to manage the new configuration. The new band leader and music arranger was an aptly named Jerry A. Ranger. He brought along a very talented singer from Bellingham named Cheryl Bentyne. Under Jerry's leadership the musicianship was top-notch and I was able to book the group into some very nice venues.

Following a three-week engagement at a five-star hotel in Vancouver, B.C., I had the group booked in a showroom in Winnipeg. After the final show in Vancouver I hit the road to Winnipeg along with the band's drummer, Michael Trullinger. Driving across Canada in the middle of the night was like being on another planet. The aurora borealis was spectacular and kept us riveted for the whole trip while Bob Marley provided the musical backdrop.

Cheryl Bentyne was a great singer with fabulous stage presence and it was inevitable that she was destined for bigger things. I had invited a REAL Hollywood agent up to Seattle to see the band in hopes of expanding our bookings. Little did I know that this agent was actually on a hunt for someone to replace Laurel Massé, who was leaving The Manhattan Transfer. Cheryl was the perfect fit for the job and we lost our main attraction. Cheryl moved to New York and has had a successful career doing what she loves to do.

♪ ♪ ♪

Seattle had sprouted another main attraction during the early 1980s, and that's what they called themselves. "The Main Attraction" was a four-man a cappella group that was getting a lot of attention around town. Knowing that I'd had some success managing The New Deal Rhythm Band, the Mains asked me to handle their business affairs for them. With Cheryl gone from the NDRB, I felt the wind had left the sails of that ship, so the opportunity to take on another project was appealing.

The Main Attraction put on a great show reminiscent of the doo-wop street groups of the 1950s. But they also brought in some a cappella arrangements of contemporary songs that made them more than a novelty act. They were good singers and captivating entertainers, and they were an easy act to stage since they required no back-up. They could perform as well on a Seattle street corner as they could on a convention hall stage.

In 1985, there was a movement afoot to adopt "Louie Louie" as the Washington State song. A local radio station arranged a concert at the Tacoma Dome to draw attention to this effort and they brought in Richard Berry, the song's author, to headline the show. The supporting acts were all the groups that had some success with the song, including The Wailers (who had the first hit record of the tune), The Kingsmen (Jerry Dennon's hit version) and Paul Revere and the Raiders. The Main Attraction had worked up a very cool a cappella arrangement of "Louie Louie" and they wowed the crowd with it that night. Even Richard Berry was impressed.

♪ ♪ ♪

After living in Belleview for a couple years, we were shopping around for a more rural environment. Carla Cross, a fabulous musician whom I'd met at U. of O., was now living in Bellevue and had gone into real estate. She found us a house on Vashon Island, a short ferry boat ride from West Seattle, and we fell in love with the place. The house was built in 1910 and still had push-button light switches, but the location was spectacular. Overlooking KVI beach in Ellisport, we had a fabulous view of Puget Sound from our deck.

Vashon Island in the '70s was a lot like Haight-Ashbury north. In fact, there was quite an influx of Californians at that time, so the lifestyle was pretty wild and crazy. Musicians and artists flourished and there was always a party going on somewhere. The annual Harvest Parties that we threw at our house were week-end-long affairs that drew revelers from all over "the rock."

The owners of the Vashon Theatre loved to put on live shows and I started presenting a series there called "Wednesday Nite Live." Wednesday was a dark night for most local and touring musicians, so they were happy to find a venue to fill an empty night. Among the acts I booked were local favorites Riley and Malone as well as The New Miss Alice Stone Ladies Society Orchestra, a seven-piece all-female campy swing band from LA. I also went out on a limb once and booked The Kingston Trio. They were in the area and had a free Wednesday and they gave me a big discount on their fee. Even so we barely made enough to pay them, but I think Bob Shane was there more for the party anyway.

After the show he and a couple of the band members came over to our house for an all-nighter. We had a lounge area up in our loft and Bob took a big mirror off the wall and laid it on the coffee table. He extracted a huge bag of coke from his coat pocket and deposited a snowy mountain onto the mirror. Then he rolled up two hundred-dollar bills, one for each nostril, and proceeded to plow right down the middle of that snow field. I looked at him in shock and said, "Bob, you're gonna kill yourself!" He looked up at me, smiled and did it again. I thought sure I'd be calling 911 soon, but as I came to find out over the years of working with him, he had a super-human constitution. As he used to say, "I plan to live forever. So far so good."

♪ ♪ ♪

Always on the lookout for some wacky way to entertain

people, I was drawn to Dick Van Dyke's character, Bert, in the *Mary Poppins* motion picture. There's a scene where Bert dons a bass drum on his back, hangs an array of horns around his neck and dances as he plays a squeeze box and bangs the bass drum. I thought *I could do that*, so I rigged up a bass drum with a strap down to my foot to beat it. Instead of the squeeze box I played the banjo and had a harmonica rack around my neck.

As I got more proficient at playing this stuff, I started adding instruments one at a time to the point where the whole rig weighs in today at just under 100 pounds. I thought it would be fun to march in the annual Strawberry Festival parade with this goofy get-up and that was the beginning of Bob O'Luney's Amazing One-Man Band. Wanting to expand on this crazy idea even further, the next year I enlisted a bunch of friends to join me in the parade and we created the Vashon Kazoo Marching Band, which became a perennial Strawberry Festival parade fixture.

♪ ♪ ♪

The hip music store in Seattle was The Folk Store out in the U District. I was a regular customer and I got to know one of the employees, "Fat" Jack Hanson. "Fat" Jack (yes, that's the name he preferred) was not only a master picker, singer and song writer, but also a fine craftsman. I had a wild hair to own a seven-string banjo and I brought the idea to Jack. He crafted a neck for me and attached it to an old rim from a dismembered banjo. It was strung like a guitar with the seventh string functioning as the drone string.

A couple months after he finished it, I had stopped by a

local venue to hear a band. I left my VW bus in the parking lot, locked and loaded with musical gear, including my new seven-string banjo. When I got back from my reconnaissance mission I found the van had been breeched and my new banjo along with my bass amp were gone. At least that was the extent of the theft, but I had fallen in love with that banjo. I called "Fat" Jack, told him my sad story and begged him to make me another one. A couple months later I had my replacement.

♪ ♪ ♪

I need to tell this story now, even though it's chronologically out of order. Years later when I was living in Colorado, I was writing a piece called "The Colorado Trail" for Allan Shaw's *Popular Folk Music Today* magazine. I would interview various Colorado performers and write their stories for publication. I interviewed Jimmy Ibbotson of The Nitty Gritty Dirt Band at his departure gate at Stapleton Airport as he was flying out on tour. That was in the days when you could still walk out to the concourse without a ticket. I interviewed John Denver by phone as he was awaiting his boarding call at LAX for a flight to China where he was touring as the first American artist to perform there. (Reprints of these interviews are included later in this book.) And I interviewed Dick Weissman in my office in Lakewood.

In the 1950s, Dick Weissman had been a member of The Journeymen, along with John Phillips and Scott McKenzie. Now he was a professor at the University of Colorado, Denver, professing musicology. He had some interesting stories to tell of those early days of the budding folk music craze in New York City. As we were finishing our chat, I picked up my "Fat" Jack second-generation, seven-string banjo and handed it to him saying, "Have you ever seen anything like this?" He took it from me, played a few licks and said, "Yeah, I have one just like this." I was a little dumbfounded because I was pretty much under the impression that I had invented the idea. So I asked him where he had acquired his seven-string banjo and he said, "I bought it in a pawn shop in Seattle." No way! The thief had hawked it to the pawn shop and...what an amazing coincidence!

♪ ♪ ♪

"Fat" Jack approached me one day and asked if I might be interested in forming a folk group with him and a couple of his friends. So along with Herb Sage (aka Bruce Kirkman) on guitar and Carey Black on bass, we began performing as The New Fireside Singers. Herb was a prolific songwriter, and Jack wrote as well, so much of our repertoire was original material with a very "folky" orientation. I don't think we did any Brothers Four material, but we did a few obscure Kingston Trio tunes. There weren't a lot of venues that would book us, but because The Brothers Four had played there, I managed to get us a two-week run at a Vegas-style restaurant/showroom on Lake Union called The Wharf. Every night was pretty much like Monday night at the Holiday Inn, although I don't recall ever falling asleep on stage there. I believe we were the last act to perform at The Wharf.

♪ ♪ ♪

In 1976, Jerry Dennon called and asked me to do a recording project for him. He had a concept in mind to market me as "The Banjo King." He paid me to arrange and produce an album of plectrum banjo instrumentals with a piano, bass and drums back-up band. Released on Jerry's First American label, the LP, entitled *The Banjo King Plays Ragtime*, had an interesting sales history. Since I was really just a hired hand on the project, I wasn't privy to the actual sales figures, but Jerry did tell me that it had sold quite well in Turkey. And a few years ago, my brother sent me copy that he'd found on Ebay that had an album jacket printed in Spanish. Apparently, sales were strong enough world-wide to warrant a Volume II, so I recorded *The Banjo King Plays Favorites* a couple of years later. I never heard any sales figures for this cassette-only release, but I did discover that Jerry Dennon, marketer extraordinaire, had sold nine cuts from the *Ragtime* album to Murray Hill Records. These cuts appear on a box LP set entitled *The Banjo – A Collector's Treasury*. The cover states: "Featuring Flatt & Scruggs, Pete Seeger, Eric Weisberg, Mason Williams, Jim McGuinn, Mike Seeger, Joe Maphis, Erik Darling, Jim Helms and many others." "Many others" were me and a guy named Denny Wright. I never saw a dime from this compilation, but who needs money when your name appears on an album with such banjo luminaries as Denny Wright?

♪ ♪ ♪

As I mentioned before, success in the entertainment industry has a lot to do with who you know and how you use those connections. Jim Bailey had connected me with Jerry Dennon who connected me with The Brothers Four who connected me with The Kingston Trio and Bob Shane. So how did I come to work with him? Well, that became the next chapter of my life, so I guess I'll make it the next chapter of this book.

BOB O'LUNEY'S AMAZING ONE-MAN BAND

Official promotional photo for
the Bo Mooney Duo.

Bo Mooney and our plywood sign at
the University Towers in Seattle.

Bo Mooney Duo on the Virginia V – a large party boat that you could rent for cruising around Puget Sound from Seattle. We would promote a party cruise, folks would pay a fee to come along and we'd play music as the fans partied. It resulted in occasional DUIs for revelers returning home on land.

New Deal Rhythm Band.

Acapella group The Main Attraction.

The New Fireside Singers. *L to R standing*: Me, Fat Jack Hanson, Cary Black. *Seated*: Herb Sage (aka Bruce Kirkman).

Bo Mooney One-Man Band
in the Vashon Parade.

CHAPTER SEVEN

The Kingston Trio: Part One

IN MARCH OF 1985, BOB SHANE called and asked if I could fill in for a hospitalized Roger Gambill. Roger, who had been the Kingston Trio's tenor and head funny man since 1973, was in the hospital after suffering a heart attack at age forty-two. He was expected to recover and be back on the road within a month, but the Trio had bookings and as Bob used to say, "No play, no pay." That not only applied to individual members, but to the entire group as well, and Bob was not in favor of canceling any bookings.

The first date was a Friday show in California, and I was available. However, I had to be back in Seattle the next day for a Saturday evening show with The Brothers Four. Luckily the logistics worked out and I was able to play both dates. I didn't have much time to prep for the Trio show, but Bob and George Grove offered to fly up to Seattle to rehearse with me. They came to my house on Vashon Island where we went through each song in the show once. That was enough to assure Bob that I was capable, so he headed uptown to play Pac-man at the local tavern. Rehearsal was not in Bob Shane's wheelhouse.

The biggest issue I had that weekend was one song that was common to both The Kingston Trio's show and The Brothers Four's: Pete Seeger's "Where Have All The Flowers Gone?" Each group had a distinctly unique arrangement of the song and it took some effort on my part to make sure I got it right on both nights. I had a few more shows with The Trio over the next couple of weeks as we anticipated Roger's recovery. Sadly, on March 20th we got word that Roger had passed away. Bob asked if I was willing to leave the Brothers Four. I told him I would have to think about it.

Every ounce of me wanted to respond immediately with an unfettered "YES!" but I had a lot to consider. I'd been a member of The Brothers Four for fifteen years and I had a strong sense of loyalty to my fellow Bros. Weighing in favor of joining the Trio was the fact that they were doing over 100 shows a year while The Brothers worked only intermittently. And although that meant a substantial increase in my income, it also meant I'd be spending a lot more time away from home. I was conflicted, but my family and the many friends that I consulted all said, "Go for it!" And so, with some sadness, I gave my notice to The Brothers Four and embarked on the next chapter of my life. My regrets about leaving The Brothers Four were greatly assuaged when I found out that Mark Pearson, whom I had replaced in the group, was back in Seattle and was eager to step back into his former role.

As I did with The Brothers Four, let me inject some history about The Kingston Trio for those who may not be familiar with the group. For a detailed account of The Trio's career, I recommend William Bush's book, *Greenback Dollar*. But briefly, Bob Shane, Dave Guard and Nick Reynolds formed The Kingston Trio in the mid-1950s while attending college in the San Francisco Bay area. A local promoter named Frank Werber discovered the group and landed them a recording deal with Capitol Records. A song from their first album about the hanging of a condemned murderer named Tom Dooley caught fire and propelled the group to stardom. They became Capitol's top-selling act until the arrival of The Beatles.

Many hits followed after "Tom Dooley," fueling the group's popularity with not only the college-aged crowd, but with the general population as well. Dave Guard left the group in 1961 and was replaced by John Stewart. That configuration rolled on until 1967, when the decision was made to disband. After a brief solo outing, Bob Shane decided to reform the Trio, but lacking exclusive ownership rights to the name, "The Kingston Trio," he rebranded the group as "The New Kingston Trio." Enlisting the services of Pat Horine and Jim Connor in 1969, this "new" version toured and recorded until 1973, when Horine and Connor were replaced by Bill Zorn and Roger Gambill. In 1976, Bob arranged to purchase the rights to the "Kingston Trio" brand from his former partners, Nick Reynolds and Frank Werber. That same year, Zorn left the group and George Grove took his spot. When I replaced Roger Gambill in 1985, I was the seventh non-original member, or as I used to say, "I'm the one, I'm the one – the one they call the seventh son."

By 1985, The Kingston Trio had evolved into a six-piece

group. In addition to Bob, George and me on the front line, we had bassist Stan Kaess, drummer Tom Green and multi-instrumentalist Ben Schubert backing us. The Trio has employed a bass player from the beginning and adding Tom Green on drums took the place of and expanded on Nick's iconic conga and bongo drums. Ben Schubert provided another musical layer that filled out the arrangements with fiddle, electric tenor guitar, banjo or mandolin.

A DAY IN THE LIFE

All of us lived in different parts of the country, so when we started a tour, we would each fly out of our home airport and meet at the closest airport to the first date on the tour. There we'd rent a van, cram our instruments and suitcases in and head for the target destination. Although I'd done many tours with The Brothers Four, there was a whole different rhythm to Kingston Trio touring. For one thing, we were doing a lot more of it than The Brothers Four!

While some tours allowed us to travel to several shows within a region via rental van, others had us traveling on a daily basis by commercial airlines. For those tours, a typical day on the road would often start with a 5:00 a.m. wake-up call for a 5:30 departure to the airport. Fly to the next city and check into the hotel by early afternoon. Maybe take a quick nap or, if I'd had enough sleep the night before, hit the hotel pool for a few laps. All of us but Shane would then head to the venue around 4:00 to do a sound check. (Just a side-note: to this day I hate drum sound-checks. If you haven't experienced one, they're hard to describe, but they epitomize for me a concept of what hell could be like.) Return to the hotel for dinner, shower and shave, then back to the venue by 7:30 for an 8:00 show. After the show, back to the hotel bar for decompression and hobnobbing with the inevitable gaggle of hardcore fans that would follow us there. Finally, hit the rack, hopefully by midnight, for a few hours of sleep, and then do it all again.

I made sure to sign up immediately for the frequent-flyer programs offered by all the airlines that we flew on. Before long, I'd accumulated enough miles to upgrade to first class on most flights, especially those five-hour cross-country trips. That provided for early boarding, free drinks and a decent meal. It was certainly a nice perk and we all took advantage of it whenever possible.

Our schedule was so intense at times that it seemed like a blur. We often joked that our booking agent booked us alphabetically rather than geographically. In one three-day period in July of 1985, we played in Colorado Springs, then the next day in Rancho Bernardo, California, followed on the third day with a trip across country to Rochester, Michigan. All in alphabetical order. We were rarely in one town long enough to do anything other than what we were there to do.

THANK YOU REPUBLIC AIRLINES

I learned a hard lesson about traveling by commercial airlines early in my stint with the Trio. Greg Deering of Deering Banjos fame had given us some instrument cases to try out and provide him with some feedback as to their reliability for road travel. He was considering adding them to his accessory product line as an optional case for his finely-crafted banjos. George was given a case for his long-neck banjo, and

I was asked to test drive a guitar case. These were not hard-shell cases, but they were made of heavy-duty Styrofoam covered with a durable vinyl material.

I was carrying my Yamaha L-53 guitar on the road at the time, and it fit very snugly into this new case that Greg had given me. Retrieving my guitar at baggage claim after a flight to San Diego one morning I noticed some damage to my new case. I was concerned and decided to open it and inspect my guitar. My heart nearly stopped when I saw what the airline had done to my beautiful instrument. The neck was totally broken off at the heel and I feared that I would never play that guitar again.

I took my mangled mess to the Delta ticket counter and filed a claim for damages. Of course, the airline initially declined to take any responsibility for their careless handling of my property, but after a couple strongly worded letters with threats to boycott their airline, they finally relented and offered to compensate me for the repair. Upon my return to Seattle from that tour I took my poor baby out to the Folk Store and asked Fat Jack if he could reattach my neck. He did a masterful job of putting it back together and suggested that I retire the Deering Styrofoam case and replace it with a heavy-duty Calton case. I was assured that I could drop my guitar in a Calton case from the Empire State building and it would sustain no damage. And true to their claim, I never suffered another mishap from mishandling of my instrument by the airlines.

But singer-songwriter Tom Paxton apparently had not heard of Calton cases until he showed up in Midland, Michigan, one evening to open for us. Tom had been one of my early folk music influences and I was excited to see him again. But the story he told us when he came into the dressing room was, sadly, one I could relate to. He had flown in on Republic Airlines and, just like my incident in San Diego, he had found a damaged guitar case at baggage claim. And just like my incident in San Diego, he had found his dismembered guitar on the inside. But being a prolific songwriter, he decided to document this sad occasion with a song. He actually performed it in his set that evening, playing George's guitar, and both he and George's guitar received a hearty and sympathetic response from not only the audience, but from the Kingston Trio as well. Here's the song he composed on his ride from the airport and regaled us with that night. He later recorded it on his album entitled, *One Million Lawyers and Other Disasters*. You can find it online at: https://www.youtube.com/watch?v=mwV8ozElNjk

Thank You Republic Airlines

Flying through the Michigan skies
With a song in my innocent heart
I placed myself in professional hands,
Masters of the traveler's art
When I opened my guitar case at the end of a beautiful flight
I'm sure you can imagine my feelings,
As I beheld this beautiful sight
Thank you, Republic Airlines,
For breaking the neck on my guitar
I arrived to do a concert with The Kingston Trio
Opened my guitar case with a smile, con brio
Thank you, Republic Airlines,
What a joy to the musician you are

What a zest you've added to pedestrian skies.
It was boring to be flying where wild goose flies
But the tedium was broken by the wonderful surprise
When you broke the neck on my guitar
Thank you, Republic Airlines,
For treating my instrument with care
There can be no greater happiness for the musician
Than to find his instrument in this condition
Ho-ho, Republic Airlines,
In the firmament of travel you're the star
For you treat each piece of baggage like a child of your own
When you come across an instrument,
It's dropped like a stone
May you wake up every morning with a new broken bone
Like you broke the neck on my guitar
Well, I've been traveling most of my life

And the thrill is a long time gone
And the sight of another DC-10 just fails to turn me on
But I feel my heart start pounding
When I get to the baggage claim
And when I see how you handled my instrument,
The thrill is still the same
Thank you, Republic Airlines,
For splintering the neck on my guitar
My guitar case was so strong
That nothing could go through it
Way to go Republic, only you could do it
Crash bang, Republic Airlines,
In the field of demolition you'll go far
For you took it as a challenge when I checked in my case
And you saw the fragile stickers glued all over the place
May a team of mad flamenco dancers do to your face
What you did to the neck of my guitar

There could be no satisfaction greater than if
You should be the next to go the way of Braniff

And it wasn't long after that night that Republic Airlines did, in fact, go the way of Braniff. I wonder if that song had anything to do with their demise.

THE PALOMINO CLUB

Shortly after I joined the Trio, we were booked at the famed Palomino Club in North Hollywood. If you've never been there, go rent Clint Eastwood's *Every Which Way But Loose* or *Any Which Way You Can*. The bar scenes in those flicks were filmed at the Palomino and you can get a good sense of the atmosphere of the place from both of those films. On any given night you might hear David Allan Coe, Jerry Lee Lewis, Linda Ronstadt or Dwight Yoakam perform, among others. But despite the level of musicianship that graced its stage from night to night, the Palomino was pretty much a country music dive, complete with a high level of red-neck testosterone.

A fair amount of beer was spilled in that place over the years. I discovered that grim reality as I was changing shoes for the show and made the mistake of walking across the dressing room in just my sox. The carpet was soaked and squishy like a sponge and by the time I had taken six steps I was ankle-deep in Willy Nelson's spillage from the night before. And I hadn't brought an extra pair of sox!

As we were tuning up and going over the set-list before the show, who should walk into the dressing room but one of folk music's all-time icons, Fred Hellerman. Fred, along with Lee Hays, Ronnie Gilbert and Pete Seeger, had formed a group called "The Weavers" in the 1950s that cracked open the door for the folk music boom that the Kingston Trio would usher in a few years later. The Trio revered The Weavers and even adapted several of their arrangements for their own repertoire. And being a long-time Weavers fan myself, meeting Fred Hellerman was definitely the highlight of the evening for me.

In the house that night was the Ragin' Cajun, Doug Kershaw, who was scheduled to take the stage at the Palomino later that week. Bob thought it would be cool to have him join us on a tune, so he invited Doug on stage. He didn't have his fiddle with him, so Shane instructed Ben to loan Kershaw his. Reluctantly, Ben handed over his fiddle and bow and we launched into an impromptu rendition of "Jambalaya." Doug Kershaw really rips into it when he plays, and note by note the hairs on Ben's recently re-haired bow began to shred. As we acknowledged the standing ovation at the end of the tune, Kershaw handed the fiddle and bow back to Ben, who looked with disgust at the mangle of horse hair hanging from his bow. Luckily he had a spare.

♪ ♪ ♪

I was sporting a full beard when I joined the group and Shane persisted in giving me crap about it, saying it made me look old. I was standing out in the parking lot of the hotel on the day of the show when Shane and Tom Green drove up, returning from a cigarette run. Shane looked at me and said, "You really oughta shave that beard, man. It makes you look really old." *Yeah, I hear you! But Roger had a beard – why pick on me?*

Well, I'd had enough of his BS (Bob Shane) and I went

back into my room and proceeded to shave only the right half of my face. Later we all went over to the show and when Shane saw me he just laughed and said, "Oh, that's cool!" Well, I was playing the thing like nothing was out of the ordinary and most of the guys noticed and got a good laugh. But oddly, apparently Ben Schubert was oblivious (I think I was fairly invisible to him anyway.)

We went on stage with my half-shaved face and I'm sure the audience was wondering, "What-the...???" But hey – it was LA after all, so maybe it was like a normal thing to those folks. As the show went on, I made a point several times to turn around and talk to Ben, consulting him about keys and capo positions. I made every effort to get him to look at me head on and even though he did, he never reacted to what he was looking at.

The time came in the show for Shane to do "Scotch and Soda," so George and I left the stage. I went to the dressing room and shaved off the other half of my face. When I came back on stage the audience reacted to my new look and Shane made a comment about it. I turned around to Ben and he finally saw me. He reacted with surprise to my clean-shaved face, but when I told him later about walking around all day and doing the first half of the show with a *schitzo* face, he couldn't believe that he hadn't noticed. Man we got a good guffaw outa that! Sing along now: "I left my beard at the Palomino..."

LOST LUGGAGE

After playing a convention date in Atlanta one evening, Bob Shane drove to his home in Alpharetta to spend the night. The rest of us retired to our hotel near the airport. The next morning we had a flight to Cincinnati, so we checked out of the hotel and took the shuttle to the airport. We checked in for the flight, got our luggage tagged to CVG and boarded the plane. So far we had seen no sign of Bob Shane. We were becoming concerned and then, just as they were closing the door for departure, in blew Bob, huffing and puffing. And he had no more plopped his butt down in his first-class seat when he jumped back up and went forward to speak with the flight attendant.

When he came back to his seat we all wanted to know what was up. He told us that he had slept through his alarm and because of his late start, he'd driven his Maserati 90 MPH all the way to the airport. He drove up to the curb-side baggage check, pulled out his guitar and suitcase and asked the Red Cap to hold them for him. He was going to park his car and he'd be back to check his bags in for his flight. Well, after parking his car and noticing the time, he went straight to the gate and forgot to check his luggage. His conference with the flight attendant was an attempt to somehow get his bags on this plane. As he was in the process of enlightening us about his predicament, the plane began to pull back and we were on our way. We were sure that we'd have to find a guitar for Bob to play when we got to Cincinnati, since there was no way his bags could have made it onto our plane.

Arriving in Cincinnati, we stood around the baggage carousel waiting for the luggage to roll in. As the belt jolted into motion our jaws all dropped at once when Bob's guitar and suitcase appeared as the first two pieces off the plane. How was that possible? It was the luck of deBobwan. (He did have incredible luck, by the way. For example, if we were driving to a specific destination in a city, such as a restaurant or a music store, he would invariably find a parking spot right in front of the place.)

Well, the rest of the Cincinnati-bound passengers started grabbing their bags as they came around the carousel and one by one they vacated the terminal. And then the carousel stopped. Wait – where are our bags? Say what? They went to Nashville? How was that possible? The luck of the rest of us!

And it wasn't the last time that happened. On several occasions over the years I had to play a borrowed or rented guitar when mine was sent to an alternate destination. And one day, all of our instruments got misdirected. We were in the middle of a two-week engagement at the Fairmont Hotel in San Francisco when we had a 1:00 p.m. show in a shopping center in Tempe, Arizona. Amazingly, the flight schedule worked out so that we could leave San Francisco in the morning, arriving in Tempe with plenty of time to do a sound check and a one-hour show. Then we would fly back to San Francisco in time for our first show in the evening.

Well, when we got to Tempe, our instruments were not on the plane. The promoter picked us up at the airport and there was a scramble to find instruments for us, but the time was too short and we were unable to play the show. But we needed to get our instruments back in time for our 8:00 p.m. show at the Fairmont, and the airline finally tracked them down in Memphis. Back in San Francisco we were on the phone with the airline hourly, pressing them to return our missing gear by showtime. Perhaps threats of canceling all our future flights on their airline were enough to kick the necessary forces into gear and our instruments were delivered to the Fairmont at 7:45. Whew – that's cutting it pretty close!

SAN FRANCISCO'S FAIRMONT HOTEL

The first time I stepped onto the stage of the Venetian Room at the Fairmont Hotel in San Francisco I was overwhelmed with a sense of history. This was where Tony Bennett sang "I Left My Heart In San Francisco" for the first time outside of his shower. And before that, Cab Calloway had bellowed out his "Heigh-dee-heigh-dee-ho!" to the hip Bay Area crowd. Known for presenting nothing but the best in entertainment acts, it was an honor to play the room where so many luminaries had graced the stage. I somehow managed to bring home the huge 4′x 2′marquee poster from our engagement there and the upcoming acts listed were Michael Martin Murphy, The Fifth Dimension and Miss Peggy Lee.

The act that preceded us was the great Captain and Tenille, purveyors of such Top 40 hits as "Love Will Keep Us Together," "Do That To Me One More Time" and who could forget "Muskrat Love"? I found out about their previous engagement in kind of an odd way. I woke up one morning and a note had been slipped under my door. It was addressed to Toni Tenille. I didn't recognize the name and when I went down for breakfast I stopped by the front desk to let them know them know that I wasn't Toni Tenille. The guy looked at the note and said, "Oh, The Captain and Tenille played here last week and Toni stayed in the room you're in. I'll have the manager pass this note along." Oh – THAT Toni Tenille. *I'm sleeping in the same bed that Toni Tenille slept* *in? I'm looking into the same mirror that Toni Tenille looked into? I'm sitting on the same toilet...*OK...never mind.

The entrance to the stage was through the kitchen. The maître d' would always greet us by the stage door and ask if we wanted anything. One night he told us that when Tony Bennett played there, he would always request a glass of Port wine before going on stage. He claimed that it calmed his nerves and loosened up his vocal cords. It sounded like great advice from the man who would know, so we all took to ordering a shot of Port just before showtime.

George and Bob had developed a bit in the show where Bob would make fun of George for being bald. George would respond that he preferred being bald to having grey hair like Bob. And anyway, baldness ran in his family. Bob: "Oh, so it's in your genes." George: "No, I've got hair in my jeans." Big laugh. Well that was the end of the bit until one night Bob turned to me after that and said, "So what about you?" Off the cuff I responded, "Oh I'm just hangin' out waitin' to see if I turn grey or go bald." Surprisingly, that elicited a big laugh from the audience. Well, as it turned out, Tommy Smothers and Henny Youngman were in the audience that night. These are two of the funniest guys in the world, so I was pretty floored when after the show Henny Youngman said to me, "That line you had about turning grey or going bald was the funniest bit of the night." Holy Moley! Praise from the world's top comic for an off-the cuff remark? Well, needless to say, the line stayed in the show thenceforth.

One of the coolest things about the Fairmont was the fact that they not only presented world-class shows in the Venetian Room but they also featured live entertainment in the Tonga Room. And not just any local band played there. During our stint the Tonga Room entertainment was none other than Poncho Sanchez and his Latin Jazz Band. What a treat to listen to some great Latin music and sip a piña colada before hitting the stage for our own show.

♪ ♪ ♪

Stan Kaess was our bass player at that time. He was an interesting character and kind of hard to get to know. He was very reclusive and pretty much stayed in his room until showtime. One day I happened to visit his room for some reason and I notice that he had a stack of room service trays, probably eight or ten of them, on the floor. Stan was a big guy but it surprised me that he would order that much room service. I later asked Tom Green about it and he informed me that Stan hardly ever ordered room service. Instead, he would scour the halls for room service trays that people had set out after having finished their meal. If there was any food at all left on a tray Stan would take that back to his room and eat it. I guess a half of a steak here and maybe a dish of peas from another room could add up to a meal. I don't know what his pay was for playing bass, but apparently he pinched every penny of it.

♪ ♪ ♪

The *San Francisco Examiner* wrote an article about us to promote our show. We had this meme about entertainment writers for newspapers that they invariably would get some detail in their article twisted. Maybe they would write that George Grove had rendered a great performance of "Scotch and Soda." Uh, no – that was Bob Shane who sang that song. Well, this reporter from the *Examiner* came over to the hotel to interview us and Bob recounted to him about how the group had started right there in San Francisco, hit records, blah, blah, blah. And then finally the reporter wanted to know all of our names. So we each gave our name and spelled it for him and told him what part we sang and what instrument we played. When the article came out the next morning we knew we'd find something amiss, and sure enough, we did. The reporter had all of our names spelled correctly, except for Ben Schubert's. Somehow his had been abbreviated to "Benubert." So Ben got a nickname.

♪ ♪ ♪

We were booked at the Fairmont on another occasion, and we ended up arriving a day early due to a dark date on the schedule. As it turned out Donovan was playing that night in the Venetian Room and we managed to finagle our way into Donovan's second show (we knew the maitre d'). I was a huge Donovan fan and I'd even tried to smoke dried banana skins, as in "Mellow Yellow." That was a myth, I'm sure – at least I derived no high from it.

We had front row seats and Donovan put on a great show. Afterwards he joined us at the bar and Bob decided that we should go down to this club where a guy we'd met on the Norwegian Cruise ship was doing a karaoke show. Donovan wasn't hip to karaoke and so he said he'd like to go with us and check it out. I was really hoping that we could get Bob and Donovan up to do a duet. Well, we got to the bar, and you know how things are – Donovan took one look at the scene and bolted. That was the last we saw of him, but I stuck around and grabbed a karaoke slot to sing "Sunshine Superman" in his place.

Speaking of karaoke, Bob Shane and his wife Bobbie were invited out by friends one night to go to a karaoke bar in Phoenix. Unbeknownst to Bob, his friend signed him up to sing "Scotch and Soda." When, to Bob's surprise, the MC called Bob to the stage, he was kinda pissed about it, but being a good sport he went up and took the mic. He did a classic rendition of his big hit, got a smattering of applause from the drunks at the bar and as he was returning to his seat, the MC thanked him and said, "Wow, that was almost as good as the original." He had no clue!

PERSONNEL CHANGES

In December of 1985, we were playing at Harrah's in Reno when Stan Kaess abruptly left for home. He said his doctor had requested that he return to Denver for some medical testing. It turns out that Stan had cancer. He rejoined us later that month for his final tour, culminating in a New Year's Eve gig in San Diego. He let us know that his condition was terminal and he wouldn't be able to tour with us any further. With tears we said our last goodbyes, and sadly, he passed away a couple of months later. That left a hole in all of our hearts, not to mention a hole in the band.

With dates pending starting in February, we needed to replace Stan. I suggested my friend Cary Black, who had been our bass player in the New Fireside Singers in Seattle. I knew that Cary was qualified and that he knew the repertoire, so without even an audition, Cary joined us for the next tour and remained our bass player for the following two and a-half years.

Finally, in the spring of 1988, Cary felt that he'd had enough of the road, and probably enough of us. He gave notice that he was leaving, but he recommended a replacement. It was another Seattle bassist named Paul Gabrielson. Paul had actually filled in for Cary on a week-long tour in the summer of 1987, so we knew he could do the job. Paul joined us in May of 1988, and he ended up occupying the position of Kingston Trio bassist longer than any other bass player in the group's history.

TV SHOWS

We were often requested (or required) to do local TV shows to promote our performances. That often involved an 8:00 a.m. departure to the studio for a 9:00 a.m. air time. Usually, we would sing one song and do a little interview with the host or hostess. Occasionally we were invited to perform on nationally-aired programs such as the PBS folk music specials or Ralph Emery's *Nashville Now*. Our first appearance on that show was a perfect example of the perils of live television.

We were scheduled to perform Billy Edd Wheeler's *The Reverend Mr. Black*, which featured George on the spoken verses with Bob and me joining in on the choruses. As we were setting up the camera shots and doing sound check, the crew asked if we wanted to have them scroll the lyrics on the teleprompter. George responded, "No, I've done this song hundreds of times and I could do it in my sleep." So when it came time for our spot on the live broadcast, we made it through the first verse and chorus as we had done hundreds of times before, when suddenly George had a serious brain fart. The lyrics were nowhere in his head, so he just started trying to make stuff up, sort of telling the story, but with no rhyme (and very little reason) just to make it to the next chorus. Luckily, the song ends with a rousing chorus with all three of us singing, so at least we finished on a high note.

Then, during the commercial break, we were directed to our seats for the interview. The seating arrangement had the three of us next to each other with Bob at the end of the line next to Ralph. When the red light came on Ralph began the interview, directing question after question to Bob Shane. Bob's one-syllable response to each question: "Yeah." "No." Yeah." "Yeah." "No." And so it went for a good four or five minutes with nary a question directed to George or me. Well, Ralph, sometimes you get what you ask for.

In May of 1986, we were invited to participate in a TV special entitled *America Votes the #1 Hits*. This was a Dick Clark production and he was one of the hosts, along with Barbara Mandrell, Tony Orlando and Frankie Avalon. We were in fine company with an impressive array of #1 hit makers, including Air Supply, Petula Clark, Dawn, Roberta Flack, The Four Tops, Mr. Mister and Frankie Valli. Pretty stiff competition and I have no idea who got the most votes, but it was fun meeting Dick Clark and hanging out with all those major stars.

A LIVE RECORDING

In early 1986, the Trio's management was contacted by Steve Vining of Intersound Productions. He wanted to propose a recording project that would result in a CD release of a live Kingston Trio performance. We had a meeting with him to discuss the details of the project and his main emphasis was on the fact that this recording was going to be "direct to digital." In other words, the audio mix would be done live on-site, and this mix would go straight to a digital file from which the CD copies would be produced. This approach would eliminate several steps in the normal recording process which may unintentionally alter the true sound of our live performance.

So Bob signed the deal and the date was set for the recording. The venue selected was Santa Ana's Crazy Horse Steak House and Saloon. It was a fun place to play and we always drew a good crowd there. The plan was to record our two shows that day and pick the best cuts from both sessions for the album. The recording crew was set up in a back room where they could control the recording mix separate from the house mix. They informed us that, rather than use the regular Shure SM-57 mics that we preferred for our instruments, they wanted us to use some high-tech condenser mics that they assured us would accurately capture the sound of our instruments.

=We did two great shows in front of two different high-energy audiences, and we felt that we had plenty of good material in the can to select from. A few days later we received a preview version of the album with the material they had selected. After giving it a listen we were all very disappointed in the sound quality and the mix. The high-tech mics they had forced on us were very thin sounding and our instruments did not sound as we had hoped. But there was no fixing this "direct to digital" recording, since the mix, including all the individual mic levels and EQs had been set prior to our performance, with a few minor adjustments made for the second show. Bob threw a fit and filed a complaint via a phone conversation with Vining. I wrote a detailed letter itemizing the issues we heard with every instrument and voice, all to no avail. There was no fix it in the mix on this one.

The CD was released with fifteen tracks under the title *The Best of the Best*. Since it was a "direct to digital" representation of our live show, we did sell plenty of them at our CD sales table. Intersound later repackage the recording as *Tom Dooley and Other Hits* with only ten tracks. I don't have any idea about the details of the contract Bob signed for this recording, but I do know I never saw any royalty payments for my contribution.

ON THE ROAD AGAIN

We occasionally played a night club in Chester, New York, called Boodles Opera House. It was a funky little country venue run by Mr. Jarvis Boone. He was a character and he put on his own shows there with his house band. The first time we played there we were a little surprised to find that our contract rider requirements had not been precisely met. Tom Green had detailed specifications as to the kind of drum kit that any particular venue was required to provide. When we arrived for sound check we saw what resembled a drum kit on stage, but it was made out of trash cans. The bass drum looked like a large wash-tub turned on it's side and the tom-toms were actual trash cans with drum heads attached. Tom looked at that drum kit and asked the manager when the real drums would arrive. He was told this was it. It seems that the house drummer had been in an accident and his spine was fused as a result. During his rehab he had put together this special drum set that allowed him to stand up when he played. But Tom Green played seated, like most drummers. Well, sometimes you just have to play with the cards you're dealt.

♪ ♪ ♪

August of 1986 took us on a month-long tour dubbed "The Grand Folk Revival." The Trio shared the bill with Glenn Yarbrough, The Limeliters (sans Glenn) and Melanie Safka. Remember Melanie? Her 1972 number one hit, "Brand New Key" (aka "The Roller Skate Song"), was kind of a novelty song but really put her on the map, selling over three million copies. Her producer/husband, Peter Schekeryk, joined us off and on over the duration of the tour and one day he showed up with some great news for Melanie. It seems that he had successfully negotiated a contract with a toy company to sell her Roller Skate song for use in their national advertising campaign. This did not sit well with Melanie and the sparks flew between the two of them. She viewed her composition as art and the use of the song in a TV commercial was, in her mind, a flagrant abuse of her work. Well, money does talk and apparently Peter had secured a nice financial benefit, so after a few days of fuming, Melanie finally accepted the inevitable.

Touring with Glenn and The Limeliters gave me a chance to really get to know these performers who had impacted my early career development. Glenn had been replaced in the Limes by Red Grammar, who was a fabulous singer and performer, and the group was in top form. Lou Gottlieb kept us in stitches on and off stage with his sophisticated humor while Glenn regaled us with stories from his days sailing the high seas. One of my favorites was his recounting of a layover he had on a small Caribbean island as he awaited favorable winds to cross the Atlantic. Glenn told us that he preferred to sail in the buff when the weather permitted, and he spent his several days on this desert island unclothed. Apparently, a company that flew tourists around the islands for aerial sightseeing excursions had somehow found out about his temporary residence. They began flying daily tours at low altitude over Glenn's encampment, identifying the buck-naked sailor below as the world-famous Glenn Yarbrough. I wonder if any of those tourists have photos!

♪ ♪ ♪

Occasionally we would be forced to deal with the cranky Bob Shane. We had a date in Decatur, Illinois, where we were scheduled to play two shows at an outdoor festival. The 4:00 p.m. show went fine, but the contract specified that Bob was to be paid after that show. The promoter failed to appear with the payment, so Bob went back to the hotel, vowing not to do the second show unless payment was forthcoming within the hour.

George and I were unsure how to handle this, but we felt that Bob could hold to his threat if the promoter reneged on the contract. So George went back over to the festival and found the promoter. He told her of Bob's threat to cancel the second show if she couldn't come up with the payment before that. I'm not sure how she pulled it off, but an hour later she showed up at the hotel with a bag full of cash – mostly ten-

and twenty-dollar bills. George took the bag up to Bob's room, knocked on the door and Bob answered the door in his underwear. When George handed him the bag, he looked at the cash and said, "What am I supposed to do with this?" He then proceeded to throw the bag into the hallway, scattering the thousands of dollars in small bills everywhere. Then he slammed the door and went back to bed.

Well, we had the payment, so technically we were obligated to do the second show. But in the meantime George rallied all of us to join him in the hallway to pick up the cash, count it and get it back in the bag. It took all five of us nearly a half hour to get all the money accounted for and somehow we did convince Bob to join us for the second show.

SYMPHONY CONCERTS

The Kingston Trio performed anywhere from four to half-a-dozen concerts each year with symphony orchestras around the country. George Grove had written scores for eight or nine songs in our repertoire, and I eventually added another three. We interspersed these numbers with non-orchestrated songs to fill out the two-hour show.

Soon after joining the Trio in 1985, we were booked to perform with the Nashville Symphony. As it turned out, it was not quite *with*. When we arrived in Nashville we were informed that the symphony was on strike. Yes, the Nashville Musicians Union Local 257 was not allowing any union symphony players (which was most of them) to perform. Well, we were non-union, we were there to do a show and people had purchased tickets. So we did our part as the symphony members picketed outside the auditorium. How ironic that we actually raised money for the orchestra as they were refusing to perform. We never heard if their effort won them any success with their contractual demands, but they sure didn't score any points with the audience that night.

When I first joined the group, I was informed that each of us would have a solo slot in the show, and Bob allowed us to perform any song of our choosing (with his approval, of course). I chose to do an original tune of mine called "Allergic To Work." It's a comedy song that gets good audience response and Bob liked it. I have a sixteen-bar instrumental solo in the middle of the tune and I'd written a clarinet part for our symphony shows. The first-chair reed player usually pulled the assignment and whenever possible the conductor would arrange for him/her to come forward for the solo.

In July of 1987, we were booked to perform with the San Francisco symphony. The guest conductor for the evening was John Dankworth, and sadly I had no clue about his resume, other than that he was married to Cleo Lane. I had no idea that he was a world-class clarinet player. At rehearsal, when it came time to run through my tune, I called for the first-chair reed man to come up and read my chart. I meant no disrespect to orchestra musicians, most of whom have devoted their lives to learning and performing classical music. But very few have the ability to improvise – they only play what's written on the music sheet. So we ran my tune and the clarinet player dutifully read my chart quite accurately, but with very little emotion.

As we were packing up after the rehearsal, Mr. Dankworth came over to me and asked if I would like to have him play that clarinet solo. I was a little perplexed, because I didn't realize that was his instrument. My reaction was to feel empathy for the poor first-chair reed man who had run the tune at rehearsal, and I wasn't confident about making a last-minute change. So I declined his offer and stuck to the original plan. To this day I kick myself for being so uninformed as to miss such an opportunity. I can only imagine how the audience would have erupted with applause after what would have been a truly amazing addition to my song. Regrets? I have a few...

Another memorable symphony concert was the night we played with the Eugene, Oregon, symphony. Several members of my family still lived in Eugene, including my parents and my younger brother, Sam. Sam's life partner, Dick Trombley, is a flautist and was a professor at the University of Oregon. He also played in the symphony and after our concert, he and Sam threw a small party for us at their home. Among those at the party was Mason Williams, who had come down from his home in nearby Oakridge to attend our concert. Somehow Bob Shane sensed that Mason had a bag of cocaine in his pocket, and he kept pestering Mason all evening about holding out. Mason never relented and Bob finally gave up. We had an early flight the next morning so we said our goodbyes and headed for the hotel. My brother told me later that as soon as we left, Mason pulled out the cocaine and the party lasted until dawn. It's probably a good thing that we left when we did.

We stopped off in Durham, North Carolina, one evening for a concert with the Durham Symphony. Governor James Martin was scheduled to conduct the orchestra's rendition of "Stars and Stripes Forever" that night, and we were in the

Green Room prior to the show when the Governor entered with his entourage. Introductions were made all around and then the Governor turned to Bob Shane (who had remained seated, puffing on a cigarette) and made the following announcement: "I've had three major ambitions in life. One was to become Governor of North Carolina, and I was elected to that position in 1985. Second was to conduct a live symphony orchestra, and I get to do that tonight. And third, to sing a song on stage with The Kingston Trio." Bob blew a lung full of smoke in the Governor's face and responded, "Well, two outa three ain't bad." Classic Bob Shane!

♪ ♪ ♪

One of my favorite symphony stories is one that was told to me when we performed with the North Carolina Symphony in Raleigh. Bob Shane had coerced me into playing a tune on my musical saw in each show, primarily, I'm sure, to give him an opportunity to leave the stage. I had written an arrangement of "America The Beautiful" for symphony and musical saw and every time I performed that with an orchestra it elicited foot stomping and bow-tapping from the musicians. The audience always got a kick out of it too.

Following our afternoon rehearsal with the North Carolina Symphony the conductor cornered me and said he had a story to tell me. It seems that in a previous season the orchestra had programmed a piece of Appalachian folk music arranged for symphony. In the middle of the arrangement was an eight-bar solo for musical saw. The orchestra cast around trying to find someone who played the saw, and they were finally referred to an elderly woman who lived up in the mountains somewhere. (She was not a union member.) They made arrangements to drive her down to Raleigh in time for the afternoon rehearsal, put her up for the evening in a nice hotel and pay her a small fee for her trouble. The rehearsal went well and the conductor was confident of a successful evening performance.

When the program came around to the Appalachian number, they brought the lady out on stage and seated her. Unfortunately, her eight bars of music did not come until about twenty minutes into the piece. It had been a long day for the old gal and as the music played on leading up to her solo she dozed off and slept right through it. I guess with my experience of playing in my sleep at the Bellevue Holiday Inn I could have given her some pointers on how to do that.

GRAMP'S SAW

I'm often asked how I came to play the musical saw, an instrument that resides in the same dark corner of oddball and obscure gizmos as the kazoo and the washtub bass. Well, the story actually starts when I was a young lad. I had the privilege to be the first great-grandchild of my paternal great-grandfather, Samuel Wimmer. Gramp, as we always called him, was a gentle soul who had spent his younger days as a carpenter in Spokane, Washington. I understand that he built many houses in the area during the 1920s and '30s, well before the advent of power tools. By the time I came into his life he had lost his sight due to some degenerative affliction, but he could tell my brothers and me apart just by touching our heads. He also played the piano by feel, and his renditions of the old hymns often filled the air in

Grandma's house. Earlier in his life he had been a member of a drum and bugle corps and his ancient bass drum resided in Grandma's attic. Retired and sightless, he had taken up residence in the back bedroom of Grandma's house, and we saw him regularly.

When Gramp passed away I somehow came into possession of the tool box he had carried from job to job in his carpentry days. There was his old wood-handled hammer, a pair of pliers, a few screw drivers, a beautiful wood plane and a 1920's-vintage Disston cross-cut hand saw, still sharp and serviceable. I often used Gramp's tools for various projects of my own, like the toy chest I built for my son, Graham.

One day I was at a party at a friend's house and his uncle began playing music by running a violin bow across the top side of a hand saw. It was an eerie sound, but I was fascinated that a saw could be used to make music. I watched and listened to this gentleman for about a half hour before finally asking him to show me how he did it. His response was, "Oh, I don't know – it just sorta plays itself." Well, thanks for the free lesson!

So when I got home, I retrieved Gramp's old saw from the garage, grabbed the violin bow from my violin case and set out to learn how to play a saw. "*Screech – scratch – squawk* and *scrumble*" – I couldn't get a note out of the thing. The cats couldn't stand the sound and went next door for several days. After a couple weeks of failed attempts, I finally got a pure note to sing. Then I figured out how to vary the pitch. After a while I found a way to add vibrato by bouncing my knee a bit and eventually, I got to the point of actually playing a whole song.

I've played many different saws over the years, but I've

never found one that sings as sweetly as Gramp's saw, and the reason is the quality of the steel. Vintage saws from the 1920s and '30s have a tendency to produce a more pure sound, while those made from the 1950s on just don't have that same quality. I've also experimented with different bows and I finally settled on a bow that I purchased from the Early Music Store in Boulder, Colorado. It's designed to play a medieval instrument called a psaltery and the shape and length of the bow allow for easy handling.

You don't run across too many people who play this instrument any more, but I have a friend in Denver, Ward Lucas, who had taught himself to play the saw and we began experimenting with playing duets. Ward was a news anchor on Channel 9 in Denver and quite well-known in the area. When the Trio was booked to play a concert at the Paramount Theatre there a few years ago, I invited Ward to join me for a saw duet. We harmonized beautifully that night and I'm sure we were the highlight of the evening.

When Gramp's saw graduated from carpentry tool to musical instrument I decided to have a case made for it. I once tried to take it aboard a plane as a piece of carry-on luggage. When it went through the X-ray machine at the check point, TSA pulled me aside and explained that, despite my contention that it was a musical instrument, it did have the potential of being used as a dangerous weapon. Well, for that matter, so does my banjo!

MERI

True confession time: I was not a model husband while out on the road. (Actually, none of us were.) I often succumbed to the enticements of female fans and Commandment #7 was not on my radar. I was aware that similar abuses of the Commandment were happening at home during my absence, and eventually my first marriage ended in the inevitable divorce.

The catalyst for that split occurred on September 6th, 1987. The Kingston Trio flew into Denver to headline a festival in Lakewood, Colorado, called Lakewood On Parade. We played an afternoon concert in the city park that was packed with folks of all ages, from kids to grandparents. We had a spot in the show at that time where we would ask the audience for requests. People would shout out their favorite Trio hit that we hadn't played yet and we'd oblige one of the requests with that song. When we opened the request line that day we heard calls for "Greenback Dollar," "Tijuana Jail," "MTA," "Wake Up Little Susie." Wait – say what? I looked over at the source of that suggestion and saw a beautiful red-haired woman who obviously had no clue about The Kingston Trio's repertoire. But I couldn't take my eyes off of her for the rest of the concert and I'm sure my horns were showing.

When we finished the show, the promoter asked us to do a meet-and-greet over by the ice cream truck and I had my eyes peeled for the red-headed lady who thought we were the Everly Brothers. And then – there she was. I introduced myself and joked with her about her request. She told me her name was Meri – spelled M-E-R-I, the Irish way. Well, that explains the red hair, I thought. We chatted a bit, and then I asked her if she would join us at a party we'd been invited to at a local restaurant. At first she declined and I was really disappointed. But as we were packing up, she came back over to our trailer and said, yes, she'd love to come along. But she needed to stop by her house first and check on her daughters.

So we all piled into the limo for a short drive to an upscale neighborhood. As we pulled into the driveway of a huge home, Meri turned to me and said, "I wish my oldest daughter was home – I'd really like to introduce her to you." I was a little surprised by her comment and I asked her, "How old do you think I am?" She said, "Well, my daughter's in her twenties and I think you're about her age." "Meri," I said, "I'm forty." Her response: "Oh shit – I'm in trouble." I took that as a surprisingly positive reply since she was still intent on going to the party with us.

Meri invited us all in while she checked on her two younger daughters. It was a beautiful home and we were all quite impressed that a single mom would have the wherewithal to own such an amazing piece of real estate. Back in the limo, I was now even more fascinated with this obviously very successful and beautiful woman. When we arrived at the party, we started to get to know each other. We danced (badly), had some drinks and I had a sense that the evening was just beginning. And sure enough – I chalked up another one-night stand. Or so I thought.

As we flew out of Denver to the next stop on our itinerary, I couldn't get Meri off my mind. I was starting to think I'd fallen in love. I felt like a high school kid discovering heart-throb for the first time. Garth Brooks had just released a song called "Baby Blue" and it became my "Meri" song: "Baby blue was the color of her eyes. Baby blue, like the Colorado skies..." Yeah, that was Meri. And I couldn't wait to see her again.

Later that month we had a two-week engagement at the Fairmont Hotel in Dallas, so I arranged for Meri to join me there. But leave it to Bob Shane to try to horn in. When he saw Meri and me in the lobby, he came right over and, looking directly at Meri's chest, said, "I remember you from Denver. What's she doin' with you, Haworth? I saw her first." And before Bob could progress to the next line: "Can I take you upstairs and..." I ushered Meri into the elevator and out of harm's way. Yes, this was definitely turning out to be more than a one-night stand.

NATIONAL QUAIL HUNT

In December of 1987, we found ourselves in Enid, Oklahoma, at the invitation of the Grand National Quail Club. This was their annual gathering of hunters from all over the country and even from across the Atlantic. It was four days of skeet shooting, quail and turkey hunting and partying. Besides The Kingston Trio, other celebrities attending included Roy Clark, Tennessee Ernie Ford and Grampa Jones.

I'd never owned a gun in my life and obviously, this event required that I have one. So Bob gave me one of his shotguns and I could only hope that everybody would stay out of my way when I had this thing in my hands. The first day we were in Enid, I got some training on firearm usage. Then it was over to the skeet range for some total embarrassment. I racked up the lowest score of all the attendees that weekend.

Over the next couple of days we were each paired up with another hunter to go out and try to shoot some quail. I'm sure the quail were not worried about my marksmanship, but I think my partner was happy for my ineptitude. It seems that when I fired my gun at a bevy of quail in the brush, it scared the birds into flight, giving my partner a clear target. So between the two of us I guess we proved to be a good team. On the last day of the event, we went out looking for turkeys, which are a much bigger target than quail. Somehow I managed to bag one, although it is possible that my hunting partner actually shot it and let me take credit.

The highlight of the event for me was the evenings. After a long day out in the fields we'd gather after dinner in the lobby of the hotel and the guitars would come out. Try to picture The Kingston Trio singing "Greenback Dollar" with Roy Clark playing back-up. And sitting right next to Tennessee Ernie Ford as he gave us a rendition of "Sixteen Tons" just gave me goosebumps. It was one of the perks of being a Kingston Trio member to be accepted into this elite circle as an equal.

ATLANTIC CITY

In early 1988, we took a contract for a four-week sit-down gig at the Atlantis Hotel in Atlantic City. Wow – a month on the Atlantic seashore in the middle of winter! Well, it was a month of work, so that was a good thing. Although I'm pretty sure Bob Shane lost a chunk of his paycheck at the blackjack tables.

We did two shows a night, 6:00 and 8:00 p.m., which allowed for us to catch some of the night life up and down the Boardwalk. Scanning the entertainment calendar one day, I saw that John McEuen was performing at one of the other casinos. As a long-time Nitty Gritty Dirt Band fan, I had to catch that show. So after our second performance, I talked the guys into joining me and we all headed over to see McEuen's late show.

This was a solo gig for John, although he had a five-piece band backing him. The band was Runaway Express, from Denver. John did a fantastic show and the band was a perfect compliment to his musical dexterity. After the show we all hung around to meet John and the band. Jim and Salli Ratts headlined the Runaway Express and from that night on, we became fast friends. Out of curiosity, realizing that they were from Denver, I asked if by chance they knew a woman in Lakewood named Meri who owned a printing company. Salli's friend Marci, who had flown out from Denver to see the band, responded, "Oh Meri from Cedar Park Printing. Yeah, I know her." Small world!

Jim was also a huge Kingston Trio fan and meeting Bob Shane was a big deal for him. He started hanging out at the bar with Bob and really got to know him over the next few days. One day he showed up and told Bob he'd written a song for him. The song was "Every Inch of the Way," with a lyric that encapsulated Bob's life as an entertainer and a Calypso musical feel reminiscent of the Kingston Trio's early days. Bob later recorded that song at Jim's studio in Denver.

♪ ♪ ♪

One day Bob told us that The Smothers Brothers were in town and Tommy had called and invited us to their late show. Over the years we were double-billed many times with the SmoBros and I never tired of their show. Even the same old jokes cracked me up every time I heard them. But on this occasion, The Smos had brought along a special guest – The Great Flydini, aka Steve Martin.

Steve had been one of the writers on the Smothers Brothers TV show, and he had invented this bizarre act where he would extract a wacky array of items from the zipper fly in his pants. Thus, The Great Flydini. He wore a coat with one fake arm, allowing his real arm to feed things like a telephone, a fry pan, a pineapple, and other odd-ball items out through his wide-open fly. Where he had them stored is a mystery, but each item he pulled out elicited uproarious laughter.

After the show, we were in the dressing room when Steve began writing a comedy bit for the Smos. The concept was that Dick had quit the act and Tommy was going out as The Smother Brother. Steve would write a line and then instruct Tommy to allow about fifteen seconds for the audience to respond before continuing with the skit. Everything was precisely timed for effect. It was quite an amazing process to watch and only served to elevate my admiration for this amazing talent. Steve Martin is not only one of the funniest men on the planet and a talented actor, but he can also play circles around most banjo players.

THE KINGSTON TRIO FREE FOOD DIET PLAN

Traveling the way we did allowed for very little sense of routine in our lives. Every day was different. The week-long sit-down gigs at the Fairmont and some of the casinos around the country did provide time to explore the town, hit the gym or the pool and eat meals on a regular schedule. But the daily grind on the road often had us grabbing a meal on the run from Wendy's and then maybe a Little Debbie's pastry before bedtime.

At one point, George and I looked at each others' growing bellies and vowed to get serious about losing some weight. We determined that our enemies were fast food and room service. So we made a pact that on the next few tours we would only eat free food. Certainly this would reduce our caloric intake and result in some weight loss.

So the next tour out we kept to our agreement and only ate the free meal in first class on the plane. Then there was the free food at happy hour at the hotel. Of course, the dressing room at the venue came equipped with trays of munchies, all at no cost. After two tours of sticking to our free-food regimen, we were both shocked to discover that rather than lose weight, we each gained five pounds that month. So much for The Kingston Trio Free Food Diet Plan.

WINTHROP ROCKEFELLER, JR.

The popularity of The Kingston Trio spanned all social strata. Most of the fans that we met at our shows were just regular middle class folks, and Bob Shane bonded easily with them, as did the rest of us. But occasionally we found ourselves hobnobbing with the upper crust and sometimes those encounters were heavily influenced by the "Mr. Bob Effect." One of the wackiest of these soirees was a booking we had in Arkansas at the ranch of Winthrop Rockefeller, Jr., who was the son of former Arkansas Governor, Winthrop Rockefeller, Sr. The Kingston Trio had been invited surreptitiously by Mrs. Rockefeller, to surprise her husband at his birthday party. The reason, we were told, was that the Trio had always been Win's favorite musical group.

We flew into Little Rock and were met in grand fashion by

the Rockefeller's private limousine service. They drove us quite a distance out of town to a beautiful agrarian complex on top of a well-placed hill overlooking the rolling Arkansas landscape. We entered the grounds and were driven to a section of buildings that was, in actuality, a private motel. We each had our own room, and the accommodations were on a par with any Holiday Inn.

About 7:00 someone picked us up and drove us to the conference hall, where the party was in progress, with about 100 people in attendance. (Bob Shane claimed, years later, that Bill and Hillary Clinton were there, but we weren't tuned in to who they were at the time.) We came in through the kitchen (welcome to show biz) and, at the appropriate moment, we took the stage and did our show. Win was duly surprised and elated at having his favorite group give him a private concert, and a great time was had by all.

After the show we were all invited up to the main house for cocktails. The main house sat at the very top of the hill with a commanding view of the entire countryside. The interior was all oak paneling and antique furniture, decorated in a southern genteel style. At one point a few of us found ourselves in the study with the birthday boy. He went over to the bookcase and picked up a beautiful hand-tooled leather case. He opened it up and extracted an exquisitely crafted throwing ax, wrapped carefully in a soft flannel cloth to protect it from scratches. He explained that this was a numbered art piece produced by some well-known ax-grinder and was probably worth a couple thousand bucks. We all admired it carefully, taking care not to leave any fingerprints on the gleaming stainless steel blade.

Bob Shane took his turn with it and grabbing it by the handle, made a motion to throw it. Luckily, he didn't let go, but I think a few hearts stopped for an instant. In response Win said, "Would you like to go outside and throw some functional throwing axes?" Of course our machos kicked in and we all said, "Let's go."

Win grabbed a couple of his kids and a ranch hand and we went out behind the house to this big field. The ranch hand drove up in a hay truck and put the headlights on high beam, illuminating a huge stump of a tree turned on its side. They brought out five or six axes similar to the one we'd been admiring in the house, but these were well-worn with many a throw under their belts. We took turns throwing these axes at the stump until we all got thirsty and decided to go back inside.

As the party was winding down, Bob announced to our host that, since we had an early flight, we should probably head back to our quarters. Win went into his study and came back out with the leather case containing the numbered art piece throwing ax. With great ceremony and awe-filled thanks for years of the best music in the world, he gave it to Bob Shane as a memento of their meeting. We were all kind of drop-jawed, but Bob accepted the gift gracefully and we said our goodbyes.

When we got back to the lodging compound, Bob invited us all into his room for a drink before bed. We were all sitting around laughing about some of the hoi-polloi we'd just been hanging with, when Bob pulled out his gift from our host, opened the case and unwrapped the beautifully hand-crafted numbered art-piece throwing ax. He kind of looked it over for a minute, admiring the craftsmanship, and then all of a sudden he just flung it at the wall. It was a good hit and the blade buried itself in the drywall about two inches. We all sat there in shock for an instant and then we just erupted in cheers and laughter. Someone pulled it out of the wall and tossed it across the room into the opposite wall. Then we each had a turn with it and by the time we were ready for bed, Bob's room was pretty much shredded wheat.

The next morning we were met bright and early by the private limousine service and they drove us back to the Little Rock airport. When we got into the waiting room inside the terminal someone asked Bob where the ax was. He said, "Oh, I left it in the limo." Huh???!!!

So, to summarize, we had come to the Winthrop Rockefeller estate as heroes and had been honored with a very valuable personal gift as a measure of Mr. Rockefeller's appreciation for our artistry. As thanks, we destroyed his property and then rudely left his now ruined and value-less numbered art-piece throwing ax in his private limousine for him to find. Do I need to mention that we never played in Arkansas again?

BILL MOREHEAD EVENT

At 6:45 a.m. on July 9, 1988, Paul Gabrielson and I left Seattle aboard Delta Flight 372, bound for Cincinnati. Long-time Kingston Trio fan and close friend, Bill Morehead, had booked us to perform for a corporate event that he was hosting at the Kenwood Country Club. We did a great show for them that evening and Bill got lots of compliments for booking us.

We had a day off the next day before traveling on to Long Island and Bill promised us a night on the town as a special "thank-you" for making him a hero. Around 6:00 p.m., we all met in the lobby of the hotel to board the limo that Bill had reserved for the evening. After we were all on board, our driver, Don, announced that he had another fare to pick up and transport before we could hit the town. He assured us that it would only take about fifteen minutes.

We drove to an up-scale shopping center and pulled up in front of Macy's where a couple of octogenarian women were waiting for their ride home. Don got out and explained to the ladies that he had another fare, specifically The Kingston Trio. He assured them that there was still room for them and he would take them straight to their destination.

It was apparent that the women were a little put off by this change of circumstances, but they had no other means of transportation, so they reluctantly climbed into the back seat next to Bob Shane. Bob immediately went to work on them with the intent of shattering any sense of decency. Offering them a joint he'd just lit, he opened with, "Here, take a hit of this – it's really good shit." Then straight into "Huh, why don't you show us your tits?" It all went downhill from there and the poor gals were duly mortified. Fortunately, the ride to their residence took less than ten minutes, although I'm sure it was like an eternity for them. We didn't hear their comment to Don as he assisted their exit from the limo, but you can bet it wasn't complimentary.

Our friend, Bill, had an itinerary planned for the evening and off we went on a tour of Cincinnati nightlife. After our stop at about the third watering hole we were all pretty well liquored and Bob's earlier improprieties began to look like child's play. I discovered the sunroof in the rear of the limo and asked Don to please open it. Why he complied, I have no idea, because now we had a whole 'nother view of the world. We were whoopin' and hollerin' and wavin' to folks as if we were in a parade. At one point a moon even appeared over the sunroof. Hello, Cincinnati!

Well, as the song says, "Ain't no such thing as too much fun." But we sure pushed the limit that night. We rolled back to the hotel around midnight, not even ruing the hangovers we were destined to enjoy in the morning. And morning did arrive with the obligation to head on to the next show. Bill Morehead had arranged for the same limo company to drive us to the airport and as we were loading our luggage, we noticed that a different driver was at the wheel. We asked why Don wasn't driving us and the new driver responded, "Don came in this morning and quit." Hmmm...I wonder what could have prompted that?

RENO AND LAS VEGAS

Bob Shane approached everything he did with gusto. His guitar strumming was loud and forceful, resulting in occasional broken strings in the middle of a song. He had developed a knack for grabbing a spare string from his back pocket, quickly removing the broken one, restringing with the new one, tuning it and jumping right back into the song. This always resulted in amazed applause from the audience. Well, George had mastered this trick before I joined the group (although it's impossible to restring a banjo in under a minute) and I quickly realized that I, too would need to carry a pack of spares.

In April of 1988, we were booked for a two-week engagement at Harrah's in Reno and Meri had flown in from Denver to join me. Our relationship was getting pretty serious at that point and we would occasionally arrange to meet up for a few days somewhere out on the road. Meri enjoyed attending our shows at Harrah's and one night she joined a table of fans right in front of center stage. We came out playing hard and heavy on "Hard Ain't It Hard" and Shane immediately broke a string. Quick change – applause – on with the show. Next up, "Three Jolly Coachmen" and I broke a string. Well before long, George joined in with a broken guitar string and we looked down on the stage in front of Shane and there was a pile of money there. Turns out Meri and the gang at the front table had started a betting pool on which one of us would break the next string. Only in Nevada.

There was something about that Harrah's gig that brought out the wackiness in us. George was doing a song as his solo number about "Jocko The Clown and the Trapeze Lady." The gist of the story line is that a fire breaks out in the circus tent and the trapeze lady (who Jocko secretly loves) is stuck in the rigging with no way to get down. So he climbs up and finds a rope to swing out to her on. She grabs the rope and slides down to safety, but as Jocko is sliding down the rigging gives way and he crashes to the ground. George takes a dramatic pause there, which on one night became a little more dramatic. Just as Jocko was hitting the sawdust, I created a loud thud backstage. Whatever I used to make the thud then rolled across the back of the stage, sending the audience into uproarious laughter and ruining the somber mood of the song. Well, of course revenge was in order, so during my solo, George broke the mood by rolling a grand piano across the stage behind me. Then he and I decided to pull one on Shane, so during "Scotch & Soda," George and I did a bit of ballroom dancing across the back of the stage. The audience thought that was hilarious, but Bob never saw us, so he didn't have a clue what they were laughing about.

Harrah's had put us up at the Ramada Inn for the duration of our gig and It turns out that Meri and I caused an evacuation of the hotel one night. Fortunately, we were never busted and we never confessed to our crime. What happened was, we had lit a little mood candle on the bedstand. It seemed like an innocent thing to do to enhance a romantic evening. But apparently there was just enough smoke emanating from the tiny flame to set off the fire alarm in our room. Well, somehow that set off the entire hotel and we were instructed over a loudspeaker to exit the building. There we all were out in the parking lot in our pajamas waiting for the all-clear, which finally came. The next night George made an issue of telling the audience about our late-night rendezvous in the parking lot of the Ramada Inn. Somehow he had obtained information that the alarm was set off by "some stupid guest with a candle in their room." Well, that was us, but we were never outed.

♪ ♪ ♪

A few months later we had a week at The Four Queens Hotel in Las Vegas. This had been a frequent stop for us over the years and we always had a good time there. Bobbie Childress was the maître d' for the showroom, and of course Bobbie being a woman, and Bob Shane being Bob Shane, he took notice of her. It eventually got serious and Bob and Bobbie were finally married in 2000.

I've never been much of a gambler, pretty much sticking

to the penny slots when I could find them. And there was very little else to do in Vegas during the day, so I was really happy when Meri decided to fly in from Denver for a few days of extra-marital dalliance. Of course all of us musicians had rooms at the Four Queens, but Meri had previously stayed and played and apparently spent a chunk of money at the Tropicana Hotel, way down the strip. She was offered a suite to stay there for the week and hopefully, in their minds, drop some more cash. Well, forget my room at the Four Queens, Meri's suite had a jacuzzi, a full bar, and a nice balcony, and not to mention – her!

Meri invited the entire group to enjoy her plush digs and one day we were sitting out by the pool with George. He began to ask some odd questions, like, "What would you do if you weren't in the Trio anymore?" Questions that were couched in idle speculation but to Meri and me, had an overtone of a change in the wind. And sure enough, a few weeks later we were playing up in Wyoming when Shane called me into his room after the show. He informed me that Nick Reynolds had been wanting to rejoin The Trio, and Bob had finally made the decision to bring him back on board. Meri and I had driven up to Wyoming from a gig in Colorado Springs the night before, and our drive back to Denver the next day was gloomy, to say the least.

Looking at this development from a business perspective, I couldn't fault Bob. Having two original members in the group was sure to command more interest from buyers as well as audience members, and possibly generate more income. And since I was a big fan of Nick's, I certainly couldn't hold a grudge against him for stealing my gig. I'd had a good run with the group but now...what's next?

Big changes were in store for me, that's for sure. My marriage to my first wife was definitely over, although it took some time for the divorce to be final. In the meantime, Meri flew out to help me pack up my life on Vashon Island and, along with Graham, we headed to Colorado to start a new chapter. Meri and I were finally married on September 6, 1990, three years to the day after our first encounter. But it took some time for me to regain my footing after losing my gig with The Kingston Trio.

The Kingston Trio promo photo.

Marquee at The Palomino for a Kingston Trio gig on the 4th of November, 1985.

"Back to Back" is my favorite photo of Shane and me. This was taken at the Palomino Club by long-time Trio fan, John August Lee.

The Trio with Tom Paxton.

The garbage can drum kit provided us at the Boodles Opera House in Chester, New York.

I may not have bagged many quail during the International Quail Hunt, but I did mangage to get this turkey on the last day of hunting.

Quail hunting with Tennessee Ernie ford (*top*) and Roy Clark (*bottom*) in Enid, Oklahoma.

Poster for the show in the
Fairmont Hotel's Venetian Room.

CHAPTER EIGHT

Life in Colorado: Part One

CONTEMPLATING AN UNCERTAIN FUTURE, I found myself in a state of depression, so I sought out counseling. I immersed myself in learning typesetting so I could help out with Meri's printing business. I was reluctant to totally abandon my music career, but Denver was a new market for me and I knew it would take time to establish myself.

Sadly, our neighbor across the back fence passed away and her husband asked me to sing at her funeral. The ceremony was held at Concordia Lutheran Church in Lakewood, and it turned out that we had several neighbors and customers of Meri's who were members there. I had a sense that God was reaching out to me after many years of being a prodigal son. Meri and I became members of the church and I definitely felt the power of the Gospel resonating in me. After attending Concordia for a couple years, I was invited to assume the role of worship team leader, directing the music for our Sunday services. Here was an opportunity to use my God-given talents in a very positive and rewarding way. My renewed relationship with Christ put me back on track emotionally and I found my way out of the doldrums of despair from losing, at least temporarily, my sense of purpose, not to mention my source of income.

Another major factor in my rehabilitation was the support I received from fans everywhere. While Nick's return to The Kingston Trio was celebrated by all, I heard from many people that they felt I had contributed in a positive way to the continuity of the group. One of my staunchest supporters was Mike Kavanagh, a highly regarded radio personality at WSB Radio in Atlanta. Mike had a weekly program called "Money Matters" which dealt with...well, money matters. He had a solid background in financial planning and he enjoyed sharing his knowledge.

Mike was also a huge Kingston Trio fan and had even booked us for an event once. When Mike heard that I had been "replaced," he was so upset that he sent back a whole collection of CDs that he had recently ordered from the Kingston Trio website. He reached out to me and offered to assist in any way to help me rebuild my career. He felt I needed a website to promote myself, so he took it upon himself to build one for me. Although we never signed a formal contract and no money ever changed hands, we both considered him to be my business manager and his continued support lasted until his untimely death in 2008.

Eventually, I began to find work in the local club scene. As a solo, I felt the need to enhance my performances with some additional accompaniment, so I invested in a Roland keyboard sequencer. I spent many hours producing backing tracks that I used in my shows. It was time-consuming work, but it did pay off. I was calling my act "The Fabulous Bo Mooney Show," reviving my stage name from the Seattle days. But I was still missing the camaraderie of working with live performers, so I decided to hire two female singers to flesh out my show.

Adding "The Luna Chicks" definitely elevated my show to another level. The original Luna Chicks (there were later incarnations) were Angie Belden and Shawn Cornish, two good friends who were involved in local theater productions. They were both good singers who understood my concept of incorporating a theatrical element to compliment the music. At great expense, we had costumes custom designed for the ladies and every song was choreographed and enhanced with props. I was fortunate to know a printer, as the promotional pieces we designed would have cost a bundle at retail prices. Every effort was made to promote this show on a highly professional level, and that did result in some nice gigs.

In 1990, Colorado legalized gambling and the mountain towns of Central City and Black Hawk became our local Las Vegases. Meri acquired the printing accounts for several of the new casinos and that kept us pretty busy. We pulled a few all-nighters getting print jobs out and delivered, but we were happy for the business. As Meri got to know the various casino managers, she began promoting our show for their entertainment stages. We did quite a bit of work in various casinos, and that eventually involved adding some personnel to the band. My son, Graham, played drums with us for a while and we also added a bass player, fiddle, keyboard and steel guitar, shifting our repertoire focus to covering the country music hits of the time. Try as I might, I never could master that little voice crack thing that Garth Brooks does.

We were riding pretty high on that concept and decided that we needed a video to promote the show. A friend recommended a local video production company, and we staged a shoot in front of a live audience at a local club. Despite the fact that our friend was able to get us a substantial discount on the production, it was still a pricey endeavor. But the final edit came out well and proved to be a good sales tool for us. Even so, I don't think we broke even on that project, considering the overhead of paying a seven-piece band. But it sure was fun!

THE LIMO

On Easter morning 1991, Meri was reading the Denver newspaper and happened on a classified ad for a 1985 Lincoln stretch limousine. I'm not sure why she felt we needed a limo in the family, but it did prove to be a novel investment. It was fun to roll up to one of my Denver gigs in a stretch limo, even if I was the driver. And the customers at Meri's printing company were quite impressed one day when I drove into the parking lot, parked the limo and opened the back door (chauffeur style) for our dog Krypto to exit.

We had no intention of starting a limousine service, but we did hire out on one occasion. Pink Floyd came to Denver in June of 1994, to play a concert at Mile High Stadium. Apparently every limo in Denver was booked for that night and out of the blue I got a call from some record producer (that's how he identified himself) from LA. He was asking – no, he was begging – to rent our limo to take some Denver friends to the show. He was quite desperate and said he'd called every limo company in town and somehow he'd gotten my number as a last resort. So Meri came up with a hefty fee, to which he agreed, and I ended up driving him and a car load of his obviously very impressed friends to the concert. He offered me a ticket to the show, but I was concerned about leaving the limo unattended in the parking lot with the other 500 or so limos that had been booked for this event. So I stayed in the car with the windows down and actually enjoyed the Pink Floyd show at a very reasonable volume level.

♪ ♪ ♪

I opened for the duo of John McEuen and Jimmy Ibbotson, of Nitty Gritty Dirt Band fame, at one of the mountain casinos one night, and after the show John was wondering how he was going to get to the airport the next day for his flight out. I said, "John, we own a limousine and I'd be very happy to drive you to the airport – no charge." John, being John, asked me a bunch of detailed questions about the age, description and condition of the vehicle, thinking, I suppose, that I might be duping him into a ride in some jalopy. I assured him that it was a legitimate stretch limo and when I showed up the next day to pick him up, he was pleasantly surprised and appreciative of the ride. As I was assisting him with his luggage at the airport, I was thinking maybe…? But no, no tip.

♪ ♪ ♪

We had purchased a ten-foot utility trailer to haul the lights, sound, props and other equipment for our show. It was quite a sight when we hooked that up to the back of the limo and drove off. Meri had booked The Fabulous Bo Mooney Show on a week-long tour around the state, and we arrived at each show in grand style. One of our stops was in Craig, where we were booked for their local summer festival. The kids were all agog at our limo/trailer combo and they gathered around to watch as we unloaded and set up. Meri had an idea to let them all take turns sitting in the back seat and watching TV. So she formed a line and had the kids enter on the starboard side, four at a time, sit and watch the tube for a couple minutes and then exit on the port side while the next four kids took a turn. It was probably the best entertainment for kids that Craig had ever had.

♪ ♪ ♪

KOOL-105, the oldies radio station in Denver, put on a big concert every year at Mile High Stadium. One year the show featured The Mamas and The Papas, America, The Beach Boys and Jan and Dean. The Trio had worked many times with a California promoter named Bill Hollingshead, and it just so happened that Jan and Dean had hired him on as their manager. I called Bill to see if we could get tickets to the show, and instead, he gave us backstage passes. We called Shawn, the Luna Chick, and invited her to drive us in our limo to the show. When we arrived at the backstage entrance we were met at the gate by a nice young man named Tyrone. We showed him our pass and he opened the gate to allow our limo to enter. Of course, if we had driven up in a Honda Civic I'm sure we would have been directed to another parking area, but no, it was, "Just drive your limo right on up to Jan and Dean's trailer if you would please."

We had front row seats, but we spent a lot of time back stage talking with many of the performers. Of course, we had to say "hi" to John Phillips and also Spanky McFarlane, who had taken over for Cass Elliot. She gave me a big reunion hug, remembering a couple shows The Kingston Trio had done with them a few years earlier. We were standing right by the stage when the Beach Boys came off and Mike Love looked at me and said, "Kingston Trio – thanks for giving us that song about the Sloop John B." Wow – turns out I was more recognizable than I had ever imagined.

As we were chatting with Jan and Dean after the show, Dewey, Dan and Gerry of the band America, came over and introduced themselves. They saw our limo and asked who it belonged to. We identified ourselves as the owners and we offered to chauffer them back to their hotel. As the three of them plus their whole band piled into the back, Shawn handed me the keys and asked if I would drive so she could ride in the back with all those guys. Before we were even out the gate a chorus of "A Horse With No Name" broke out and we all sang along as we headed for their hotel.

Tyrone, the young man who had been manning the back-stage gate that night, had taken a shine to our limo. He told us that he would watch it while we enjoyed the show and it was obvious that he was fantasizing about driving it. As we were loading up to leave, he handed Meri his phone number and said that he'd bc happy to drive for us any time. His dream came true a few weeks later when we called and invited him to drive us to one of my shows. From that point on he became our regular driver and he took on the responsibility as if the limo were his own.

♪ ♪ ♪

My thirtieth high school class reunion was scheduled for July of 1995, and we were thinking it might be fun to show up in our limo. We asked Tyrone if he would like to go to Oregon with us and he was all in. He said he'd never been west of the Rockies and he was thrilled with the invitation. The drive out to Oregon from Denver is two days at best, and Meri couldn't afford the extra time away from her printing business. So we arranged for Tyrone to drive alone out to Oregon and we would fly out in a couple of days to meet up with him. Amazingly, it all worked out and we drove up to my reunion in style, only to be outdone by one of my classmates, John Case, who owns a limousine service in Portland. He showed up in a classic 1965 (our graduation year) Lincoln stretch that put our '85 stretch to shame. Still, we had a great time and I had a chance to reunite with John Eads and entertain our class with some tunes from The Kinsmen.

Since Tyrone had never seen the ocean, we decided to take a day and drive to the coast. The weather was perfect for a beach run and we ended up renting some dune buggies before heading back to Medford for our flight home. Two days later Tyrone showed up with our limo, having washed and detailed it after the long trip. Well, all good things come to an end, and after enjoying that car for a good five years and several thousand miles, we sold it for exactly what we'd paid for it. What a fun toy it was!

THE DENVER FOLK MUSIC SCENE

Denver, being a large metropolitan area with a diverse

population, featured an amazing variety of entertainment venues. On any given weekend night you could find a place to enjoy jazz, rock, punk, Goth, Latin, country and even folk music. Swallow Hill Music was Denver's folk music mecca, and they presented concerts by both local and national recording artists. One evening Tom Paxton invited me on stage there to harmonize with him on "Bottle Of Wine."

Just down the street from Swallow Hill was Denver's premier acoustic music store, the Denver Folklore Center. Owned and operated by Harry Tuft, the Folklore Center was the gathering place for local folkies and I dropped plenty of money into Harry's cash register over the years.

One day when I was hanging out there sampling some Deering banjos, Harry asked me to come over and meet a fellow who had just walked into the store. It was Walt Conley, a local legend who had jumped on the folk music bandwagon back in 1958. We hit off immediately and became good friends.

After a gig at Sheabeen's Irish Pub in Aurora one evening, I sat down with Walt for some beer and conversation. He was recounting his early days booking entertainment for Denver's Satire Lounge. It was 1960, and one of the first acts he booked there was a duo he'd met in Aspen, The Smothers Brothers. And an as-yet-unknown local singer named Judy Collins also performed there regularly.

Well, one night Walt had the Smothers Brothers on stage for two shows and in walks this scruffy kid with a guitar case. He introduced himself to Walt as Bob Zimmerman (later to be known as Bob Dylan) and he asked if Walt would let him do a set between the SmoBro's shows. So, Walt let him play a few tunes and nobody was much impressed with him. But he decided to hang around Denver for awhile and he begged Walt to let him sleep on his couch. Bob was looking for gigs in the Denver area and Walt landed him a booking at a sleezy bar in Central City called the Guilded Garter. (It's gone now, but I actually played there a couple of times.)

One night Walt got a call from the owner of the Guilded Garter telling him that Bob Z. had stolen some money from her purse as he was leaving after his gig. She knew that Bob was still sleeping on Walt's couch so she asked him to get her money back. When Bob got "home" Walt confronted him about the theft. He finally confessed and coughed up the stolen cash, but Walt said – that's it – you're outa here. He told Bob to go get a room downtown at some flea-bag cheap hotel.

Walt and his roommate, Dave Hamil, had a duo at the time and one night they went out for a gig. When they got home later they noticed that about half of Dave's record collection was missing. They immediately homed in on Bob Z. as the culprit and they went down to the hotel to confront him. When they knocked on the door of his room he didn't answer but apparently he'd peeped thru the peep hole and saw who was at the door. Well, Walt and Dave went back downstairs and as they walked out of the lobby, they heard this "plop-plop-plop" sound coming from the alley around the corner. So they followed sound and saw Bob Z. three floors up throwing all the stolen albums out the window to avoid being busted. Oops! Busted he was. They called the cops, collected the stolen albums and suggested that Bob hit the road. Which he did, only to eventually return to Denver as a big star!

RECORDING, PRINTING AND SHUTTERS, OH MY!

I had done a lot of songwriting over the years and after relocating to Colorado, I felt I had enough decent material to record an album. I contacted Jim Ratts and arranged to hire him to record my tunes. Jim was in the process of moving to a new house and he was often unavailable to act as recording engineer, but he trusted me with his equipment. He allowed me to come in and work on my project when he was otherwise occupied, and I actually recorded a lot of the vocal tracks on my own. The final product was released on cassette in 1989 under the title *Home Made – A Baker's Dozen*. There were thirteen original tunes, but alas, none made it to the airwaves.

Since I wasn't on the road at this point, I spent a lot of time helping Meri with her businesses. I did design work for the printing company and I often worked the counter at both her copy center and the shipping and packaging company. As if that wasn't plenty of business to take care of, through an odd set of circumstances, we acquired a shutter and blinds company. Meri had ordered shutters from a company that was a printing customer of hers, and the owner fell on hard times, leaving us and other customers without the product that we had ordered. Meri, being the consummate business person, felt she could resurrect this company and fulfill the delinquent orders. Jumping in with both feet, I learned how to measure windows and order shutters and blinds to fit. We hired an experienced installer who taught me that trade and I embarked on a whole new career.

One afternoon I was measuring windows for shutters in a home and my attention was drawn to a very nice acoustic guitar that was on a stand in the family room. I asked the owner if I could play it and it turned out to be a Stuart Mossman Great Plains model with excellent tone. The owner indicated that he was considering selling it, so my interest was piqued. I told Meri about it and we discussed the economics of adding another guitar to my collection, which we determined was not in the cards at that time. Well, Fathers' Day arrived a couple weeks later, and Meri surprised me with a very special gift. It turns out she had negotiated with our shutter customer to accept the guitar as part of the payment on his order. And what a gift that turned out to be! To this day that Mossman is my everyday working guitar and to be honest, it is very comparable in tone and playability to my Yamaha L-53 and my Martin HD-28.

Stuart Mossman left Martin Guitars to start his own company in Kansas. He developed his own designs and bracing techniques and his guitars were highly regarded in the boutique market. Bob Shane knew Mossman well and they often shared a bindle when they got together. At one point Bob ordered a custom guitar from him and the specs of the order included a secret compartment in the heal, accessed through the fingerboard, that was just the right size to hold a vial of cocaine. To hide this stash hole, Bob had Mossman install a removable vintage Hawaiian coin as a cover. It was not only a very beautiful and playable instrument, but more importantly, it served as an effective way to transport Bob's stash.

♪ ♪ ♪

Bob O'Luney's Amazing One-Man Band put on some miles during this period. I was booked most every summer to play at the Parades of Homes, the homebuilders association's annual showcase. I played at shopping malls, birthday parties and even in the parking lot as fans were coming into the arena for a Colorado Avalanche hockey game. I also played quite often at Elitch Gardens Amusement Park and I once did a seven-hour stint at the Denver Zoo. I went straight to the chiropractor after that gig. Occasionally our golden retriever, Krypto, would accompany me. He was famous all over town as a singing dog, responding to my harmonica playing with a soulful howl, quite often in tune with me!

♪ ♪ ♪

October 9, 1996, was a landmark day for me. It was my fiftieth birthday and, while I still claim every birthday is my twenty-eighth, this one, I guess, had to be acknowledged as a milestone. Meri, ever the discreet party planner, had organized a huge event behind my back. She arranged for some friends to invite me on a hike in the morning while she staged the party. When I got home from our hike I was met at the gate by fifty or more friends and neighbors holding life-size photo copies of my face in front of theirs and singing "Happy Birthday." Wow, a whole yard full of fifty-year-old Bob Haworths! Well, it was a fun time for sure, but the next day I went back to being twenty-eight.

PINCH HITTER

When Nick rejoined the Trio in 1988, Bob Shane whispered to me as I walked out the door, "Keep your bag packed – you never know." Yeah, right, was my internal response. But then in November of 1991, Bob called to inform me that Nick was having surgery and would be out of commission for a while. So off the bench I came to pinch-hit for the Nickster. Then again in 1996, Nick was once more going under the knife, so I did another several weeks until he was able to hit the road again. Each time I filled in, it was like I'd never left – we blended just like before. Years later, Bob's wife, Bobbie, told me that Shane often commented that, "Bobby Haworth saved our ass so many times." Well, that's what pinch-hitters do. Maybe you don't hit a home run, but at least a single.

Mr. Bob called again in late June of 1997, informing me that Nick was scheduled for rehab and would not be able to join the Trio for a week in July at Bohemian Grove. The Bohemian Club began in San Francisco in 1872 as a gathering place for journalists, artists and musicians. It was initially an environment where journalists could escape the office, exchange ideas and develop new relationships. They identified as "Bohemians" and welcomed poets, artists and musicians as their peers. The club later purchased a 2,700-acre parcel of land in the redwood forest of northern California and established an elaborate summer camp facility called Bohemian Grove for members and guests. It's virtually an up-scale summer camp for adults.

The Kingston Trio was invited on many occasions as camp guests and it was a unique experience. There are several different campsites throughout the Grove and each one has its own theme and membership. We were guests of the Aviary Camp and we were treated like royalty. I had an actual bedroom in their clubhouse – not the way I remember Scout camp. But some of the activities were somewhat "scoutish" and each day was packed with an interesting array of educational and entertaining offerings.

Here's a sample schedule of a typical day:

7:00 – 11:00 a.m. Breakfast
9:00 a.m. Trap and skeet shooting
10:00 a.m. Museum Talk: "Sea Birds of the World"
NOON Organ Concert at the Lake
12:30 p.m. Lakeside Talk: "What Jack Nicklaus and Beethoven Have in Common"
3:30 p.m. Museum Theater Stage: "An Afternoon of Music for Violin and Piano"
4:00 p.m. Fly Fishing Demonstration at the Lake
6:30 p.m. Great Organ Concert at the Grove Stage
7:00 – 9:00 p.m. Dinner
9:15 p.m. Campfire Show: "Ghost Stories"
10:15 p.m. Afterglow at the Grill: "Fred Radke and Friends"

We did a campfire show one evening and then a Friday afternoon show for our hosts at the Aviary Camp. Our opening act on Friday was The Tree Frogs, Aviary's in-house folk group. The whole Grove was invited to attend, and in the audience that day was former President George H.W. Bush. He didn't ask to join us on stage, but he did sing along and he was very warm and complimentary when we met him. We were told that Henry Kissinger was also in the crowd, although we didn't have a chance to meet him. I would have loved to hear him sing "Tom Dooley" with his German accent!

Then it was back to Denver and relative obscurity. In addition to The Fabulous Bo Mooney Show featuring The Luna Chicks, I experimented with several different combinations of musicians and musical styles. I had a five-piece country band for awhile called "Coyote Moon." Graham played drums in that band in addition to a bass player, keyboard and fiddle. Then there was "Bob Haworth and The Heart of America" with an eclectic repertoire of folk, classic rock and 1940's swing tunes. And soon to be forgotten was "Biggs & Little," a very short-lived duo with a talented entertainer named Stan Orlow.

Bob Shane had introduced me to Stan, who was a huge Kingston Trio fan. And I mean "huge" – Stan weighed over 300 pounds and when he strapped on a guitar it literally looked like an ukulele on him. Stan held forth for many years at a club called The Beachball in Newport Beach. He had a four-piece band and his show was the extreme definition of the term "blue." Among the songs in his repertoire was a version of "Greenback Dollar" that featured the line, "...I don't give a fuck about a greenback dollar." I think Bob Shane wished that we could sing it that way and he would haul us down to the Beachball to catch Stan's show anytime we were in the area.

Stan and I became good friends over the years and we thought it would be fun to sing together. So we concocted this wacky idea to call ourselves "Biggs & Little" to play on our obvious difference in size. Of course, I was Bobby Biggs and he was Stan Little. Stan came out to Denver and we threw together a show, including as many crude tunes as we could squeeze into a four-hour gig. Meri booked us at a local venue called The Emerald Isle, so we added a filthy version of "The Irish Washerwoman" to the set. On our opening night we came out of the chute with "The Rodeo Song," followed by "Asshole from El Paso," "Dolly Parton's Tits" and of course, "Greenback Dollar." I think the audience was kind of stunned and the management was mortified. I don't remember if we got paid, but we were asked not to return. Poor Meri was quite embarrassed and promised never to book us again. Well, it was fun while it lasted. Stan went back to California and we buried Biggs & Little with some regret.

♪ ♪ ♪

My first stab at a Kingston Trio tribute group was "The String Alongs." Hereford Percy was a Denver banjo player in the highly-regarded Southern Exposure bluegrass band. He was also a Kingston Trio fan and had actually booked us for a show with the Longmont, Colorado, symphony several years earlier. I asked him if he'd like to put together a show of Kingston Trio material and he was all in. Our third guy was Ernie Martinez, probably the hottest acoustic musician in Denver. We did one show at a little theater in Golden and then wouldn't you know it...Bob Shane called again.

The Fabulous Bo Mooney Show hits the road.

The Limo. Chauffeuring our friend, John Wagner,
Denver's Warwick Hotel GM.

Presenting Bo Mooney and the Luna Chicks!
The bottom photo was our Western version.

Tom Paxton, Meri and me at Swallow Hill in Denver.

Biggs (*on the right*) & Little.

CHAPTER NINE

The Kingston Trio: Part Two

I **WAS EXPECTING ANOTHER FILL-IN** date, but this time Bob informed me that Nick had decided to hang it up for good. Would I be willing to come back in as his replacement? Well, duh! So Nick picked his last date and Shane asked me to join them in Arizona for his final show. Tom Green had retired to his home in Wisconsin back in 1994, and Paul Gabrielson had left the previous month to play jazz, leaving Ben to play bass with the Trio. Bob had decided to downsize the entourage, returning to the original configuration of the Trio plus a bass player. But on Nick's last show, Bob asked me to play bass, allowing Ben to play his fiddle and electric tenor guitar one more time before switching back to bass going forward.

The next night we were off to Idaho, and I was back on the front line. Just like riding a bicycle – it all comes back to you as soon as you jump on. We had a fairly full schedule from that point on and it didn't take long before I had slipped back into the rhythm of touring.

In May of 1999, we took a week-long booking at a club called Sweet Basil in Tokyo. I hadn't been back to Japan since my Brothers Four days, so this was maybe a little bit nostalgic for me. I had a chance to see my cousin, Sammy Smith, and his wife, Kozy. I was surprised at how quickly my Japanese came back to me. Yes, the *benjo*/banjo joke still had legs. The Japanese fans love their sake and at the end of one of our evenings there, we were followed to the parking garage by an entourage of very happy revelers singing, "Riss rittre right of mine, I'm gonna ret it shine..." And we couldn't resist – we joined in and sang "arong" with them. (OK, I'm probably in trouble now with the PC Police.)

♪ ♪ ♪

The Kingston Trio virtually put Martin Guitars on the map in the late 1950s. Because they had big hits with songs that were easy to play, and because they played Martin Guitars, every wanna-be folk singer had to have a Martin Guitar. Due to the demand, Martin was backlogged for years trying to keep up with production. So in honor of The Kingston Trio's 40th Anniversary in 1997, Martin Guitars issued a special Limited Edition consisting of forty sets of three different instruments. Each set included a special Kingston Trio D-28, a custom 0-18T tenor guitar and a Vega long-neck banjo, produced by Greg Deering. These were replicas of the instruments that the original Trio had played and the sets originally sold for $12,500. Bob Shane received set #1 and set #2 was split up with Bob getting the D-28, the 0-18T tenor went to Nick, George received the Vega long-neck banjo #2a and John Stewart got banjo #2b. When Bob invited me to rejoin the Trio, I think he felt bad that I had missed out on this special commemoration. To make up for it, he had Dick Boak select the finest HD-28 from inventory and then he ordered "The Kingston Trio" inlays on the 11th, 12th and 13th frets to match the inlays on the special edition D-28. In addition to that, he ordered my name to be inlaid at the 20th fret. This was a very special "welcome back" gift from a very special friend. I doubt if it has any resale value though. Who would want a guitar with my name on it?

As it turned out, that guitar didn't spend much time on the road. In fact, now it never goes out of the house. But in pursuit of Bob's vision to return the Trio to its original instrumental configuration, I suggested that I should play tenor guitar as Nick had done. Bob found me a 1930's-vintage Martin tenor, for which I paid him $800 in installments. I studied Nick's capo positions on different songs and tried to emulate his relentless rhythmic patterns. I found that tenor guitar, even though Nick used standard guitar tuning, was quite a different animal than the six-string I'd been playing all those years. But eventually I began to catch on and it did serve to more accurately represent the original Trio sound.

♪ ♪ ♪

In the spring of 2000, Bob decided that we needed a CD to represent the group's configuration at that time. We spent two days at a studio in Phoenix basically recording our show. It was mostly done live, with very few overdubs and we released it a couple months later under the title, "By Special Request." The repertoire held true to the title, as the song selections were primarily the tunes that audiences hoped to hear at our shows. It proved to be a big seller at our post-concert sales table.

♪ ♪ ♪

Back on the road, we were booked to sing one song (guess which one...) at the 125th Anniversary Gala for the New York "Y." We were taken by surprise when we were introduced to the other celebrities that were on the program that night. Carol *Hello Dolly* Channing, song-writer Sheldon *Fiddler on The Roof* and *Merry Minuet* Harnick, Broadway star Mike Burstyn, jazz pianist Dick Hyman, father and son guitar duo, Bucky and John Pizzarelli, opera star Marilyn Horne, TV and movie actor Bob Sherman, soul singer Ella "Big Momma" Mitchell and appropriately, Tom "Happy Birthday" Chapin. Oh, and the MC was Kitty "To Tell The Truth" Carlisle. Holy Moley – did I leave anybody out? I'll bet I won't get a party like that for my 125th birthday!

Two weeks later we were on the Millennium Stage at the Kennedy Center for two shows. To this day none of us have a clue what the occasion was, but on our itinerary it states that Senator Ted Kennedy made the opening remarks before the first show at noon. A Kennedy speaking at the Kennedy Center – what a coincidence! Actually, it was sometimes the case that we would be hired as the entertainment for a special event and not be informed as to what the event was. Speculation: Hmmm...Kennedy Center, so something to do with the arts; Kingston Trio, so something to do with American Music as an art form? Well, we got paid, so that's all that mattered.

BUSTED!

Occasionally our manager managed to put together a tour that allowed us to stay on the ground for several days. We'd rent a van or two cars and drive the tour. Obviously, there were a few days off here and there to allow us to cover the mileage to the next venue. On one of these tours we ended up with a day off somewhere in North Carolina and a friend of Bob's who lived in the area invited us to a party.

I need to preface this story with the revelation that Bob Shane hated seat belts and refused to use them. When we'd rent a car, he'd find some way to disable the seat belt so that the alarm wouldn't ring even though he wasn't wearing it. So when Bob's friend showed up at the hotel to lead us to the party, Bob decided to ride with him and he asked me to drive the other boys and follow in the rental car. When I got into the car, I tried to undo the seat belt so I could use it, but it was taking too long and the lead car was getting impatient. So off we went with me wearing no seat belt.

As fate would have it, we came upon a state patrol check point of some sort and I got busted for not having my seat belt on. Bob did offer to pay the ticket ($40 or something) but somehow that never happened and, seeing no upcoming dates in North Carolina, I just blew the whole deal off. Well, sometimes things come back to bite you and years later, this one did. Hold that thought for the next chapter.

WAKE UP LITTLE SUSIE

By early 2000, Meri had divested herself of all her businesses, allowing her to travel with me more often. The Kingston Trio was booked for two shows in Massachusetts opening for The Everly Brothers in August. I wanted Meri to join us on that tour because our chance meeting in Colorado back in 1987 had been a result of her calling out a request for "Wake Up Little Susie," obviously mistaking us for a bar band. I thought she would enjoy hearing her request from the original performers.

We had rented our own car for the tour and we pulled up early to the first venue, parked and went inside to locate our dressing room. The place had three dressing rooms – one marked "Kingston Trio," one marked "Everly Brothers" and the third designated as "Everly Brothers Band." We were tuning up in our dressing room when the road manager for the Everly's came in and asked me to move our car. The Everly's had arrived – in two separate buses – and they needed room to park them.

So I went out and moved our car and when I came back to our dressing room – it wasn't our dressing room anymore. Not only had Don and Phil arrived in separate buses, but they also demanded separate dressing rooms. The KT had been moved to the Everly's band's dressing room to allow Don and Phil to each have their own space. At first I was somewhat put off by that, but as it turned out, we had the privilege of hanging with the EB band. The line-up for that tour included Albert Lee on guitar, Buddy Emmons on pedal steel and Jamie Hartford on guitar. WOW! What a crew to hang with!

Meri was really hoping to get a photo taken that night with the Everly Brothers, so I went to their road manager and asked if that was possible. He said it wasn't likely, because the only time the brothers ever wanted to be in the same room with each other was when they were on stage performing. But he said he'd ask. And for some odd reason they consented, even autographing the photo after we ran out and had it printed quickly before the next day's show. And what a show they put on! You would never have guessed how much they hated each other.

On our return trip home following this short tour, Meri and I were routed through Dallas. As we were waiting at the gate for our connecting flight to Denver, a gentleman approached me and said, "You're with The Kingston Trio, aren't you?" As I focused on the person in front of me, I blurted out, "Yes, and you're Doug Kershaw, aren't you?" Indeed, it was The Ragin' Cajun who was also returning home after a tour. I was not aware of the fact that Kershaw had moved to Greeley, Colorado, and it was great to reconnect with him. We traded phone numbers and promised to keep in touch.

NORTH TO ALASKA

In September of 2001, we were booked along with the Limeliters on a Holland America cruise to Alaska. We departed from Vancouver, B.C., on September 3rd aboard the SM *Volendam* for a one-week cruise. In addition to a couple shows we did for the insiders who had booked the cruise specifically for our entertainment, there were nightly jam sessions with the fans, many of whom had brought along guitars and banjos. Meri came along, as well as her parents, Ed and Evelyn Vohs. We had a great time and saw parts of Alaska that I'd never seen before.

Returning to Vancouver on September 10th, we disembarked and bid farewell to our fellow shipmates. Meri and I caught a flight that day back to Denver and her parents headed back to Oregon. Some of the cruisers decided to stay in Vancouver for a day or two for some local sight-seeing, to their unexpected dismay. The next morning I was fixing breakfast when my son, Graham, called and told me to turn on the TV. We were stunned to learn that the Twin Towers in New York had just been destroyed by a couple of passenger planes. It was 9-11 and the nation fell into a state of shocked disbelief. All air flights were cancelled nationwide, leaving many of our friends stranded for days in Canada.

The Trio was scheduled to perform at the University of Wisconsin on September 14th, and word was that air travel could be shut down for several days. Our travel agent finally found an airline that was being allowed to operate, so she got us all booked on flights to Wisconsin. The audience that night was so ready for an evening of musical escape from what the country had just suffered, and it was apparent that we provided exactly what they needed. I had written a song on the plane, "United States Are We," with a very positive, "we will survive" message and I opted to sing it as my solo that night. It got a good response and I continue to sing it year after year on that sad day in our history.

HAIL TO THE CHIEF

There were many professional politicians who were big fans of the Trio and we sometimes encountered them in our travels. Just after Thanksgiving in 2001, we were booked to perform in New York City for a gathering of politicians honoring Senator Hillary Clinton with some award. When we arrived at the venue, we were informed that Hillary was in Washington, D.C., and unavailable to appear in person to accept her award. Instead her husband, former President Bill Clinton, would accept the honor on her behalf.

We did a brief show to warm up the crowd and then left the stage as the ceremony began. To the roaring applause of the crowd, in came Bill Clinton, escorted by Mayor Rudy Giuliani. There was a bit of speechifying relative to Hillary's award and then the President asked if The Kingston Trio would come back on stage and join him in a rendition of "God Bless America." Bob Shane was a little hesitant (I don't think he was a Clinton fan), but you don't turn down a request from a former President. Fortunately I knew the song pretty well in the key of D, so I grabbed my guitar and we made our way back to the stage to join the President. The whole room sang along, and after we finished, Bill shook our hands and thanked Bob for his contribution to the American music scene. As we all left the stage, I had to bite my tongue to avoid turning to Clinton and thanking him for clarifying to the world that fellatio was, in fact, not really sex.

D-U-N-N-DONE!

February weather in Colorado can certainly raise havoc with air travel. We had played a date in Beaverton and the next day we had a flight out of Denver heading to Cerritos, California. Denver was pretty well frozen over and flights were being delayed due to planes having to be de-iced before take-off. We sat in the waiting area until they finally called our flight to board. We got buckled in, expecting to be off the ground shortly, but NO! Sit and wait, sit and wait. Finally,

Benubert got up out of his seat, collected his carry-ons and announced, "This sucks! I am D-U-N-N done!" He walked off the plane and called his wife for a ride home to Estes Park.

Well, that didn't sit well with Mr. Bob, and after a fairly loud phone call, he was able to get Ben to commit to one more week with us until he could be replaced. Catching an early morning flight the next day, Ben rejoined us for a few more shows before heading back to Colorado for good. Luckily, Paul Gabrielson was ready to hit the road again, so even though the bottom almost fell out on us, everything worked out well.

PBS LOVES FOLK MUSIC

PBS called and invited us to participate in a show they were planning called (thank you, Woody Guthrie) *This Land Is Your Land*. Judy Collins and the Smothers Brothers were scheduled to be the hosts and the cast was a veritable who's-who of popular folk music. In addition to The Kingston Trio, there were performances by The Brothers Four, the Limeliters, John Sebastian, The Highwaymen, Glenn Yarbrough, Roger McGuinn and Randy Sparks and The Minstrels, including Barry McGuire.

The production was scheduled for two days at Carnegie Mellon University in Pittsburgh. Waiting in the Green Room for our segment to be taped, I struck up a conversation with Roger McGuinn. I asked him to show me how he played "8 Miles High," and he obliged with a quick guitar lesson. When I got home I tried it out on my Yamaha twelve-string, but I discovered that you can't replace the sound of a vintage Rickenbacker.

Back at the hotel there was always a jam session going on

somewhere. I got wind of a rehearsal that Randy Sparks was holding in his room, so I headed up there to be a fly on the wall. Years earlier, Randy had sold his rights to the name "New Christie Minstrels" to a group of attorneys, so the *decet* (a musical group consisting of ten musicians) he was rehearsing that night was dubbed simply "The Minstrels." It was the same configuration as the original group, with some long-time members and others who were more recent additions. I think over the years somewhere in the neighborhood of 500 performers walked on stage as either a "New Christie Minstrel" or simply a "Minstrel." Among the group's alumni were such luminaries as Kenny Rogers, Kim Carnes and Gene Clark.

A few months after this taping for PBS, a motion picture came out called *A Mighty Wind,* which was a parody of the folk music era. One of the fictional groups in the film was The New Mainstreet Singers, which bore a striking resemblance to the Randy's Minstrel groups. There's a scene in the movie depicting a rehearsal of The New Mainstreet Singers, and it occurred to me that there must have been another fly on the wall that night in Philadelphia. Someone involved in scripting the film had somehow duplicated that rehearsal for the movie. If you've never seen *A Mighty Wind* I recommend it for a good laugh. And watch for *This Land Is Your Land* to air on your local PBS station. It usually makes an annual fund-raising appearance.

BOB SHANE'S HIGH SCHOOL REUNION

Bob Shane graduated from Honolulu's Punahou School in 1952. His fiftieth class reunion was scheduled for two days in June of 2002. Of course, his class requested that he bring the whole Trio to the reunion party, and we were always more than happy to spend a few days in Hawaii. One of Bob's classmates was Richard Kelley, owner of the Outrigger Hotel chain, and he generously offered us deluxe suites at his Waikiki Beach Hotel. It was a great get-away, although we wished we could have stayed longer. And no, Barrack Obama was not in attendance. He didn't graduate from Punahou until 1979.

AFTER ALL THESE YEARS

Since my last recording project in the mid-'90s, I had continued to write, and by 2001, I felt that I had enough decent new material for another album. I wanted this to be a professionally produced and polished CD with all the bells and whistles, so I went shopping for a producer. I was referred to a guy in LA with some good credentials, and I had a sense that he would be a great person to work with. Matt Cartsonis had not only worked with Pete Seeger and John McEuen, among others, but he was also at that time Warren Zevon's band leader. Yeah, I could work with this guy!

We spent some time planning the arrangements and then I layed down the basic tracks at Jim Ratts's studio in Denver. Matt then took those tracks back to LA and worked on fleshing out the production. John McEuen played banjo on a couple of cuts, George Grove played on one tune and Van Dyke Parks, former Beach Boys member and brother of Carson Parks, played piano. One song ("Right Smack Dab") has kind of a Cajun feel and I called Doug Kershaw and asked if he would saw his fiddle for me. He kindly obliged and when I asked him what his fee was, he said, "Oh, just bring me a can of Red Bull." No way – I brought him a whole case.

By the summer of 2003, the album was finished and packaged under the title *After All These Years*. We arranged to have the CD release party the day after the Kingston Trio played at Denver's Hudson Gardens in July. We rented a party room not far from our home and we had over a hundred friends and neighbors as our guests. My son, Graham, played drums, Matt, my producer, played, and Bob Shane and George Grove joined us for some tunes, allowing all the musicians on stage to now boast of having played with The Kingston Trio.

SWEET JUDY BLUE EYES

A month later, we were booked to perform at the Minnesota State Fair. We shared the bill with Judy Collins, who was also showcasing a couple of up-and-coming female performers. The plan was for Judy and her acolytes to open the show, then we would take the stage for a set, followed by a rendition of Judy's signature song, "Amazing Grace," featuring the whole ensemble.

We all took turns with a sound check and then Judy directed how she wanted to stage the finale. We ran through "Amazing Grace" one time and then broke for dinner. As we were tuning up for the show, I approached Judy's manager and asked him if he thought Judy would mind if I played my musical saw on "Amazing Grace." He said, "That sounds like a great idea, but let's not tell her." So at the end of the show as Judy came back out to join us, I moved over to the chair that we'd set up with a mic for me to play the saw.

As Judy began to sing, I played some long, sustained harmony notes that really sang out on top of everything. Judy heard what I was playing but couldn't figure out what it was or where it was coming from, although she seemed to be OK with it. She finally looked stage left where I was seated and "saw" what I was up to. She kind of laughed and then asked me to take a solo. I obliged her with a cross-cut rendition of the tune, which elicited a rousing response from the crowd. After the show, she gave me a hug and said, "Thanks for that nice surprise!" Ah, that's sweet, Judy!

CHRISTMAS IN BETHLEHEM

Capitol Records released The Kingston Trio's Christmas album, *The Last Month of The Year,* in 1960. While the songs they recorded were mostly obscure, they were well-arranged and performed. Since I had been with the Trio, we had never performed any of these songs in concert, but December of 2003 was, in fact, "The Last Month of The Year." We were booked at the State Theatre in Easton, Pennsylvania, for a Christmas show, and we decided to include several songs from the album in this show.

We had flown in a day early and, appropriately, we were lodged in a hotel in nearby Bethlehem, PA. And it was snowing like crazy. This was shaping up to be a Christmas experience to remember. As I was settling into my room, George called and told me that Dick Boak, our artists rep at Martin Guitars in nearby Nazareth, had invited us to lunch. I looked out my window and saw snow piling up pretty fast. At that point we didn't have a ride available. This was often the case when we were at the mercy of the concert promoter for ground transportation. We often missed out on interesting local attractions just because we either had no time in a day or no transportation available. In this case, we were determined to get to Nazareth if we had to walk. As it turned, our friend, Mac Carter happened to be at the factory when George called Dick Boak, and Mac very generously offered to brave the white snows of winter to make the half-hour drive to pick us up and bring us back to Martin.

Once at the Martin factory we were treated like royalty and Dick gave us the full tour. I had toured the Yamaha factory in Japan a couple times, but this was my first visit to the Martin factory. I was quite fascinated by the integration of modern guitar-building techniques (automated lacquer sprayers, for example) with the tried and true methods developed by C.F. Martin in the 1800s that are still in use. We saw ancient irons used to heat and bend the sides of D-28s that continue to be state-of-the-art. The only difference now is the use of electricity to heat the irons as opposed to hot coals. I gained a whole new respect for my Martin guitars after seeing the care that goes into the construction of each individual instrument.

We saw guitars in various states of construction and saw some beautiful wood in the process of becoming somebody's lifetime musical companion. But the one single guitar that I wanted to take home with me was out of my reach. At each milestone in the Martin history a special instrument has been built to commemorate the event. We saw serial #500,000, which is on display in the Martin Museum. We saw serial #750,000 – The Peacock (because of the inlay) – which Dick Boak displayed at our concert that evening. But the crown jewel in the collection is serial #1,000,000. I was in such awe that I didn't pay much attention to such details as the model number, type of woods used, etc. Dick did tell us that Chris Martin had selected a particular piece of spruce for the top that had exceptionally wide grain, as opposed to the tight grain we normally associate with good tone. Apparently, Chris's grandfather was of the opinion that the wide grain offered better tone, and in this case he was certainly right on the mark.

As they unlocked the humidified vault and gently removed this recently finished instrument, we stood in amazement. The inlay on every portion of the guitar was exquisite – almost garish, but not. George and I were each allowed a couple minutes to fondle and strum, wishing all the time that our pockets were big enough to hold a guitar. Apparently we were among the first non-Martin employees to handle this guitar and we felt very honored.

After one last strum and some fond farewells, they locked up #1,000,000 and we followed Dick Boak (heads still swimming with excitement) across the street for lunch. Dick's a very funny guy with lots of amazing stories. He had been at Martin for twenty-eight years at that point and had stories to tell about so many huge stars who have played Martin guitars: Johnny Cash, Jimmy Buffet, Paul McCartney, Willie Nelson, Eric Clapton, The Kingston Trio…he could go on for hours and never lose our attention. But finally, there were no

Me with Serial #1,000,000!

more crumbs on my plate and it was time to head back for sound check.

The winter storm was in full fury as we arrived at the State Theatre in Easton. Meri had booked this event capitalizing on the fact that this was to be The Kingston Trio's first ever Christmas show and the weather was certainly contributing to the ambience. We'd been working for months to re-learn and polish seven songs from *The Last Month Of The Year* album plus "Glorious Kingdom" from the *Close Up* album. It was a perfect night for this music, and the audience (minus a few no-shows due to the weather) was warm and toasty in this beautifully restored turn-of-the-century venue. We coaxed the folks into a mass sing-along on "A Round About Christmas," and I saw many lips moving as we made our way through such favorites as "Go Where I Send Thee," "All Through The Night" and "We Wish You A Merry Christmas."

The snow was still coming down as we drove back to Bethlehem that night. Our itinerary called for a 10:00 a.m. flight the next morning from Philadelphia to West Palm Beach, Florida, for a show at a private residence on Saturday evening. Saturday morning dawned to treacherous roads, canceled flights and basically no way to get to Florida. Luckily, our host for that evening had access to his corporate jet, which he sent over from Cleveland to pick us up in Philadelphia. I was personally a little apprehensive about this: small plane – bad weather – Buddy Holly – hmmm....

As it turned out, the pilots of this craft were very professional and did a fantastic job of transporting us comfortably down to FL. They had a nice meal on board for us, we didn't have to go through any security checks and we got to load our own luggage. I dropped Shane's guitar a couple times just to get the feel of being a real baggage handler.

From that point on we had smooth sailing. We had a nice show that night at a lovely Palm Beach residence. It was a birthday party for this gentleman's wife, with about 150 guests attending. Our opening act was the five daughters of this couple, who sang a song for their mother. We were told that The Kingston Trio had been a household staple during the years that these girls were growing up and they knew all of our songs. Sure enough, they sang along on everything, and as we started "MTA," one of the daughters jumped up on stage and sang my part. She brought down the house!

We very rarely (if ever?) did a private concert in someone's home. Although The Kingston Trio could draw a crowd of 4,000 people to a concert venue and keep their attention for two hours, a private party is a whole ' nother animal. While I stop short of accusing the audience that night of being rude, there were several factors at play that created an entirely different set of circumstances for us. First of all, this was a family affair with people of all ages. The attendees came to this party to honor the lady of the house on her birthday, so it's not like we were the main attraction. Our music was recognizable, at least, to most of the guests, but we found ourselves in the position of a hired band as opposed to concert artists. People wanted to talk as we performed and, oddly, they wanted to dance to our music. It took us a few minutes to realize that they didn't want to hear us talk. In fact, several people even admonished us to stop talking and just play music. Bob, being the comedian that he was, felt somewhat baffled by this and after telling a few more jokes despite the crowd's lack of response, he finally settled into a different pace with less verbal communication. All I can say is, they paid for us to be there – they even sent a private plane to make sure we got there. It was their party – they can dance if they want to.

END OF AN ERA

On April 23, 2004, we played the Carlisle Theatre in Carlisle, Pennsylvania. Before the show, Bob Shane was having some breathing issues and we were concerned that he was catching something. The show went off without a hitch and the next day we were off to Cedarburg, Wisconsin. Bob was still having some difficulty, but being the ultimate showman, he forged ahead and again, gave a stellar performance to the crowd at the Cedarburg Performing Arts Center.

The next day at the airport, we could tell that Bob was not well. Upon his arrival in Phoenix that day his doctor immediately checked him into the Mayo Clinic with congestive heart failure. The smoking, cocaine and alcohol had finally caught up with him. Not wanting to cancel any upcoming dates, Shane immediately called Bill Zorn and asked him to stand in for him. Our next date was on May 1st in Waco, Texas, so we didn't have much time to prepare a show. George and I met Bill in Phoenix and we rehearsed for a couple days before hitting the road. Changes were in the wind.

NO BANJOS IN THE *BANIOS* OF NAPOLI

One of the fascinating things about show business is the variety of venues that we've had the opportunity to play. We've performed in brand new, state-of-the-art theaters, tiny little night clubs, restored vintage vaudeville theaters, outdoor arenas and parks – yes, and even in private homes. We've performed all over the United States and Canada, and occasionally we're called to perform internationally. Such was the case when we received an offer to play a one-nighter in, of all places, Italy!

This booking came on rather short notice, but it came at a good time for us – right in the middle of a six-week break in our schedule. We were all glad to have a chance to stretch our vocal cords again, and the prospect of visiting Italy was intriguing. We were asked to be the entertainment at the fiftieth wedding anniversary party for Jim Morris, formerly "the voice" of Notre Dame football, and his lovely wife, Leahray. The party was going to be held at a mountaintop resort in Ravello, about an hour from Naples which apparently was the location of their wedding a half-century previously.

We left our respective homes with the plan of meeting in Newark to catch a Continental flight to Madrid, connecting to Rome and then on to Naples. Paul had it easy, taking the train from his home in The Big Apple down to the Newark airport. George flew from Las Vegas to Phoenix, meeting up with Bill for their flight on to Newark. They arrived around 5:15 p.m., allowing plenty of time before our scheduled departure at 8:25. My situation, however, proved to be quite a bit more hair-raising.

I flew from Denver to Chicago Midway and had a three-hour layover before my flight on to Newark. My scheduled arrival in Newark was 6:55, giving me an hour and a half to make my connection to Madrid. They started boarding my flight from Midway at 3:00 and then, without warning, asked us all to deplane. The explanation was that there was bad weather in Newark and the FAA was delaying all inbound flights due to the traffic that was building up. We were told that our flight would be delayed by two hours. Hmmm... there goes my comfy layover –now, how do I get to Madrid?

I called Nikki Gary, our manager, and she found me a seat on a later flight from Newark to Rome, where I could hook up with the other boys and fly on to Naples with them. This, however, was an economy class seat, as opposed to the business class seat on our scheduled flight. Bummer!

As it turned out, they ended up boarding our plane around 4:30 and there appeared to be some hope that I could possibly make my international connection. I arrived in Newark and was off the plane at 8:00, leaving me twenty-five minutes to make it. I noticed on the reader board that they had delayed my departure by ten minutes – even better! I caught the train from A concourse to C concourse and headed for security. There I was informed that I didn't have a boarding pass, so I had to go back up to the Continental ticket counter and beg the other customers to let me go to the head of the line. The agent informed me that the flight was closed – no way would I make it. I asked her if she could call the gate, as I'd noticed a ten-minute delay, and she obliged. Good news – they were still boarding and they were holding the door for me.

Back down to security, where they tore my carry-on apart while I sweated bullets. I crammed everything back in and did the O.J. down to the gate. True to their word, the door was still open and I fell into my seat with a huge sigh of relief. We were finally all on board and as they closed the door we toasted our impending adventure.

Being a mostly vegetarian (I do eat fish), I had ordered vegetarian meals for all my flights on this trip. Dinnertime came and, as Murphy would have it, there was no vegetarian meal for me. I decided to order the halibut, which turned out to be rather unappetizing. In fact, I think it was bad, because by the time we got to Madrid I was living up to my nickname, "Chunks." The rest of the trip to Naples was pretty miserable for me and all I could think about was getting into my hotel room and lying still.

Our connection in Madrid went smoothly and we were off to Rome on Alitalia Airlines. Everything was going like clockwork until we were starting to board our flight from Rome to Naples. Paul suddenly realized that he'd lost his boarding pass. As George and I boarded the bus that drove us out to the plane, Bill waited with Paul's luggage as he retraced his steps looking for his boarding pass. No luck! I'm sure this could only happen in Rome, but somehow Bill and Paul were able to persuade the airline to let Paul board the plane, despite his missing boarding pass

Just to backtrack a little, the weekend before this trip, Meri and I had been the guests of Richard and Linda Kelley at their ranch in the Rockies outside of Granby, Colorado. Richard went to school with Bob Shane in Hawaii and his father owned the property where the elder Shane had his sporting goods store on Waikiki. The Kelley's are the owners of the Outrigger Hotel chain, with properties all over the Pacific Rim. As world travelers, they advised me that if I checked any luggage I should not expect to see it after landing in Rome. I took their advice and arranged to carry everything with me in a small roller-board and a gig bag for my guitar.

Paul was also traveling light with a backpack and a gig bag for his bass. However, Bill had checked a suitcase and his guitar, and George had checked his guitar and banjo.

And just as I had been warned, their checked luggage was nowhere to be found once we landed in Naples. They filed their lost baggage claims and hoped for good news before the next day when we were scheduled to perform.

Upon exiting the baggage claim area, we came to the conclusion, after about a half hour of searching and waiting, that our pre-arranged ground transportation was non-existent. We decided to brave a cab ride into town, which proved to be an adventure in itself. The driver spoke a little English, and as he was trying to impress us with his language skills he was doing his best imitation of James Bond, whipping through the narrowest streets at break-neck speeds. Luckily, he didn't take the shortcut down the stairs. We were so thankful to be alive when he pulled up in front of our hotel that we tipped him big – something, he told us, that only Americans do. We weren't quite sure how to take that.

We checked into our cubicles (our rooms were literally ten feet square plus a small *banio* (aka bathroom), and I tried to fight off the jetlag and the food poisoning. Paul and Bill did go out for pizza and beer, but I just wanted to sleep.

The next morning we faced the lost baggage issue, with still no information from the airline as to where it might be. With the uncertainty of that issue, we were advised by our local contact that perhaps we should consider borrowing or renting instruments. He gave us directions to a street where there were several music stores, and we set off to see what we could see.

Napoli, as the locals call it (and why don't we?) is a dirty, busy city, very reminiscent of New York City to me (and Paul concurred.) There are street vendors everywhere and cars speeding every which way with no concern for pedestrians.

We quickly learned to cross streets in large groups to allow a buffer against the traffic. Following our noses and a map written in Italian we found our way to several music stores. Bill and George bought guitar straps, picks, extra strings and capos. We'd been told that the sound company would bring some guitars, but they didn't know where to get a banjo. Actually, the word "banjo" is awfully close to "*banio*", so I don't know if they really knew what we were looking for. In any case, we saw only one tenor banjo and a couple of banjolas, lots of accordions and mandolins, but nary a five-string banjo.

We decided to give it up and have lunch. We found a nice open-air pizzeria and ordered the local cuisine. According to the travel brochure, pizza was actually invented in Napoli, and it was delicious, that's for sure!

Back at the hotel there was still no word from Alitalia about the lost luggage. Bill had purchased a new shirt to wear that evening (no stripes) and we decided, even though George and I did have our show clothes, to wear a variety of attire so Bill wouldn't stand out so much. Our ride to the gig arrived at 7:00 and we hit the road for a spectacular drive to Ravello. Once out of Naples the scenery became very lovely, with views of Mt. Vesuvius and the sea, mountain cliffs and quaint little villages. Our route wound for many miles up into the mountains, eventually spilling out into the town square of Ravello. From there we had to walk about a mile to the villa where the party was being held. George was thanking the airline for losing his instruments, as lugging a guitar and banjo all that way would have made the trek a lot more tedious.

We were scheduled to play after dinner in a beautiful garden, and there we found the sound system, a plywood platform as a stage and a variety of guitars for us to use. Don't tell anybody at Martin, but Bill played a Fender acoustic and George used some brand of acoustic/electric cutaway. We planned a show and George went over his banjo parts on his borrowed guitar.

Showtime! We opened with "Corey Corey," with George doing a very respectable banjo imitation on that red guitar. Well, the audience loved it and before we knew it, people decided they wanted to dance. They were a little timid at first, but two tuxedoed gentlemen got the ball rolling by doing some kind of Greek two-step punctuated with belly-bumping. The women couldn't stand it so they joined in and we became a dance band for the evening. That was alright with us – no striped shirts, no banjo – why not just have fun with it? As we began to play "Scotch and Soda" everybody got up to dance. We noticed one elderly lady walking ahead of her aged husband towards the dance area. As he was lagging far behind, she walked over to a small tree, grabbed ahold and began dancing with the tree. We were all laughing so hard that we barely made it through the song..

After our show we had a chance to chat with the guests, all of whom had thoroughly enjoyed our performance. One of the guests was Paul Hornung, a former Heisman Trophy winner from Notre Dame and Hall of Fame running back in the '60s for the Green Bay Packers. George had actually met and partied with him several years ago, and he was in rare form on this particular evening. The Morris's had flown most of their guests (around forty people) over from Michigan on a chartered 747, and the party was scheduled to continue for another couple of days. We said our farewells, got the check and headed back to Napoli.

The next morning we arrived plenty early at the airport to allow George and Bill time to deal with their lost luggage. It had, in fact, shown up the night before, but not in time to be of any use to us. Now they had to recheck it all back to the U.S. I spent the time shopping in the duty-free store and roaming around the airport. At the Alitalia ticket counter I thumbed through a promo brochure for the airline and discovered one very interesting page. It was a picture of a woman playing the violin in front of several instrument cases. The caption read: “We transport the most delicate musical instruments there are: the musicians. Alitalia is pleased to place its love for music at everybody’s service.” Well, they did take good care of us, I will admit – but I wish they’d put the same effort into transporting our instruments!

Finally they called our flight to Milano (Milan in English) where we connected with our trans-Atlantic flight back to the good old U.S. of A. As we sat on the plane heading for home, I pulled out the map that we’d used the day before to find our way around Napoli. I noticed a rather odd statement on the back of the map, which read: “It is written: See Napoli, then die.” Well, okay, then – take me away! Been there – done that.

BACK IN THE U.S. of A.

October took us to Mesquite, Nevada, for a one-nighter at the Casablanca Resort and Casino. We’d been looking forward to this date, as Bob Shane and his lovely wife, Bobbie, were planning to drive up from Phoenix. They were able to arrange for an oxygen tank that would fit into the car and supply Bob with three days of air.

Our show that night was a double bill with Glenn Yarbrough and The Folk Reunion. The group consisted of my ex-Brothers Four partner, Dick Foley, along with Rick Dougherty of Limeliters fame. Doug Barnett filled out the group on keyboards, bass, guitar and vocals. Glenn and Company opened the show to the delight of the packed house, playing a mixture of Limeliters and Glenn Yarbrough hits along with some really wonderful new songs.

After a brief intermission we took the stage and proved once again that the music of The Kingston Trio is destined to live forever in America. Bob and Bobbie were sitting back stage and seemed to be very pleased with what they were hearing. This was the first time ever that Bob had been to a Kingston Trio show that he wasn't suited up for. It was also the first time the Shanes had ever heard us perform, and we were in top form that night. Toward the end of the show, George stepped up to the mic and, with great reverence and fanfare, introduced Bob Shane, who came out and sang his signature, "Scotch and Soda" to many cheers, tears and a standing ovation! He was truly missed by not only the fans, but by us as well and it was a thrill to hear him sing that night.

RED SOX

The next day, we headed back to Las Vegas to catch a flight to Boston. The Boston Red Sox had called and invited us to sing "The National Anthem" and "MTA" at one of their playoff games against the New York Yankees. The Kingston Trio was proud of the fact that every time we had sung the

Anthem at a major league ball game the home team had won. As it turned out, we were scheduled to sing for game #4, the crucial "make-it-or-break it" game for the BoSox, who were down three games to zip in the play-off series.

We went down to Fenway Park on Sunday afternoon for a sound check. This particular park has about a 2.5 second delay on the sound bounce-back coming from the outfield wall, which they call the big green monster. We tried singing the Anthem once and it was terribly distracting and hard to keep our place with that 2.5 second echo. They offered us wireless in-ear monitors, which saved the day for Bill and me. They had a volume control on the receiver box, so you could adjust the level and hear the mics really well. I couldn't have done it without the monitor, but George wasn't comfortable with his and he decided to tough it out.

That evening, after we sang our two numbers, they marched us straight up behind home plate through the crowd and out into some secret passageway. All the way up through the stands we were getting high-fives from fans of all ages, many of whom were too young to remember Charlie or even the MTA (it's now the MBTA), but they all knew the Anthem and they all knew that the home team had to win that night! We were there to bring them good luck, and we didn't disappoint. At 1:30 in the morning, after twelve nail-biting innings, Boston finally won!

There is a maze of back hallways and secret passages in the bowels of Fenway, and we hiked through many of them that afternoon and evening, going between the field and the green room. You can really feel the history of that building when you get down into the areas where they keep the lawn mowers and the sod. Then up through another ancient hallway, running your hands along bricks that have seen generations of fans, players, hot-dog vendors and beer schleppers. What a rush!

The team treated us like royalty, presenting us with Red Sox jerseys, caps and team jackets. They fed us well, too, with a sumptuous spread of clam chowder, lobster, exotic cheeses and desserts. After our performance we watched the game from the 600 Club, with endless supplies of beer, popcorn, shrimp and hot dogs. America is the greatest place on Earth, and baseball is the greatest game! We were part of history that night! We'll be bragging for years about how we broke "the curse of the Bambino" and sent the Red Sox on to an eight-game winning streak and the World Series Pennant. Yeah – it was The Kingston Trio who did that!

THIS LAND IS YOUR LAND TOUR

We flew home for three days before heading back out on a ten-day package tour under the moniker (thanks again to Woody Guthrie) the "This Land Is Your Land Tour." On the bill were Glenn Yarbrough and The Folk Reunion, The Brothers Four and The Kingston Trio. Kind of like the Monsters (or Dinosaurs?) of Folk. We had seven shows between October 22nd and 30th in various towns in Ohio, Michigan and Indiana, and we traveled that ribbon of highway aboard a forty-passenger bus. There were only fourteen of us (including Glenn's wife, Kathleen, and my wife, Meri), so there was plenty of room to spread out. It didn't take long to break out the instruments and make a little travelin' music. It was great fun hanging out with old friends for a few days.

This tour was like a folk music group-swap, considering the backgrounds of many of the participants. Of course, Glenn Yarbrough was an original member of The Limeliters and along side him was Rick Dougherty, who had taken Glenn's part in that group in a later iteration. Another Folk Reunion member was Dick Foley, a founding member of The Brothers Four. Bill Zorn had been with The New Christie Minstrels when I first met him. He then joined The Kingston Trio before moving to England for several years. Upon his return to the United States he had joined The Limeliters and now was back with The Kingston Trio. And, as you already know, I was a previous member of The Brothers Four. It was like a folk group tossed salad!

Bill and Rick had worked together as members of The Limeliters and they had become close friends. I had no idea how deep that friendship was at the time, but there was one incident on the road that would have been a clue, had I picked up on it. Rick played any instrument on demand, including guitar, banjo and bass. At that time there was a possibility that Paul was considering leaving the group to play jazz in New York which meant we might be looking for a bass player. As we were exiting the bus at a hotel one day, Meri turned to Bill and suggested that maybe Rick could become our bass player. Bill responded, "Oh, I have bigger plans for Rick." Meri said that he quickly ducked away, as if to avoid any explanation of the comment. Months later we would understand.

For the most part, this tour went smoothly except for one stop in Ohio. For some reason the promoter had booked us rooms at a funky "resort" that was comprised of several separate cottages around the property. When we entered our cottage, we found it to be far more funky than the outside. Apparently it had rained the day before and the carpet was squishy like a sponge from where the ceiling had leaked. There was also a big wet spot in the middle of the bed, cockroaches were running around and we were never able to get the heat to work. Other than that, it was a pretty crappy place. When we got over to the venue for sound check we complained to the promoter but all he could say was "oh well."

Back in our cottage after the show, Meri and I found some extra blankets in the closet and we somehow managed to curl up on a dry corner of the bed with all our clothes on. But we didn't get any sleep that night, and as we were boarding the bus the next day everybody had similar complaints about the place. To add insult to injury, someone informed us that there was a perfectly good Radisson Hotel right across the street from the venue and room prices were comparable. Grumble and groan...off to the next show.

We returned home from that odyssey with only a couple days to do our laundry and repack for a five-day jaunt back to New England. The first show on November 5th was a special night for us. We were performing in the venerable Providence (Rhode Island) Performing Arts Center, a vintage vaudeville house with ornate gilded walls and vaulted ceiling. Our opening act was one of my all-time musical heroes, John Sebastian. I was a huge Lovin' Spoonful fan, but John was the talented one, in my estimation. He wrote great songs, had a cool voice and played guitar, harmonica and autoharp, which was a very unusual instrument for a group with drums and electric guitars. John played all his hits that night and brought back a lot of memories. We also had the honor of having him join us on harmonica for our rendition of "Lookin' For The Sunshine."

THE CHARLIE CARD

On Sunday we drove to Boston for a day off. Our hotel and meals were being comped, so we decided to take ourselves out to McCormick & Schmidt's, a fabulous seafood restaurant in the Park Plaza Hotel building. As luck would have it, on a night when everything is already free for us, we were informed by the maître d' that the restaurant was offering a free entrée to all veterans. George was the only vet among us, so he got his free entrée that he didn't have to pay for anyway. The best part of it being free was – it was absolutely delicious! There's nothing worse than a free meal that's inedible.

It was back to work on Monday with a special event for the Massachusetts Bay Transit Authority, formerly the Metropolitan Transit Authority, aka the MTA. We'd been invited to sing "The MTA" for the unveiling of the "Charlie Card," the MBTA's new fare system. They had initiated a debit card that can be activated in various increments and then swiped at the turnstile whenever you ride the subway. Advice was solicited from several sources as to what to name this card and the overwhelming response was to call it the "Charlie Card," acknowledging the character in our hit song. We had been given Red Sox jackets when we sang the National Anthem at their playoff game in October, and in honor of their World Series win we were asked to wear them for this ceremony.

The event was scheduled to be held at the location of the old Scollay Square station, which is mentioned in the song as the place where Charlie's wife handed him his daily sandwich. We were met at the hotel by a group of executives from the MBTA who escorted us to a nearby subway station for the short ride to the former Scollay Square. Joining us on the ride was Governor Mitt Romney, who would officiate the ribbon cutting. As we approached our destination the Governor leaned over to me and asked if we would allow him to join us for our rendition of the MTA song. The memory of Bob Shane's comment to Governor Martin crossed my mind, but I dismissed the temptation to resurrect that response. So when it came time to recount the story of Charlie on The MTA, Mitt grabbed a mic and sang along. And he did a very fine job, too. He claimed that he'd wanted to do that ever since he was five years old and heard "MTA" on the radio. Five years old??? Young whippersnapper! I was thirteen when that song came out.

DAVID PEEL SUBS

Bill Zorn and his wife had planned to visit family in England over the Christmas holiday, leaving us in a quandary as to how to deal with two December shows. Bob Shane suggested that we get David Peel to fill in. David had sung with Bob in a group called The Shane Gang after the Trio had disbanded in 1967, and Bob had actually touted him as his potential replacement before Zorn came back into the picture. David and I had connected in Nashville and become friends, so bringing him in for these two shows was a perfect fit. He had recently relocated to Colorado, so we imposed on George to fly in from Las Vegas to rehearse. Since we'd had such a good reaction to our Christmas show in 2003, we decided to use the same set list for these performances, one in Cheyenne, Wyoming, and the other in Newberry, South Carolina. The shows went well, and I was actually wishing that David could stay on as our Shane replacement.

THE LONG AND WINDING ROAD

January of 2005 opened with a hometown show for me at Denver's Paramount Theatre. Bill had returned from England, so we were back to "normal," I guess you could say. But I had a sense that there was some friction developing between Bill and me. It was hard to put my finger on it, but there was just something "off" in our relationship.

In April we were booked for another ten-day tour under the banner, "This Land Is Your Land Tour." Once again we were on the bus with The Brothers Four and Glenn Yarbrough and The Folk Reunion. Then the Trio was off to Japan for a two-day tour playing one date in Osaka and one in Tokyo. I had a sense that Bill and George were avoiding me for some reason. They would go off together to grab lunch and not invite me. And I just felt something was up. At the Tokyo concert when it came time for my saw solo, Bill walked by me on his way off stage, stage-whispering a snide remark: "It's Howdy Doody time." Well, on with the show, but that didn't sit well with me.

Back in the States we had a concert in Irvine, California, with the Pacific Symphony, and Pat Sajak was the MC for the show. Bob Shane had driven up from Phoenix and it was great to see him. But I walked into the dressing room to witness a hasty scramble among Bill, George and Bob, as if I had barged in on a secret meeting. Was I just being paranoid? No, as it turned out Bob informed me later that evening that

Bill and George had requested that Bob let me go so Rick Dougherty could take my place. Booted out again? Really? Well, now all of Bill's odd innuendos made sense. Apparently this had been in the works for some time.

My pink slip didn't take effect immediately. We had a show with The Smothers Brothers at Meadowbrook Farm in Gilford, New Hampshire, on July 17th and it proved to be the gig from hell for me. Not only was I depressed about my impending termination, but now I had to do another show with these guys. I was starting to understand how Don Everly must have felt about Phil.

My trip to New Hampshire on the 16th started with an overbooked flight out of Denver. I somehow got bumped onto a later departure to my Chicago connection. Once in Chicago I was then faced with a cancellation of my flight to Manchester due to a mechanical failure. (The plane's, not mine – although I was starting to fall apart.) I was rebooked on an early morning flight which required sleeping for a few hours on the floor of the airport waiting room. I had to rearrange my ground transportation from Manchester up to Gilford, and if all went well from that point on, I'd arrive at the venue barely in time for sound check.

Now, don't get the idea that nothing else could go wrong, because upon arriving in Manchester I found that my guitar had been routed elsewhere. There was no guarantee that the airline could retrieve it and deliver it to Gilford in time for the show, so I called the promoter and asked him to round me up a guitar. I knew there was no way they could find me a tenor guitar, and sure enough, the best they could do was a Takamine six-string with a cutaway.

After the show I had a farewell drink at the hotel with Tom and Dick Smothers, who were sorry to hear about my termination. But they wished me well and honored me with a photo. I'm pretty sure I slept through my return flights to Denver the next day, and I was happy to find my guitar waiting for me at baggage claim.

Coincidently, Meri had booked what was to be my last date with the Trio on July 22, 2005. We were scheduled to play the Britt Music Festival in Jacksonville, Oregon, the site of that summer job I had back in 1963. My high school buddy, John Eads, was dying of cancer and I had spoken to him by phone several times telling him to hang on – I'd be there soon. Sadly, he passed away just a few hours prior to our arrival. I dedicated that show to him, as many of the audience members knew John. Another of our classmates, Ron McUne, was the director of the Britt Festival at the time, and he and I sang a duet together in John's honor. After the show, Carroll Graber, my choir director from Hedrick Junior High, found me and we had a nice chat. The following day it was back to Denver to see what the next phase of my life would be like. I'd already been through this before, so I knew I would survive.

Meri, me and the Everly Brothers.

With the one and only John Sebastian.

Matt Carstonis (*in hat*) and Jim Ratts at work on my 2003 album *After All These Years.* Originally recorded at Jim's studio in Denver, then mixed and finalized in LA by Matt.

Mitt and me at the MTA event.

The MTA's "Charlie Card."

The Ragin' Cajun, Doug Kershaw.

On the Bus. "This Land is Your Land Tour" with Glenn Yarbrough, The Brothers Four and The KT.

The Trio performing at Fenway Park before the critical fourth game of the 2004 American League playoffs against the NY Yankees. We'll be bragging for years about how we broke "the curse of the Bambino" and helped the Red Sox to become World Champs!

Me with John McEuen of the Nitty Gritty Dirt Band (*left*) and Matt Carstonis during a break from recording my album, *After All These Years.*

Bob and Meri aboard the SM *Volendam* with Meri's parents, Evelyn and Ed Vohs.

Alaska Cruise with The Limeliters in 2001.
Front row, L to R: Bob Shane, Alex Hassilev.
Middle row, L to R: Bob Haworth, George Grove, Rick Dougherty, Bill Zorn.
In the back: Ben Schubert, aka "Benubert."

The Smothers Brothers.

The Smothers Brothers sound check at
Meadowbrook Farm in Gilford, New Hampshire.

CHAPTER TEN

Life in Colorado: Part Two

MERI BEGAN BOOKING ME AT retirement homes and assisted living facilities from Colorado Springs to Boulder. This proved to be a perfect market for me, as the residents of these establishments loved my repertoire of folk music and pop songs from the 1940s and '50s. It was also a lucrative market, since I was often booked for a show every weekday, and occasionally even for two shows in a day. Well, maybe "lucrative" is not exactly accurate. At $100 per show, my income was far less than I'd been making with the Trio. But it was enjoyable work and it kept my fingers and voice limber.

Our good friend, Richard Kelley, owner of the Outrigger Hotel chain, was sadly suffering with Parkinson's disease. We also knew other friends around Colorado who had Parkinson's and it occurred to us that we might be able to assist with a fund-raising effort. We explored potential venues where we might be able to promote a concert and we contacted my old buddies, The Brothers Four, to see if they might be interested in headlining such an event. As it turned out, they were very enthusiastic about the idea, so we forged ahead with plans to make it happen.

We dubbed our effort "Concerts For A Cure," and we booked the first show in Colorado Springs at the Pikes Peak Center on December 1, 2005. We had met a young Denver-based comedienne named Lucy Roucis, who was also living with Parkinson's, and we asked her to open the show. I did a short set and then I introduced The Brothers Four. Toward the end of the show, Mark Pearson and I made Dutch Groshoff proud by playing a medley of ragtime banjo tunes together. After that, Lucy and the rest of the group came back out for a couple of closing songs. The next night we repeated that show in Denver. I hope our efforts helped to draw attention to the need to find a cure for Parkinson's.

♪ ♪ ♪

The Kingston Trio had done a couple shows with We Five and I had kept in touch with their bass player, Terry Ragno. Terry worked as an audio technician for different venues in Southern California, and occasionally we found him in the mixing booth at one of our shows. Terry called me one day to tell me about a new project he was involved with. He had teamed up with some other musicians who had credits with a variety of different hit bands. They were calling the group "Icons Experience," a name that didn't grab my attention immediately.

The lineup included Merrilee Rush of "Angel of the Morning" fame; lead guitarist Richard Moore, a former member of the Troggs; keyboard man, W. Michael Lewis, an alumnus of Quicksilver Messenger Service; Mark Tulin of The Electric Prunes on rhythm guitar; Terry Ragno of We Five on bass; and a real pain-in-the-ass on drums, Duane Waider, who had no major band credit but had an ego to make up for it.

Terry asked me if I might be interested in managing this group, and the idea did intrigue me. I hadn't dabbled in management since my Seattle days, but with Meri's business acumen and sales expertise combined with my connections to venues and buyers, we felt we could find a market for this unique concept.

I began by nixing the name "Icons Experience" – I just didn't feel it had any punch. I suggested "The Radio Idols featuring Merrilee Rush" and everyone agreed to the name change. I developed a logo, put together a press release and then started contacting some venues. It was taking time to get things up and running and I wasn't getting any strong interest from buyers yet. Duane started harassing me about not doing my job and I told him I'd be happy to back out of the project. Well, Terry stepped in and tried to calm Duane down, but to no avail. Duane finally decided to quit, which was fine by me.

On the hunt for a new drummer, I thought of Steve Peterson, who was the current drummer for The Kingsmen ("Louie Louie"). He was a perfect fit and the Kinsgmen credit enhanced the Radio Idols concept. About this same time, Mark Tulin suddenly passed away and Michael Lewis decided to quit. Merrilee's husband, Billy Mac, volunteered for the keyboard spot, and although he didn't have any major band credit, he had once backed Chuck Berry, so we listed him as a veteran of the Chuck

The Radio Idols. *L to R*: Steve Peterson (The Kingsmen), Richard Moore (The Troggs), Billy Mac (The Chuck Berry Band), Terry (We Five), Terry Lauber (The Brothers Four) and Merrilee Rush in the foreground.

Berry band. To replace Mark Tulin, we initially enlisted the services of Barry McGuire's guitarist, John York, but scheduling conflicts with McGuire's bookings took him out. Merrilee then suggested former Brothers Four member Terry Lauber, and I concurred that he would be a good choice. I knew Terry pretty well, since he had replaced Dick Foley in the Brothers Four and that added another major act name to the billing.

At this point we were virtually starting over with three new musicians, so we scheduled a combination rehearsal/video shoot at a studio in the Seattle area. Billy knew a video crew that he trusted, so we hired them to do the shoot. The band was now virtually a Seattle-based group, with Steve, Terry, Merrilee and Billy all living in the area. Terry, Richard and I flew to Seattle and we spent several days rehearsing and shooting video and promo photos.

The video featured a hit song from each group represented by the Radio Idols, so the repertoire was "You Were On My Mind" (We Five), "Wild Thing" (The Troggs), "Louie Louie" (The Kingsmen) and of course "Angel of The Morning." Billy Mac did Chuck Berry's "You Never Can Tell," but unfortunately, Terry was sick in bed with the flu that week, so he wasn't able to do the video shoot. We later photo-shopped his picture into the group photo.

With video in hand, a Facebook page for promotion and an interesting product to sell, Meri and I went to work on booking this band. We contacted several casinos where the Trio had played, a few theaters where we knew the buyer and got the word out to some booking agents that we thought could help. Then I got a call from Billy Mac. Apparently he had heard from two agents that we had contacted who happened to have booked Billy as a solo. They convinced him that they could work directly with him and Merrilee to book the band and cut us out of the process. Well, by this time, Meri and I were kind of burned out with all the ups and downs of this project. We'd invested a lot of time and about $700 of our own money into this, but it did appear that we'd hit a dead end. We told Billy to go for it and he agreed to reimburse our out-of-pocket investment when the band started working.

Weeks went by and I finally got a call from Terry telling

me that Richard had passed away and that the whole project was on the verge of collapsing. I told him how sorry I was that all this effort had been for naught and I filed The Radio Idols away in that category of "nice try."

♪ ♪ ♪

Remember that incident I told you about regarding a seat belt infraction I had incurred in North Carolina? Remember how I said that sometimes things come back to bite you? Well, it was October of 2011, my birthday was approaching and my Colorado driver's license was up for renewal. I went down to the DMV, and after the eye test the clerk was looking up my record in the computer and he says, "Oh, I see you have an outstanding warrant in North Carolina. I can't issue your license until that's cleared up."

So I came home and Meri called the North Carolina DMV. They informed her that in order to clear my record I owed them $360 (on a $40 ticket!). Well, we freaked out, because we didn't have that kind of money. Problem was, we were headed to Oregon in a few weeks and we were renting a car to drive out there. I needed my driver's license before that trip.

Meri, ever willing to try and solve any problem, asked who we could speak with about this. The DMV gave her the phone number for the DA in the jurisdiction where this happened, and Meri called him. Turns out he was somewhat of a Kingston Trio fan, and since I had no other record in North Carolina and since he believed Meri's story about Bob Shane making me drive the rental car with the disabled seat belt, and since Meri offered to send him an autographed picture of The Kingston Trio, he decided to dismiss the charge against me. But he said it could take a couple weeks for this to go through the system.

So I waited the two weeks and went back to the local DMV to get my license. The eye test went fine, but when my record came up on the computer – oops! I still had that outstanding warrant in North Carolina! Why?! I came home and we called the DA in North Carolina to see what was up. He said that the charge had been dismissed and it probably just hadn't made it through the system yet. I gave it another week, went back to the DMV and – nope – still had that ticket on my record. They gave me another phone number in North Carolina to call and the woman I spoke with said, yes, the ticket had been dismissed but in order to clear my record I had to pay a $50 reinstatement fee. Well, why didn't they tell me that before?!

By this time we were within just a few days of our Oregon trip and I was really getting concerned that I wasn't going to get my license in time. The woman at the North Carolina DMV told me I had three options: (1) I could have somebody I know in North Carolina come in and pay this reinstatement fee by cash in person. (I don't know anybody in North Carolina, so that was not an option.) (2) I could send them a personal check and wait about a month for that to clear. (Again, not an option as our Oregon trip was looming.) (3) I could send them a cashier's check overnight and allow three business days for that to clear and go through the system. This was on Wednesday, Nov. 9th and Friday was Veteran's Day – government offices closed!

So we went to the bank, got the check and sent if off overnight to North Carolina. We confirmed that it was received the next day, but with Friday being a holiday, there went one of my three days. I waited through the weekend on pins and needles – even waited through Tuesday just to give it the full three days. On Wednesday I got up bright and early full of hope that I would finally be able to get my license. I got to the DMV and stood in line for twenty minutes until they opened.

When my turn came, the eye test went fine, but then when my record came up in the computer the clerk looks up and says, "Is your name Robert Haworth?" I confirmed that it was. And she says, "Well that doesn't match the name on your Social Security card and I can't issue you a license." My heart sank, my knees went weak and I nearly cried. "So what do I have to do to get a license in this state? And how did I ever get one before now? I've had my Social Security card under the name *Bob* Haworth since I was fifteen." She responded, "Well, you'll have to go to the Social Security office and have them change the name on your S.S. card to Robert."

I dashed back home, grabbed my birth certificate from the safe (as well as my expired passport just in case) and Meri and I headed off to the Social Security office. After about a half-hour wait we were called to a window and I explained this whole thing to the lady behind the glass. She said, "No problem, we can take care of this." So I handed her my birth certificate for proof of who I was and she said that wasn't sufficient proof of my identity. She asked for my driver's license. "Oh – no – can't accept that – it's expired. Oh, and so is your passport. Well, I'm sorry – I can't help you."

I blurted out, "There's got to be a way. I need to renew my driver's license!!!" So she said if I bring in my medical records signed by my doctor that would be acceptable. OK, OK – Meri was actually planning on seeing the doctor that day anyway. I'd just gotten my Medicare card in the mail and this would be a good opportunity for me to get signed up with the same doctor. But wait – I'd never seen him before, so how would he have any records on me? Worry and fret all the way down to the doctor's office.

I got signed up with the doctor on my Medicare card and after about twenty minutes they called us into the exam room. He took care of Meri's issue first, and then I went through this whole story with the doctor. He said, "Well, we can write up something official-looking and I'll sign it as your physician and we'll see if that works."

Back to the Social Security office with my "medical records" in hand, only to wait in line again. Finally back to the same window and the lady looks over the document from the doctor and says, "OK – this works. We'll change your name to Robert." (My mother will be thrilled!) She said it would take twenty-four hours to get that info into the system and I'm thinking - *Yeah, right*!

Next morning I was third in line at the DMV when they opened. Eye test went fine and, lo and behold – my name was now Robert, which matched my old driver's license record, the North Carolina issue was gone and so, Mr. Robert Haworth, you may now have your driver's license.

And not a moment too soon! We had to pick up the rental car for our Oregon trip that afternoon, and finally I had a valid driver's license in hand. It took me six weeks to accomplish what I originally thought would take me an hour. What did I learn from all this? A couple of things. First, if you're on the road with Bob Shane, say "no" to driving the rental car. Second, if you get a ticket in a foreign country such as North Carolina, PAY UP!

♪ ♪ ♪

Meri's brother, Bill Leep, had been diagnosed with cancer and that was the reason for our Oregon trip. He had been transported to OHSU in Portland for treatment, and Meri had arranged to stay with friends in Lake Oswego to be close to Bill. After dropping Meri off there I headed down I-5 to Jacksonville to visit Meri's parents. Her stepfather, Ed, was leaving to visit his son in North Carolina (wish I'd known about him six weeks earlier!) and I was going to stay with her mom while he was gone. We had a good visit and after Ed returned, I hit the road to Colorado to fulfill some bookings that were on the calendar.

Meri was scheduled to fly home a few days later, and when I picked her up at the airport she had the most amazing story to tell me. It seems that her Lake Oswego host had driven her to the airport, dropped her off and left. When Meri got to the ticket counter to check in for her flight she discovered that she had left her wallet in her friend's car. She had no I.D. with her, and by 2011, TSA was pretty strict about their rules for flying. Well, I've often joked that Meri has an element of witchcraft in her DNA and she can sometimes pull off things that can only be explained that way. Somehow, she had bewitched TSA into letting her board that plane without her I.D., which is something that I've never heard of. Only Meri could have pulled that off!

Sadly, Meri's brother passed away in June of 2012. The

whole family was devastated, especially Meri's mother. Bill was her baby, and she took his passing pretty hard. A year went by after his death, and we knew that Mom was still in mourning. We had a sense that she needed us to fill the void of losing him. After a lot of consideration, we decided to pack up and move to Oregon.

Meri found a house for us to rent on a beautiful rural property nestled among acres of vineyards. It was walking distance to Mom's house and to the historic town of Jacksonville. And amazingly, it was also walking distance to the Britt Festival grounds where I had a summer job in high school and where I later played my last show with The Kingston Trio. As Harry Chapin sang, "All my life's a circle..."

CHAPTER ELEVEN

The Kingston Trio: Part Three

OUR LIFE WAS NOW FOCUSED on taking care of Ed and Evelyn Vohs, Meri's mother and stepfather. Ah, but once an entertainer, always an entertainer. Chatting with the vineyard owner over the fence one day, I asked if they had live entertainment in their tasting room in Jacksonville. Well, yes they did, and knowing the owner of the winery, I started performing there regularly, once again proving that it's all about who you know. And bit by bit I began to get bookings at some of the other wineries in the area.

Promoting myself locally I always mentioned my past affiliation with The Brothers Four and The Kingston Trio. And just like Rick Nelson's "Garden Party," I found that my audiences wanted to hear the music I'd been playing on the road over the past forty years. It was obvious that there was still a market for "folk music" and I decided to capitalize on that.

JOHN HOLLIS

I conceptualized a show called "Tales & Tunes of The Folk

Music Era" and I selected music from Woody Guthrie, The Weavers and many of the popular folk groups of the 1960s, including, of course, The Kingston Trio and The Brothers Four. I had a story to tell with each song, thus, "Tale & Tunes." But I needed someone to harmonize with, so I began auditioning local musicians, none of whom shared my vision for a show about folk music. Then one day I heard an ad on the radio for Callahan's Mountain Lodge on Mt. Ashland here in Southern Oregon. The singer had a great voice and at the end of the ad he plugged his performances at Callahan's. John Hollis was the name behind the voice and I made plans to go check him out.

I was immediately impressed with John's voice, guitar skills, repertoire selections and professional appearance. When we chatted on a break he indicated that he had grown up listening to folk music since his dad had been a big fan. He was definitely interested in my show concept, so I told him I'd email a song list to him.

A couple days later I sent him my show list of twenty-three folk music hits from various artists along with links to videos and recordings on the internet for reference. I guess I wasn't prepared for his response: Replying to my email he wrote: "Bob – I don't want to do this gig. Hopefully I will get a chance to sing with you again." I was absolutely deflated and I thought of every possible bribe to get him to change his mind. I'm not sure which one finally worked, but after some sweet-talking I convinced him that we could put this show together over time, song by song.

And so we did, eventually taking "Tales & Tunes of The Folk Music Era" on the road to as far north as The Island

Theatre on Vashon Island and as far south as the Woodland Opera House in Woodland, California. Locally we presented our show at libraries and Grange Halls, gradually establishing a strong loyal following.

SURPRISE!

Always keeping my ear to the ground about the latest news in the folk music world, I heard that Josh Reynolds, the son of original Kingston Trio member, Nick Reynolds, was trying to break into show business. He had formed a Kingston Trio "clone" group called "The Lion's Sons" along with his cousin, Mike Marvin, and a friend of Mike's named Tim Gorelangton. Although this didn't come to light until months later, Josh and Mike had managed to get Bob Shane to lease the Kingston Trio name and brand to them for ten years. The price they offered was $100,000 to be paid in four $25,000 installments. The contract was signed on August 4, 2016, and it was scheduled to take effect as of August 1, 2017.

For some reason, George, Bill and Rick, the group known as The Kingston Trio since 2005, had not been informed of this turn of events. The first they heard of it was when they got an email from Josh in May of 2017, a full nine months after the deal had been signed. Josh stated that he hoped they would embrace this change and support the new group as they embarked on the next leg of The Kingston Trio journey. Say what? The Shane's downplayed this communication and told the Grove/Zorn/Dougherty trio not to worry about it. Nevertheless, the group decided to hire an attorney to look into the matter and they found that, in fact, they were about to be replaced.

Apparently Josh and Mike felt the need to intimidate the GBR Trio into accepting this reality, so they decided to file a lawsuit against them. On July 28th the boys were doing sound check at the Franklin Theatre in Tennessee when they noticed a gentleman standing in the wings. Calling each of them by name, he announced that they'd been served. Really – just before a show? Could there have been some malicious intent in that timing? Well, the guys took the high road and put on two professional shows that day, with no hint of concern about the matter. But after that second show they were forced to deal with reality.

The lawsuit that was served on them alleged, among other things, "Trademark Infringement." For what, they wondered. As independent contractors, they were performing as The Kingston Trio under the full authority, they assumed, of Bob Shane. And they had four important dates coming up in August and September that had already been sold out in anticipation of the George/Bill/Rick Trio appearing. In fact, the two September dates in George's home state of North Carolina (September 22nd in Charlotte and the 23rd in Asheville) were being presented as tributes to George as a Tar Heel celebrity. Accolades were to be presented by no less than the Governor, the president of George's Alma Mater, Wake Forest University, and songwriter Billy Edd Wheeler. What would be the point of The Lion's Sons (excuse me, "The Kingston Trio") showing up for that?

George, Bill and Rick demanded the right to fulfill those contracts, and after lawyers on both sides had made a ton of money, an agreement was reached to move the take-over date to October...with the stipulation that they could only call themselves "The Kingston Trio" on the specific day of each of those shows. And they were additionally banned from ever referring to themselves individually as "...formerly of The Kingston Trio." George's forty-one year career resided in those words...never to be uttered again? It was a tough nut to swallow, but worth it, apparently, to end the lawsuit.

I had been following this turn of events through various message boards, and I was quite curious to see if this new configuration could faithfully represent The Kingston Trio. After watching a couple of "Lion's Sons" videos on YouTube I was not impressed, but I wanted to see them in person. As luck would have it, their first two shows as "The Kingston Trio" were right here in Oregon. We made plans to catch their second performance in Bend and I called Josh to let him know that John, Meri and I would be in the audience that night. He was happy to hear that we were coming and he kindly offered us complimentary front row seats.

This group had adopted the single-mic approach that was reminiscent of the original Trio, but it wasn't working that night for a couple of reasons. Mainly, the vocal / instrument balance was not well-mixed. Additionally, our front row seats on stage right only allowed us an on-going view of Tim's butt since he was turned toward the mic for the entire concert. After the show we met Mike and Tim, and as we were chatting with Josh, he pulled out a pouch attached to a leather thong around his neck. Tapping the pouch to our foreheads we were suddenly enveloped in a cloud of...ash! Josh informed us that the pouch contained his dad's ashes, which we had just inhaled. It took several days before my taste buds no longer detected the essence of Nick Reynolds in my mouth.

On the drive back to Medford, we all voiced our opinions that this group was not The Kingston Trio. Yes, they played the hits (along with an odd selection of John Stewart songs that the Trio had never done). And yes, the octogenarian audience loved them to the point of a standing ovation. But to our trained ears and eyes, they just didn't have "it."

CAMELOT THEATRE

The Camelot Theatre in nearby Talent, Oregon was creating shows based on the music and careers of various artists in a series called *Spotlight On....* They had produced *Spotlight On Aretha Franklin, Spotlight On Barry Manilow, Spotlight On Peter, Paul and Mary*" and many others. I approached the theatre with my proposal to present *Spotlight On The Kingston Trio* and they loved the idea, particularly in light of my personal connection to the group. I offered to write the script and structure the show, although we were assigned a director. The basic concept of the *Spotlight* series was to present the music of the chosen artist and string the songs together with a scripted narrative telling the story of the artist's career.

John was excited to play the role of Bob Shane in this production, and he fit the part well. We looked high and low for a banjo player who could play the Dave Guard/John Stewart part, but having no success, I took that role. Then we needed someone to play Nick Reynolds, and without hesitation I called my friend Andrew Brock. Andrew was the choir director at our church, a music teacher in the local school system and a veteran of many theatrical productions. Although he was only vaguely familiar with The Kingston Trio and had never played a tenor guitar, he jumped right in and learned it all in just a few weeks.

While we were in the middle of rehearsals in preparation for our three-week run at the Camelot, I got a call from Mike Marvin. As a holder of the rights to use of the Kingston Trio name, Mike was seeking to block the production of our show. I told him to call the theatre's Executive Director, as this show was being presented under the auspices of the Camelot Theatre as part of their *Spotlight* series, and I was merely a contracted performer. I never heard any more about that threat, so I assumed there had been some resolution of the matter. We sold out twelve shows at the Camelot and added hundreds of more names to our contact list. It proved to be one of the Camelot's most successful productions of that season.

HERE WE GO AGAIN

Less than a month after the show closed, I got another phone call from Mike Marvin late one Friday afternoon. I think I was even more surprised about the reason for this call than I'd been about the reason for his first call. "Bob, can you be in Maine tomorrow? Josh is out and we have gigs." Irony of ironies, I had replaced Nick Reynolds in The Kingston Trio and now I was being asked to replace "the Lion's son" in this new version of the group.

Well, I couldn't possibly get myself ready for the road that quickly, so they asked me to join them in York, Pennsylvania, the following Wednesday. In the meantime they brought in Don Marovich, who had been singing with The Limeliters, for the date in Maine. I flew out to Pennsylvania the next Wednesday and we rehearsed the show. I had to scramble to learn the non-Trio John Stewart songs they were doing and I suggested that audiences might relate more to other Trio tunes that were not currently on their set list. But I quickly realized that the level of musicianship in this group was far from professional, with the exception of long-time Kingston Trio bass player, Paul Gabrielson.

The single mic staging was uncomfortable for me and it took several shows before I was able to hear the vocal and instrumental mix in the monitor and adapt my singing and playing to blend with Mike and Tim. And harking back to my first encounter with the group in Bend, I was conscious of a large portion of the audience off to my left as I faced the mic. I would make every effort to acknowledge that section of the crowd when I didn't have to be right on mic. Tim, on the other hand, rarely turned to the audience on his right, thus providing folks seated to stage right with the same constant view of his butt that we'd had that night in Bend. So I could not refrain from bursting out laughing when an elderly lady approached us after a show in California one day and, wagging her finger at Tim, she said, "I am so mad! I paid $30 for a front row seat and all I saw was your butt!" Still glaring at him, she spun her walker around and stormed off.

Perhaps it was hubris on my part to think that I could inspire a desire in these guys to strive for a higher level of professionalism. My repertoire suggestions (parroted from audience requests) were summarily rejected. Quite often I was asked after a show, "Why didn't you guys do 'The Sloop John B.'?" Or "They Call The Wind Maria"? How about "The Zombie Jamboree"? And as December approached, I suggested, and even wrote charts for, "We Wish You A Merry Christmas" and "The Last Month of The Year" from the Trio's 1960 Christmas album. No, they'd rather stick to the show they knew. Nothing new, thank you. So with my hopes of actually upgrading this show dashed, I resigned myself to being whored in return for a very nice paycheck at the end of each tour. That may sound harsh, but that's how I felt, along with a whole lot of sympathy for those audience members who had paid good money for what we were offering.

Coming home from a tour late in December, I had a two-hour lay-over in Seattle. I sat down with my laptop and wrote a pretty long email to Tim and Mike addressing my grievances and proposing how we might work together to improve the show. I expressed my disappointment in Mike's decision to cancel a four-day rehearsal over the Christmas break. I thought that would have helped us immensely. But rather than hear my hopes and enthusiasm for better times ahead, Mike took all my criticisms to heart and fired me. *What? Another pink slip? Can't I ever quit on my own terms?*

Well, except for the loss of income, I was not disappointed. To be honest, the rigors of the road, even for just those few months, had taken a toll on me, physically and mentally. Add that to my artistic frustrations and I had every reason to walk away without any regrets. I subsequently heard from a number of Kingston Trio fans who told me they were surprised that I'd toughed it out as long as I had. Mike and Tim hired Don Marovich to replace me and as of my writing this, "The Kingston Trio" continues to hardly resemble the original article.

AND THE BEAT GOES ON

Back home in Oregon, John, Andrew and I began booking our Kingston Trio tribute show under the moniker, "Remembering The Kingston Trio." I guess I should have known that this would get Mike's attention, even though the venues we were playing were local Grange Halls and retirement homes. His attorney sent me a strong letter threatening a law suit if I persisted in using the Kingston Trio name in any advertising. I called Bobbie Childress to ask her opinion and she did feel that the word "Remembering..." implied that the Trio was no more. Well, that's the way I and many fans feel, but respecting her interest in the Trio's legacy and the small percentage she receives from the current group, I once again rebranded our show as "Tales & Tunes of The Kingston Trio." Now, I don't know how you present a show about The Kingston Trio without mentioning the group's name, so I guess we'll take our chances.

♪ ♪ ♪

Bob Shane passed away on January 26, 2020. The world was in the middle of a damn panic, also known as a "pandemic," and we were told to lock ourselves in our homes to keep from spreading the dreaded virus. As a result, Bob's memorial was postponed until August of 2021. John Hollis and I flew to Phoenix to attend this special gathering of friends and fans, and it truly was a memorable memorial. But getting on a commercial airline brought on a bad case of *deja vu* and I was glad that this trip had used up all my frequent flyer miles.

♪ ♪ ♪

Branding ourselves as "Hollis & Haworth," John and I expanded our repertoire and began booking other venues as a duo. One day Meri had a brainstorm to have us perform right in our own back yard, so, building on the model of House Concerts, we began producing summertime Yard Concerts. With our amazing rural setting as a backdrop, we built a 12 ft. by 12 ft. wooden gazebo as a stage. We put up four 10 ft. X 20 ft. canopies side by side and bought seventy-five folding chairs and a dozen six-foot tables. Sending out email invitations to our extensive list of friends and fans, we regularly attracted anywhere from fifty to one hundred guests to each concert. Meri dressed the tables with beautiful tablecloths and folks brought their own food and wine to enjoy as we performed. We usually made a little pocket money for our efforts by passing the hat at the end of the show, but the smiles on peoples' faces were our biggest reward. Admittedly, it was a step down from my days of playing 4,000-seat venues for big money, but one big bonus was being able to walk out my back door right onto the stage.

♪ ♪ ♪

Meri's mother, Evelyn Leep Vohs, turned 100 in April of 2020, and I guess that was a far as she wanted to go. The next month she passed away, and her husband, Ed, followed her to heaven a few months later. Relieved of our caretaking duties, Meri and I began to focus on our own life here in Oregon. Hollis & Haworth continue to perform occasionally and our "Tales & Tunes of The Kingston Trio" is available for bookings, as long as I don't have to get on an airplane. I plan to keep writing songs, serving the Lord as a musician on our church's worship team and sharing my accumulated musical knowledge with my guitar, banjo, bass, ukulele and harmonica students. Oh, and if you want to learn to play the musical saw, I can help with that as well.

♪ ♪ ♪

I wrote a song several years ago called "Who Really Knows" that addresses the reality of an uncertain future. When we moved to Oregon and settled into our rental home on a fifty-acre agricultural property, I thought I would spend the rest of my life there. Ah, but "who really knows" what the future holds? To our surprise, the property was leased to a new vineyard owner who has plans to redevelop the acreage. He issued an edict that we could no longer hold our Yard Concerts there and we were informed by the property owner that we were going to be evicted. Where would we go now? We'd been casually looking for a home to purchase for some time, yet we could find nothing in our price range that suited our needs. But our faith in God's plan for us was realized when the next day after hearing of our impending eviction, we found the perfect home that we can now call our own. A beautiful gated property with plenty of yard for Yard Concerts, plenty of square footage to challenge Meri's decorating skills and a separate "moon cave" where I can spend time on music projects without disturbing the cats. So that's where I've landed at age seventy-six. Could there be more to my story? Time will tell. But I think one book about me is enough, so you can catch any future news on my website: *www.bobhaworth.com*. For now, I think I'll get back to doing...uh, what was I doing?

Gibson
Hollis & Haworth

Hollis & Haworth

TALES & TUNES
of
The KINGSTON TRIO

As portrayed by *L to R*: Andrew Brock,
Bob Haworth, John Hollis.

Top: Yard Concert setting.
Bottom: Our Yard Concert Trio during a performance.

Top: A typical Yard Concert audience.
Bottom: Hollis & Haworth (and ducks) in concert.

ENCORE!

SO, YOU DIDN'T GET ENOUGH? I'm always happy to respond to the applause and give up another tune or two. In this case, I've saved a few more tales that didn't really fit into the rest of the book. So keep reading – there's more to tell...

BOB'S JOKES

From the beginning, Kingston Trio shows have featured humorous interludes between songs. Dave Guard's obtuse humor was a hallmark of the early shows and a prime example is his spoken intro to "When The Saints Go Marching In" on the...from the *Hungry i* album: "So if you'd like to help out, the key is maybe E this time. Or if you're more manually oriented, perhaps some clapping in 4-4 time would be a boon, because we play anywhere from 2-4 to 7-5. It gets pretty Raggedy Andy up here. Or a third alternative is, ya wanna help, ya know, but you can't because you're with somebody cool tonight. Ya know, 'tonight's the night' type thing? So the thing to do is suck on ice cubes in 4-4 time and this satisfies, ya know, inner needs, as well as sociological demands."

John Stewart assumed the front-man role when he stepped into Dave's shoes in 1961. He took Dave's obtuse approach to humor to another level with his wild story-line inventions. One of my favorites is his introduction to "Chilly Winds" on the *College Concert* album: "Up in San Francisco, about a month ago, we were out one night researching with our tape recorder and automatic copyrighting machine, when we stumbled into the local coffee house. I didn't stumble in. In fact, I would have made it in alright if Nick hadn't stepped on my hand. There was a group on stage, singing and playing, and we thought they were quite unusual. They had four zithers, a clavichord, and a phonograph, which made a wild ensemble. They did the next song and we were so taken by it, we requested they sing it again, because, for one, we didn't get a good tape the first time through. I don't want you to think we steal songs, because we actually traded it for two that they didn't have: "John Henry" and "The Blue-Tailed Fly." (Bob Shane chimes in: "There was one more song, John.") Yes, there was one more we threw in for free: an ethnic version of "Roll Me Over In The Clover."

Roger Gambill took the job as head comic in 1973. His wacky southern humor included such classic quotes as: "The other night I was out with a bunch of friends and I got so high I could duck-hunt with a rake."

When I joined the Trio I certainly wasn't prepared to be a funny-man, although over time I learned or created a few bits of humor that got laughs. But Bob Shane would use the space between songs to tell some often pretty hilarious jokes. As far as I know, they were all "borrowed" from other sources, but Bob's delivery sold them as if they were his own.

THE TALKING DOG

I remember a concert we did at Mercyhurst College in Erie, Pennsylvania, and in the front row was a woman with her seeing-eye dog. Bob used to tell a story about a travelling salesman driving around on a back-country road in Tennessee and he sees a sign in front of a broken down shanty-style house that says: "Talking Dog for Sale."

So the guy pulls into the driveway, goes up and knocks on the door and a farmer comes to the door. The guy says "You got a talking dog for sale?" The farmer says, "Yeah, he's out back."

Salesman: "Can I talk to him?"

Farmer: "Sure just go out there and you can talk to him over the fence."

The guy goes out back and he looks over the fence and sees this mutt sitting there. He looks around to make sure nobody's looking and he leans over the fence and says, "You talk?" And the dog replies, "Yep." And the guy says. "So, what's your story?"

The dog looks up and says, "Well, I discovered that I could talk when I was just a puppy and as I grew older, I decided I wanted to help the government, so I got ahold of the CIA and they hired me as a spy-dog. In no time at all they had me jetting from country to country, sitting in on meetings with spies and world leaders; and because no one figured a dog would be eavesdropping, I was one of their most valuable spies for eight years running. And I got a lot of medals for my work, but I got tired of all the traveling, so I came back here and went to work for the local police department. I was working on drug busts and other undercover work and I got some more medals, but after a while I just decided to retire. So I settled down, got married, had some puppies and here I am.

The guy is amazed. He goes back to the house and says, "How much do you want for the dog?" The farmer says, "Ten bucks." The guy is shocked and says, "Ten bucks? For a dog like that with such an amazing story?"

Farmer says, "Ah, he's such a liar! He's never done any of that stuff.""

So the punch-line hits and the audience roars with laughter, but the funniest thing of all was that the seeing-eye dog in the front row went nuts with a sound that seemed very much like dog laughter. Apparently Bob spoke Dog.

TELL ME IN THREE WORDS

A man is sitting at the bar having a cold one when a beautiful woman walks in and sits next to him. He is quite taken with her and he begins buying her drinks and carrying on conversation.

The evening is progressing nicely and at one point the somewhat tipsy young lady leans in close and whispers, "I'll do anything you want, but you have to tell me in just three words what you'd like."

The guy is taken aback and stammers, "Y-y-you'll d-d-do anything I w-w-want? A-a-anything at all???"

"Yes," she replies, "but you have to tell me your desire in just three words."

So the guy thinks for minute, takes a swig of beer and turns to her and says: "Paint my house."

THE HELICOPTER RIDE

Morris and his wife Esther went to the state fair every year. Every year, Morris would say, "Esther, I'd like to ride in that helicopter." Esther always replied, "I know Morris, but that helicopter ride is 50 dollars and 50 dollars is 50 dollars."

A few years later, Esther and Morris went to the fair. Morris said, "Esther, I'm 85 years old. If I don't ride that helicopter now, I might never get another chance."

Esther replied, "Morris, that helicopter ride is 50 dollars and 50 dollars is 50 dollars."

The pilot overheard the couple and said, "Folks, I'll make you a deal. I'll take both of you up for a ride. If you can stay quiet for the entire ride and not say a word, I won't charge you! But if you say one word, it's 50 dollars."

Morris and Esther agreed – and up they went.

The pilot did all kinds of fancy maneuvers, but not a word was heard. He did his daredevil tricks over and over again, but still not a word.

When they landed, the pilot turned to Morris and said, "By golly, I did everything I could to get you to yell out, but you didn't. I'm impressed!"

Morris replied, "Well, I was going to say something when Esther fell out, but 50 dollars is 50 dollars!"

FIVE SHOTS OF CROWN ROYAL

A man walks into a bar. He sits down and asks the bartender to pour him five shots of Crown Royal – quick! So the bar tender pours him five shots of Crown Royal and the man downs one, two, three just like that. The bartender says, "Sir, that's really expensive sipping whiskey. Why are you drinking it like that?" The man downs the fourth one and says, "You'd drink it this way too if you had what I've got." The bartender says, "What have you got?" The man downs the fifth shot and says, "Thirty-five cents."

THE LAUGH METER

I started doing a bit when Bob would tell a joke. I would play the part of the laugh meter. I'd use one arm as the base of the meter and the other arm would be the arrow, rising to indicate the level of audience response to his joke. So Bob would tell three jokes in a row to see which one would get the best response.

Joke #1: A guy sitting at home is feeling lonely and he

decides he needs a pet. He goes to the pet shop and tells the owner he wants the most unusual pet he can get, and cost was not an issue. He settles for a talking centipede. He takes the centipede home in its little centipede house, the size of a shoe box with a roof on it. He puts in on a table next to a nice warm lamp and goes in to get dressed to go out to a bar. He walks back by the shoe box and looks down at the centipede and says, "Hey, do you want to go down to Frank's and have a beer with me?" No answer. So he continues getting dressed and comes back again and says, "Hey, do you want to go down to Frank's and have a beer with me?" No answer. So he gets his coat and he's ready to walk out the door and decides to try one more time. He walks back over to the shoe box and says, "Hey, do you want to go down to Frank's and have a beer with me?" And a little tiny voice comes out of the box and says, "I heard you the first time – I'm just putting on my shoes."

The laugh meter rises to about 75 %. Next...

Joke #2: A guy goes to the ticket counter to check in for his flight. The agent says, "Sorry sir, but you can't take the dog on board." The guy says, "It's my seeing-eye dog." The agent says, "Oh, that's OK, then. You can board." The next guy in line has a pair of shades on and a chihuahua on a leash. The agent says, "Sir, you can't take the dog on board." The guy responds, "It's my seeing-eye dog." The agent says, "A chihuahua?" And the guy says, "Is that what they gave me?"

About the same response – 75% on the laugh meter.

Joke #3: Two soldiers at an army base are out in a field and they find a dead animal. One says it's a mule, the other says it's a donkey. The colonel comes by and says, "You're both wrong...it's an ass. Now get some shovels and bury it." So they're digging away and a nurse drives up and says, "Hi fellas, you diggin' a fox hole?" And they say, "Uh...no..."

100% on the laugh meter.

CAN YOU GIVE ME A PUSH?

It's 3:30 in the morning and a guy's wife wakes him up and says, "There's someone at the door – you better go see who it is." So he puts on his robe and goes downstairs, opens the door and there's a drunk standing there. The drunk says, "Hey buddy, can you give me a push?" The guy says, "It's 3:30 in the morning, it's cold and raining and you're drunk. No." He slams the door and goes back upstairs. His wife says to him, "Hey, I remember when you were in trouble once and you got help." He says, "Yeah, you're right." So he goes back downstairs, walks out on the porch and calls out to the drunk, "Hey, are you still here?" A voice comes back, "Yeah." The guy says, "Do you still need a push?" The drunk responds, "Yeah." The guy says, "Where are you?" Drunk: "Over here – on the swing."

A DUCK WALKS INTO A BAR

A duck walks into a bar. He says to the bartender, "Give me a ham sandwich and a beer, please." The bartender says, "B-b-but you're a duck." The duck says, "Well, you've got good eyes." The bartender says, "B-b-but you can talk." The duck says, "You've got good ears too. Now how 'bout a ham sandwich and a beer?" So for five days in a row the duck comes in, orders a ham sandwich and a beer, pays for it and leaves. On the sixth day the bartender's curiosity gets the best of him and he says to the duck, "You know, we don't get many ducks around here. What brings you to our part of town?" The duck says, "Oh, I'm working a construction site across the street." Bartender: "O...K..."

The next day a guy from the circus happens to stop in and the bartender tells him about this amazing talking duck that comes in for lunch every day. The circus guy is quite impressed with the bartender's story and he says, "You know, we could use a duck like that. I could offer him a high-paying job with the circus. Next time you see him, give him my card."

So the next day the duck comes in for lunch and bartender tells him about the guy from the circus offering him a really high-paying job. And the duck says, "The circus? Isn't that something that goes on in a big tent?" Bartender: "Yes, that's right." Duck: "What would they want with a dry-waller?"

A SONG BY GORDON LIGHTFOOT

George: "We'd like to do a song now by our good friend, Gordon Lightfoot. Gordy is considered the greatest song writer to come out of Canada."

Bob: "No, you're wrong. Duke Ellington was the greatest song writer to come out of Canada."

George: "Duke Ellington wasn't from Canada"

Bob: "Yes he was. He wrote "Take The Train, Eh?"

George: "Bob, your IQ test came back – it was negative."

AUDIENCE GREETING

Here's how Bob would sometimes greet the audience after our opening song: "Hi, it's really a pleasure to be here. I know a lot of acts will stand in front of you and say 'Hi, it's really a pleasure to be here' but they don't mean it. Well, we're no exception. No, it really is a pleasure to be here, 'cause we flew in on Hughes West, and believe me – it's a pleasure to be anywhere!"

WHERE'D YOU COME FROM?

A friend of mine worked at the Fox Theater in Atlanta. It's a vintage theater from the 1930s and seats about 3000 people. One night they had a rock concert there and my friend was ushering. A group of four people came in to be seated and as my friend shined his flashlight down the row where their seats were, he saw this guy sprawled out across all four seats. So he says, "Sir, those seats are taken. You'll have to move." The guy looks up and stammers, "Uh, but, uh...I... uh..." So once again my friend says, "Sir, those seats are taken. You'll have to move." Again the guy says, "I...well... uh...I'm..." My friend, now growing impatient, says, "Sir, where'd you come from?" The guy points up and responds, "The balcony."

A SNAIL AT THE DOOR

A guy hears a knock at the door, but when he opens it, he doesn't see anybody there. He looks down and sees this snail on the door mat, so he picks it up and tosses it out into the yard. A year later he hears a knock at the door, and again, nobody there. He looks down and sees the same snail there from the year before and the snail looks up and says, "So what was that all about?"

QUICK THINKING

A guy is working in a super market up in Idaho along the Canadian border there and a customer comes in and says, "I'd like to buy a half-a-head of lettuce please." So the guy says, "Well I'll have to go ask the manager." So he walks back to the back of the store not realizing that the customer is following him. He says to the manager, "Some jerk out there wants to buy half-a-head of lettuce." And just then he sees the customer out of the corner of his eye, so he says, "And this gentleman wants to buy the other half."

So later the store manager says to the guy, "I know what you did there and I like the way you think on your feet. Where'd you come from anyway?" And the guy says, "Well, I came down here from Canada." Manager: "What brought you down here?" The guy responds, "Well, Canada's just full of whores and hockey players." The manager says, "Hold on now – my wife's from Canada." The guy says, "Oh? What team does she play for?"

CHICKEN LEGS

A salesman is driving along on a back-country road when he looks in the rear-view mirror and sees a chicken running up the road behind him. He looks down at the speedometer and sees that he's going 45 miles an hour. So how could a chicken be out on the highway running 45 miles an hour? He's a little freaked out by this so he steps on the gas and speeds up to 55. Next thing he knows he sees the chicken pull up along side him and just pace him. Now he's really freaked out so he puts pedal to the metal and gets it up to 70 miles an hour. Amazingly the chicken passes him and heads off down the road. About a half mile up the road he sees the chicken turn into a driveway going up to a farm house. So the salesman follows the chicken up the driveway and stops by the house. The farmer comes out and says, "Can I help ya, mister?" The guy says, "Well, I was driving down the road there and all of a sudden this chicken passes me doing 75 miles an hour and I saw him pull into this driveway. Do you own that chicken?" The farmer says, "Yeah, that's one of my five-legged chickens." "Five-legged chickens?" says the salesman, "I've never heard of such a thing." The farmer says, "Yeah, well I did some market research and discovered that people preferred drumsticks over any other chicken part. So I did some cross-breeding and came up with a five-legged chicken." The salesman is amazed and responds, "Well, with your ability to supply so many drumsticks to the market you must be pretty rich." The farmer says, "Nope – ya can't catch the little buggers."

QUICKIES AND ONE LINERS

• I asked my wife what she wanted for her birthday and she said, "Oh, I don't know – get me something really expensive that I don't need." So I signed her up for radiation therapy.

• This next song was written by John Stewart, who used to sing with this group, and John Phillips of The Mamas and Papas. It's called "Chilly Winds" – it's a song about standing outside a Mexican restaurant.

• Yesterday a little old lady called in to the fire department and said, "Help! Help! I have a fire! Send somebody." They said, "How do we get there?" She says, "Don't you have that big red truck anymore?"

• Do you know why beer goes through you so fast? It doesn't have to stop and change color.

• The difference between a viola and a violin is that a viola burns longer.

• The definition of perfect pitch is throwing a banjo down a mine shaft and missing all the accordions.

• God gave drummers 25% more brains than horses so they wouldn't poop during the parade.

• Remember one thing in life – any one thing.

• I plan to live forever. So far, so good.

• It's much better to be rich and healthy than poor and sick.

• You don't have to be black to sing the blues, you just have to be married.

• Birds do it and fly, bees do it and die. But I don't do it 'n' I'll tell you why. Cuz I promised her that I'd be true. But I'll tell what I'll do – I'll lie down and I'll let you. If I don't move I ain't cheatin' (All spoken rapidly in one breath with no pauses.)

• When you're up to your rear end in mud, it's OK to wet yer pants.

• Remember: Eagles may soar, but weasels don't get sucked into jet engines.

• Viagra for me would be like putting a brand new flag pole on a condemned building.

• They found a good use for Viagra – they give it to old guys at old folks' homes – it keeps them from rolling out of bed at night.

• They have a liquid form of Viagra now – you can go home and pour yourself a stiff one.

• The longer the limo the easier the target.

• You can pick your friends and you can pick your nose, but you can't wipe your friends on your saddle.

• The problem with political jokes is they quite often get elected.

Bob Haworth

POETRY

I've written a lot of songs over the years, but sometimes I write lyrics and just can't come up with a melody that fits. Here are a few examples of some of my unsung poems.

MY LITTLE RED PILLOW

Every night when I crawl into bed
I have my little red pillow tucked under my head
On my little red pillow I fall asleep
Never any need for counting sheep
My little red pillow is my best friend
At night it carries me home again
Like a magic carpet it helps me fly
Into your arms in the wink of an eye
On my little red pillow I'll dream tonight
That I'm cuddled up cozy in your arms so tight

PLURALITY

LET'S START WITH A BOX – AND THE PLURAL IS BOXES
BUT MORE THAN ONE OX IS OXEN – NOT OXES
YOU MAY HAVE ONE GOOSE – BUT TWO ARE CALLED GEESE
AND IF YOU SEE A MOOSE DON'T CALL HIS FRIENDS MEESE

YOU'LL SEE ONE GREY MOUSE IN A NEST FULL OF MICE
YET HOUSE AFTER HOUSE IS HOUSES – NOT HICE
IF A MAN IS A MAN THEN MEN WILL BE MEN
BUT MORE THAN ONE FAN IS NOT SEVERAL FEN
I CAN HOP ON ONE FOOT – THEN LAND ON MY FEET
IF I PUT ON A BOOT WOULD A PAIR BE A BEET?

YOU MIGHT LOSE A TOOTH FROM A MOUTH FULL OF TEETH
CAN YOU SIT IN A BOOTH IN A ROOM FULL OF BEETH?
ONE ITEM IS "THAT" WHILE SEVERAL ARE "THOSE"
BUT THE PLURAL OF CAT IS CATS AND NOT COSE

WE SPEAK OF A BROTHER AND MANY ARE BRETHREN
BUT THOUGH WE SAY "MOTHER" WE NEVER SAY "METHREN"
AND THE MASCULINE PRONOUNS ARE HE, HIM AND HIS
BUT IMAGINE THE FEMININE: SHE, SHIM AND SHIS

THE TYPEWRITER REPAIRMAN (In honor of Austin I. Gomes)

HE'S THE LAST OF HIS KIND, A DYING BREED
IN THE BLINK OF AN EYE THERE'LL BE NO NEED
FOR A MAN WITH HIS SKILL WHO DOES WHAT HE DOES
NO ONE WILL REMEMBER WHAT A TYPEWRITER WAS

WITH DEFT AND PRECISION, REPLACING A SPRING
ADJUSTING THE ACTION – IT'S A DELICATE THING
IF THE CARRIAGE IS STUCK, HE KNOWS WHAT TO DO
AND LIKE MAGIC HE'LL MAKE THE BELL RING ON CUE

THERE'S NOBODY LIKE HIM – HE MAY BE THE LAST
HE'S HISTORY FADING INTO THE PAST
IF OUR TECHNO-SOCIETY FAILS IN THE END
I'M KEEPING HIS NUMBER – I MIGHT NEED IT AGAIN

HEY THERE, MOON

Hey there, Moon, you big old Moon -
I caught you sleepin' at the crack of noon!
Your old pal, Sun, was high in the sky
While you were catchin' a little shut-eye.

Hey there Moon, you big old Moon –
Now you're up there floatin' like a bright balloon.
Will you follow my boat all through the night?

And keep on shinin' your guiding light?
Hey there Moon, you big old Moon –
Why are you leavin' me way too soon?
It's not yet dawn and I'm far from home.
Come on back – don't leave me alone!

Hey there Moon, you big old Moon –
You must be eatin' at some greasy spoon!
You keep getting' fatter night after night.
I hope you don't POP! Now that'd be a sight!

BANJO PICKIN' FOOL

Buck-toothed and be-goggled, a banjo I once ogled
It sent a thrill of joy right up my spine
My daddy said, "Well, hey, son – think you could learn to play one?"
I said, "Why, sure!" and that banjo was mine

I played it in the shower and on the Eiffel tower
I played that banjo everywhere I'd go
I never was without it, and if by chance you doubt it
Just ask anyone I used to know

CHORUS:
I'm a banjo-pickin' fool who never went to school
I got all my learnin' on the road
I never took to readin' – I just pick it 'til I'm bleedin'
That's the only life I ever knowed – yes –
That's the only life I ever knowed

And then by chance one evening a stripper in her G-string
Took me to her room above the bar
She gave me milk and cookies and then a little nookie
We really made a mess of her boudoir

I kept up my Don Juan-ing until the day was dawning

And as she lay there in the afterglow
I had an inclination – a fatal inspiration
I started softly strumming my banjo

CHORUS:
Cuz I'm a banjo-pickin' fool who never went to school
I got all my learnin' on the road
I never took to readin' – I just pick it 'til I'm bleedin'
That's the only life I ever knowed – yes –
That's the only life I ever knowed

I saw her eyelids flutter, and then I heard her mutter
Something like, "My God – what is that noise?"
I started playing faster – I hoped I could outlast her
But all I did was make her more annoyed

So when my song was ended I saw she was offended
I grabbed my clothes and headed for the door
And as I made my exit she said, "I must express it -
Next time bring a tuba por favor."

CHORUS:
Yes I'm a banjo-pickin' fool who never went to school
I got all my learnin' on the road
I never took to readin' – I just pick it 'til I'm bleedin'
That's the only life I ever knowed – yes –
That's the only life I ever knowed

So I headed to Kentucky, I thought I might get lucky
Those Bluegrass girls have heard it all before
It didn't take me long there to gather quite a throng there
They clapped and clogged and shouted out for more

CHORUS:

Bob Haworth

Now I'm a banjo-pickin' star – they come from near and far
My Foggy Mountain Breakdown draws a crowd
I keep pickin' and a-grinnin'and the ladies' hearts I'm winnin'
I'm sure my dear old daddy would be proud
Yes I'm a banjo-pickin' star – they come from near and far
My banjo prowess has 'em all beguiled
I keep pickin' and a-grinnin'and the ladies' hearts I'm winnin'
This banjo-pickin' fool just drives 'em wild – yes
This banjo-pickin' fool – who never went to school
This banjo-pickin' fool just drives 'em wild

PARODIES

There are often occasions when something in the news or some wacky idea will remind me of an existing song that, with just a slight twist, might serve as the basis for a great parody. I always credit the composer of the original tune, with hopes that he might see the humor in my appropriation of his music. And by the way, I make no apologies for my political views.

MTA REVISITED

(My answer to why Charlie's wife didn't give him a nickel along with the sandwich. Based on the 1865 song "The Ship That Never Returned" by Henry C. Work. Parody Lyrics by Bob Haworth & Matt Cartsonis, © 2002 Three Cats Music, BMI)

DO YOU REMEMBER THAT STORY 'BOUT A MAN NAMED CHARILIE
AND HIS RIDE ON THE MTA
JUST ONE MORE NICKEL WOULDA STOPPED HIS RAMBLIN'
BUT HE'S RIDIN' THERE STILL TODAY

CHORUS:

THEY SAY HE NEVER RETURNED, NO HE NEVER RETURNED
BUT HIS FATE MAY NOW BE LEARNED
HE'S BEEN RIDIN' THAT TRAIN BENEATH THE STREETS OF BOSTON
HE'S THE MAN WHO NEVER RETURNED

NOW I WENT DOWN TO THE SCOLLAY SQUARE STATION
AND I BOARDED THE 2:15
AND CHARLIE'S WIFE WAS RIGHT THERE AT THE WINDOW
YES, IT'S STILL THE SAME ROUTINE

CHORUS:

THEY SAY HE NEVER RETURNED, NO HE NEVER RETURNED
BUT HIS FATE MAY NOW BE LEARNED

HE'S BEEN RIDIN' THAT TRAIN BENEATH THE STREETS OF BOSTON
HE'S THE MAN WHO NEVER RETURNED

CHARLIE GRABBED HIS SANDWICH THEN TO MY AMAZEMENT
HE PICKED UP AN OLD GUITAR
THEN HE STARTED SINGIN' AND A-PICKIN' AND A-GRINNIN'
AS HE STROLLED UP AND DOWN THE CAR

THERE WAS NO STOPPIN' CHARLIE
AS WE ZOOMED THROUGH THE TUNNEL
AND HE PUT ON A HECK OF A SHOW
HE REALLY HAD 'EM GOIN' THEY WERE ROCKIN' AND A-ROLLIN'
AND HIS HAT WAS OVER-FLOWIN' WITH DOUGH

CHORUS:
THAT'S WHY HE NEVER RETURNED, NO HE NEVER RETURNED
BUT HIS FATE MAY NOW BE LEARNED
HE'S BEEN GETTIN' RICH BENEATH THE STREETS OF BOSTON
HE'S THE MAN WHO NEVER RETURNED

NOW THE BOSTON SUBWAY IS CRAMMED WITH PEOPLE
WITH NO SPECIAL PLACE TO GO
THEY STAND IN LINE TO PAY A BUCK AND A QUARTER
TO SEE CHARLIE'S SUBTERRANEAN SHOW

CHORUS:
THAT'S WHY HE NEVER RETURNED, WHY SHOULD HE EVER RETURN?
BUT HIS FATE WE NOW HAVE LEARNED
HE'S AN UNDERGROUND HIT BENEATH THE STREETS OF BOSTON
HE'S THE MAN WHO NEVER RETURNED

BIMINI REVISITED
(A tribute to Gary Hart. Based on The Kingston Trio recording, "Bimini," from the album, *Sold Out*. Original music and lyrics by Bill Olofson and Mark McIntyre. Parody lyrics by Bob Haworth)

WOE TIL I GO DOWN TO BIMINI
NEVER GOT IT LICKED UNTIL I GO DOWN TO BIMINI

I TOOK A CRUISE ONE SUMMER DAY
ABOARD A YACHT BOUND FOR BIMINI BAY
MS. DONNA RICE CAME ALONG FOR THE RIDE
BUT STILL I TELL YOU I GOT NOTHIN' TO HIDE

CHORUS:

SEND MY MAIL DOWN TO BIMINI
PLEASE DON'T FORGET TO WRITE
THEY CLOSED THE CUSTOMS OFFICE
NOW WE'RE STUCK HERE ALL NITE – STUCK HERE ALL NITE

"MONKEY BUSINESS" WAS THE NAME OF THAT YACHT
WHO WOULD'VE GUESSED I'D EVER GET CAUGHT
THEY BUSTED NIXON AT THE WATERGATE
NOW THE SCANDAL IS TAIL-GATE

CHORUS
I STILL WOULD LIKE TO BE THE PRESIDENT
'CAUSE THAT'S MY ONLY HOPE FOR PAYIN' THE RENT
BUT IF I LOSE THEN I'M ON MY WAY
BACK TO 'MONKEY BUSINESS' DOWN IN BIMINI BAY

CHORUS:
WOE TIL I GO DOWN TO BIMINI
NEVER GOT IT LICKED UNTIL I GO DOWN TO BIMINI

THE WRECK OF THE ELEPHANT GERALD
(To the tune of "The Wreck of The Edmond Fitzgerald" by Gordon Lightfoot. New lyrics and story by Bob Haworth, © 2004 Three Cats Music, BMI)

THE LEGEND LIVES ON OF AN OLD CIRCUS CLOWN,
WHO WAS KNOWN IN THE BUSINESS AS HAROLD
HE WAS GOOD AT HIS CRAFT, HE COULD MAKE PEOPLE LAUGH
AND HE WAS FRIENDS WITH THE ELEPHANT GERALD
AS ELEPHANTS GO, GERALD WAS BIGGER THAN MOST
AND TO SOME HE SEEMED QUITE ENORMOUS
HIS TRUNK IT WAS LONG – BOTH SUPPLE & STRONG
AS HE PROVED AT EVERY PERFORMANCE
IT COULD WRAP TWICE AROUND OLD HAROLD THE CLOWN
AND THEN AS THE PEOPLE APPLAUDED
WITH A HEAVE AND A HO, STRAIGHT UP HE WOULD GO
LIFTING HAROLD TEN FEET OFF THE SAWDUST

BUT AFTER THE SHOW THE TWO LIKED TO GO
INTO TOWN TO DRINK AT THE TAVERN
THE CLOWN DIDN'T DRINK MUCH BUT THE BEAST WAS A LUSH
WITH A HOLLOW LEG DEEP AS A CAVERN
WHEN THEY GOT TO THE BAR –WELL, YOU KNOW HOW THINGS ARE
GERALD COULDN'T SQUEEZE IN THROUGH THE ENTRANCE
HE BELLOWED, "I'LL BE DAMNED! I JUST HADN'T PLANNED
TO GO OUT FOR AN EVENING OF TEMPERANCE!"
THEN HAROLD SAID, "HEY - IT'LL BE OKAY
YOU CAN STICK YOUR TRUNK IN THROUGH THE WINDOW
THOUGH YOUR SIZE IS A FLAW YOU'VE GOT YOUR OWN STRAW
AND YOU WON'T HAVE TO TALK TO NO BIMBOS!"

AND SO THE NIGHT WENT WITH GERALD CONTENT
TO GUZZLE HIS WHISKEY LONG-DISTANCE
BY THE TIME HE WAS DRUNK, POOR GERALD'S LONG TRUNK

WAS LIMP AND REQUIRED ASSISTANCE
WHEN THEY GOT IT OUTSIDE HE SAID, "HAROLD, WANNA RIDE?"
AND THEN TO THE PEOPLE'S AMAZEMENT
HE WRAPPED HIS TRUNK 'ROUND OLD HAROLD THE CLOWN
AND PICKED HIM STRAIGHT UP OFF THE PAVEMENT
WITH THE CLOWN ON HIS BACK HE BEGAN TO MAKE TRACKS
AS OFF DOWN THE HIGHWAY THEY HEADED
GERALD SHOUTED WITH GLEE, "PINK PEOPLE I SEE!"
AND IT WAS JUST WHAT OLD HAROLD HAD DREADED
AT THE CROSSROADS THAT NIGHT GERALD SHOULDA TURNED RIGHT
AND 'TWAS THEN THAT THEIR TRIP WAS IN PERIL
UP AHEAD LOOMED THE DITCH AND BEFORE HE COULD SWITCH
CAME THE WRECK OF THE ELEPHANT GERALD

THE PATROL CAR ARRIVED AND FOUND THEM ALIVE
THO THEY WERE BRUISED AND BATTERED AND DENTED
"IT'S ALL VERY CLEAR!" SAID THE COP WITH A SNEER
"THIS ACCIDENT COULDA BEEN PREVENTED!"
THEN HE HAND-CUFFED THE CLOWN AND SAID,
"I'M TAKIN' YOU DOWNTOWN
'CAUSE WE DON'T TAKE DRUNK DRIVIN' HERE LIGHTLY!"
BUT GERALD YELLED, "HALT! IT WAS REALLY MY FAULT!
I'M THE ONE YOU SHOULD PROSECUTE RIGHTLY!"

THE COP LOOKED CONFUSED 'CAUSE HE KNEW HE SMELLD BOOZE
COULD IT BE? A PACHYDERM JUICER?!!
THEN HE TURNED TO THE CLOWN WITH A VERY STERN FROWN
AND SAID, "LET'S HEAR THE STORY FROM YOU, SIR!"
HAROLD SWAYED TO AND FRO THEN SAID, "WELL, ALL I KNOW
IS I LANDED RIGHT ON MY CABOOSE, SIR
NOW THAT MAY SOUND UNCOUTH BUT TO TELL YOU THE TRUTH
WE BOTH HAVE HAD QUITE A FEW, SIR."
SO THE COP SAID, "OH HELL! I DON'T HAVE A CELL

TO ACCOMMODATE PRISONERS HUMUNGUS
I'LL JUST LET YOU GO, BUT I WANT YOU TO KNOW
WE DON'T TOLERATE DRUNKARDS AMONG US!"

AS THE COP DROVE AWAY THE FIRST LIGHT OF DAY
WAS COMIN' UP OVER THE HOUSES
AND THE DAWN'S EARLY LIGHT REVEALED A STRANGE SIGHT
AN ODD COUPLE OF LATE-NIGHT CAROUSERS
THE PAPER THAT DAY RAN A PHOTO DISPLAY
AND THEIR CAREERS WERE TARNISHED FOREVER
THE CIRCUS CLOSED DOWN AND THEY HAD TO LEAVE TOWN
IN SEARCH OF OTHER ENDEAVORS
SO, REVELLERS ALL – IF YOU DRINK ALCOHOL
AND STRAY FROM THE PATH STRAIGHT AND NARROW
TAKE A CAB – PARK THE 'VETTE – AND DON'T EVER FORGET
THE WRECK OF THE ELEPHANT GERALD!

DON'T TOUCH MY JUNK

(A comment on TSA's intrusive screening procedures. To the tune of "Don't Fence Me In" by Cole Porter. Parody lyrics by Bob Haworth, © 2010 Three Cats Music, BMI)

YOU CAN MAKE ME STAND IN LINE FOR AN HOUR – I DON'T MIND
BUT DON'T TOUCH MY JUNK
TAKE MY BELT, TAKE MY SHOES – EVEN THAT I WON'T REFUSE
BUT DON'T TOUCH MY JUNK
WITH YOUR HAND ON MY THIGH YOU SAY
YOU'RE LOOKIN' FOR EXPOLSIVES
THAT LOOK IN YOUR EYE MAKES ME QUESTION YOUR MOTIVES
MY HEART'S POUNDIN' LIKE A LOCOMOTIVE
SO DON'T TOUCH MY JUNK

AND NOW YOUR HAND'S GETTIN' CLOSER
I SAY "NO SIR" BUT YOU SAY I MUST COMPLY

YOUR GENTLE TOUCH MAKES ME NERVOUS
IT'S A SERVICE THAT IS HARD TO JUSTIFY
IF I HAD BOMBS IN MY SHORTS I THINK YOU'D KNOW IT
THE LOOK ON MY FACE WOULD SURELY SHOW IT
JUST GET ME ON MY FLIGHT NOW BEFORE I BLOW IT
AND DON'T TOUCH MY JUNK

CORONA, CORONA

(To the tune of "Corina Corina." With apologies to Armenter "Bo Carter" Chatmon. Parody lyrics by Bob Haworth, © 2020 Three Cats Music, BMI)

THE WORLD HAS CORONA – IT'S THE LATEST FLU
THE WORLD HAS CORONA – IT'S THE LATEST FLU
YOU BETTER KEEP YOUR DISTANCE
OR YOU MIGHT CATCH IT TOO

CHORUS:

CORONA, CORONA – CORONA, CORONA
CORONA, CORONA – IT'S THE WUHAN FLU

WE HAD THE SWINE FLU BACK IN 0-9
WE HAD THE SWINE FLU BACK IN 0-9
WE DIDN'T SHUT THE WORLD DOWN & EVERYTHING WAS FINE

CHORUS

THEY SENT CORONA FROM ACROSS THE SEA
CHINA SENT US CORONA FROM ACROSS THE SEA
AND NOW THE WHOLE WORLD IS ON ITS KNEES

CHORUS

Bob Haworth

ME AND MY BANJO

(Inspired by the Covid lock-down. Based on "Me and My Shadow," Music by Dave Dreyer, © 1927. Parody lyrics by Bob Haworth, © 2020 Three Cats Music, BMI)

ME AND MY BANJO
STAYIN' HOME LIKE WE'VE BEEN TOLD
ME AND MY BANJO
THIS SOCIAL DISTANCING IS GETTIN' OLD
OUR GIGS HAVE ALL DRIED UP – WE'RE BROKE AS HELL
WHEN WILL THIS END? WELL NO ONE CAN TELL
SO IT'S JUST ME AND MY BANJO
ALL ALONE AND FEELIN' BLUE

I CAN BREATHE FREELY NOW

(In celebration of the end of the Covid mask mandate. Based on "I Can See Clearly Now" by Johnny Nash. New lyrics by Bob Haworth, © 2021 Three Cats Music, BMI)

I CAN BREATHE FREELY NOW, MY MASK IS GONE
I'VE WAITED SO LONG TO FINALLY SEE THIS DAY
BRING ON THE FRESH AIR MY LUNGS ARE SCREAMING FOR
NOW THAT MY MASK (MASK) MASK HAS GONE AWAY

I THINK I CAN MAKE IT NOW MY MASK IS GONE
I MIGHT HAVE TO SHAVE MY FACE BUT THAT'S OKAY
WILL YOU STILL RECOGNIZE YOUR OLD PAL BOB
NOW THAT MY MASK (MASK) MASK HAS GONE AWAY

LOOK ALL AROUND – FACES WITH BIG SMILES
LOOK ALL AROUND – NOTHIN' BUT BIG SMILES

I CAN BREATHE FREELY NOW, MY MASK IS GONE
I FEEL THAT WARM SUNSHINE ON MY FACE
AND MAYBE OUR LIFE GETS BACK TO NORMAL NOW
NOW THAT OUR MASKS (MASKS) MASKS HAVE GONE AWAY
NOW THOSE DARN MASKS (MASKS) MASKS HAVE GONE AWAY

ALL I HAVE TO DO IS DREAM
(A song for "Dreamers. "Based on the Everly Brothers hit written b Boudleaux Bryant. Parody lyrics by Bob Haworth © 2018

DREAM – DREAM, DREAM, DREAM
DREAM – DREAM, DREAM, DREAM

WHEN I CAME HERE AS A YOUNG LAD
I CROSSED THE BORDER WITH MOM & DAD
THEY SAID WHEN I GOT HERE
ALL I'D HAFTA DO IS DREAM – DREAM, DREAM, DREAM

THE USA IS MIGHTY GOOD
GOT A FREE EDUCATION, HEALTH CARE AND FOOD
WHAT MORE COULD I ASK FOR
AND ALL I HAFTA DO IS DREAM

I DON'T WORK TOO HARD – MAYBE MOW A YARD
THEN SIESTA THE REST OF THE DAY
ONLY TROUBLE IS – GEE WHIZ
TRUMP WANTS TO TAKE IT ALL AWAY

THE DEMOCRATS SAY THAT I'VE GOT RIGHTS
THEY WANT MY VOTE, SO THEY'RE GONNA FIGHT
TO MAKE SURE I STAY HERE
AND ALL I HAFTA DO IS DREAM – DREAM, DREAM, DREAM...
"z z z z z z z z z z z z z z z"

HOW MUCH IS THE FINE FOR DOGGIE DOO-DOO?
(Based on my experience as HOA president for our neighborhood. To the tune of "How Much Is That Doggie In The Window?" Words & Music by Bob Merrill, © 1952 Golden Bell Songs. Parody lyrics by Bob Haworth, © 2013 Three Cats Music, BMI)

CHORUS:
HOW MUCH IS THE FINE FOR DOGGIE DOO-DOO?

'CAUSE YOUR DOG LEFT A PILE IN THAT YARD
HOW MUCH IS THE FINE FOR DOGGIE DOO-DOO?
YOUR HOA'S COMIN' DOWN HARD

LAST WEEK WHILE YOU WERE WORKING IN YOUR GARDEN
OLD ROVER DECIDED TO ROAM
HE SLIPPED OUT THE GATE UNDETECTED
AND WANDERED AWAY FROM HIS HOME (DOG GONE!)
NEXT MORNING YOUR NEIGHBOR DISCOVERED
A MESS ON HIS LAWN – SO HE COMPLAINED
THE HOA CAME AND GOT A SAMPLE
AND THE LAB SAYS YOUR POOCH IS TO BLAME, SO

CHORUS

YA KNOW, YOUR DOGGIE'S DNA IS ON RECORD
SO THERE'S NO GETTING 'ROUND IT THIS TIME
THE HOA KNOWS THE POOP-A-TRATOR
AND YOU'RE ON THE HOOK FOR HIS CRIME, SO

CHORUS

POSTIN' POTUS
(A comment on President Trump's use of Twitter. To the tune of "Rockin' Robin" by Leon Rene. Parody lyrics by Bob Haworth © 2019 Three Cats Music, BMI)

TWEEDLE-EE-DEE-DEE-DEE, TWEEDLE-EE-DEE-DEE (2x)

HE TWEETED IN THE MORNIN' – HE TWEETED AT NIGHT
HE TWEETED WHEN HE HAD TO SET THE FAKE NEWS RIGHT
ALL THE DEPLORABLES UP AND DOWN THE STREET
LOVED TO HEAR THE POTUS GOIN' "TWEET-TWEET-TWEET"

POSTIN' POTUS – TWEET-TWEET-TWEET
POSTIN' POTUS – TWEET - TWEEDLE-EE-DEE
GO POSTIN' POTUS – TELL US WHAT'S ON YOUR MIND

NOW TWITTER CLAIMED THE POTUS VIOLATED THEIR RULES
JUST FOR TWEETIN' HOW THE LEFTIES ARE A BUNCH OF FOOLS
THEY BANNED HIM FROM TWEETIN' FOR THE REST OF HIS LIFE
SAID HIS TWEETS WERE CAUSING TOO MUCH STRIFE

SO HE'S LOOKIN' FOR ANOTHER WAY REACH HIS BASE
HE NEEDS TO KEEP HIS MESSAGE IN PELOSI'S FACE
BUT PARLER'S GONE LIKE A BIRD ON THE WING
GUESS A CARRIER PIGEON IS THE NEXT BEST THING

POSTIN' POTUS – TWEET-TWEET-TWEET
POSTIN' POTUS – TWEET - TWEEDLE-EE-DEE
GO POSTIN' POTUS – TELL US WHAT'S ON YOUR MIND

INSURRECTION

(My take on January 6, 2020. To the tune of "Fascination." Music by Fermo Dante Manchetti. New Lyrics by Bob Haworth © 2022 Three Cats Music, BMI. Apologies to Nat King Cole

IT WAS INSURRECTION, THEY SAY
AND IT MIGHT HAVE ENDED RIGHT THERE AT THE START
THE WARNING SIGNS WERE CLEAR BUT NO ONE SEEMED TO HEAR
THE CALLS FOR MORE COPS TO KEEP LAW AND ORDER

IT WAS INSURRECTION, THEY SAY
PELOSI STOOD BACK AND JUST LET IT HAPPEN
SHE COULD HAVE CALLED UP THE GUARD IF SHE WANTED
BUT INSURRECTION WAS HER GOAL

OPEN BORDERS

(To the tune of "Oklahoma. "Music by Richard Rodgers (used without permission. New Lyrics by Bob Haworth © 2007 Three Cats Music, BMI)

O---PEN BORDERS
WHEN YOU COME WE'LL LOOK THE OTHER WAY
WE'VE GOT JOBS FOR YOU THAT WE WON'T DO
FOR THE LOW-DOWN WAGES THAT THEY PAY

O ---PEN BORDERS
IT'S THE LAND OF OPPORTUNITY
OH, AND BY THE WAY – WHEN YOU COME TO STAY
YOU'LL GET LOTS OF BENEFITS FOR FREE
DON'T SPEAK ENGLISH? NO PROBLEM AT ALL
JUST PRESS 2 ON YOUR PHONE WHEN YOU CALL

AND CAN YOU SAY:
"N – A – F – T – A"? IF SO WE KNOW THAT
YOU'RE GONNA LOVE OPEN BORDERS
OPEN BORDERS   – OK!

KABUL
(Based on the song "Brazil" by Ary Burroso. Parody lyrics by Bob Haworth ©2021 Three Cats Music, BMI)

KABUL – WHERE BIDEN LOOKS LIKE SUCH A FOOL
THE RUSSIANS AND THE CHINESE DROOL
AND EVEN ALLIES RIDICULE
THE WAY THIS CLUSTER-F**K WENT DOWN
AND NOW OUR PRESIDENT'S THE CLOWN
THE BIDEN CIRCUS CAME TO TOWN
AND TURNED KABUL UPSIDE-DOWN
NOW – THE TALIBAN HOLDS ALL THE CARDS
AND THEY WILL SURELY DISREGARD
WHATEVER BIDEN SAYS '
CAUSE NOW THEY RULE IN OLD KABUL

SMOKE GETS IN YOUR EYES
(A comment on the annual summer forest fires in Southern Oregon. Music: Jerome Kern / Lyrics: Otto Harbach. From 1933 musical "Roberta" Parody lyrics by Bob Haworth, © 2015 Three Cats Music, BMI)

THEY ASKED ME HOW I KNEW THE SKY'S NO LONGER BLUE
I OF COURSE REPLIED, "SOMETHING THERE ON HIGH

CANNOT BE DENIED."
THEY SAID SOMEDAY YOU'LL FIND SUDDENLY YOU'RE BLIND
THE WOODS ARE ALL ON FIRE AND YOU REALIZE
SMOKE GETS IN YOUR EYES

SO WE COUGH AND SADLY WATCH OUR WOODS GO UP IN FLAME
DAY BY DAY OUR FORESTS BURN AWAY
IT'S JUST A CRYIN' SHAME

NOW I CAN'T SEE THE SKY SO I RUN AND HIDE
WHAT ELSE CAN WE DO WITH THE FLAMES SO HIGH
SMOKE GETS IN YOUR EYES - SMOKE GETS IN YOUR - EYES

THE FOSBURY FLOP

(An ode to my high school buddy and high-jump super-star, Dick Fosbury. Parody of "The Monster Mash" by Bobby "Boris" Pickett. Parody lyrics by Bob Haworth, © 2018)

WHEN DICK WAS KID HE WANTED TO JUMP
BUT HE COULDN'T GO HIGH, HE WAS IN A SLUMP
AND THEN ONE DAY HE WAS OUT ON THE TRACK
AND HE CLEARED THE BAR LAYIN' FLAT ON HIS BACK

CHORUS:
HE DID THE FLOP – HE DID THE FOSBURY FLOP
FOSBURY FLOP – IT STARTS WITH A HOP
HE DID THE FLOP – HE WENT OVER THE TOP
HE DID THE FLOP – HE DID THE FOSBURY FLOP

NOW THE COACH WASN'T SURE IF THE FLOP WAS LEGAL
CAN YOU FLY THROUGH THE AIR LIKE AN UPSIDE-DOWN EAGLE?
BUT WHEN HE CLEARED 6'-10" AND NO ONE COMPLAINED
THE WHOLE TEAM CHEERED AND SAID "DO IT AGAIN!"

CHORUS

AT OREGON STATE FOZ PERFECTED HIS STYLE

THEY KEPT RAISIN' THE BAR AND AFTER A WHILE
HE CLEARED 7 FEET AND HE KNEW HE COULD TOP IT
AND HIS HIGH JUMPIN' FAME TOOK OFF LIKE A ROCKET

CHORUS

IN MEXICO CITY DICK HIT HIS STRIDE
HE TOOK HOME THE GOLD AND WE ALL BURST WITH PRIDE
RIGHT HERE IN MEDFORD IS WHERE IT BEGAN
NOW THE FOSBURY FLOP IS THE HIT OF THE LAND

CHORUS

AUDITIONS

As a folk musician, how do you top being a member of The Brothers Four and The Kingston Trio? I count myself quite blessed to have spent several years with both groups. That having been said, I did audition for two other folk groups over the years. I can't recall what prompted these forays into uncharted territory, but neither of them panned out, and I can only thank God for guiding me in the right direction.

During the 1970s, The Brothers Four often had long stretches of inactivity between shows or tours. We had our annual Japanese tour, lasting anywhere from a few weeks to three months, and that often provided a year's salary for me. But during those down-times I pursued other activities. I had a duo with Gary Ballard for many years. We played all the hotel lounges around Seattle and did pretty well. The duo was called "Bo Mooney," after the cartoon character that I had been drawing for years. Gary played electric guitar and five-string banjo. I played acoustic guitar, plectrum banjo, harmonicas, foot-bass (right foot) and high-hat cymbal (left foot.) We had a really full sound for a duo. This was prior to the advent of digital back-up tracks.

At some point we added my ex-wife to the "band," which split the paycheck 1/3 to Gary and 2/3 to the Haworth family. But I was always looking to increase my income and at one point I took a day job as bookkeeper for LS Cedar Company, a local lumber yard on Vashon Island. Then an opportunity presented itself to audition for The New Christie Minstrels. I can't recall what prompted that – perhaps my connection with Bill Zorn, whom I had met when he was a member of that group.

I don't recall anything about the audition – where it took place, what the audition entailed, etc. But my ex and I auditioned together, hoping they'd take us both. My only recollection about the outcome of that was that they called us back and said they'd love to have us in the group, but that we were too old. We had not yet hit age thirty, but they were not taking anybody over the age of twenty-five. So we didn't get that gig (thankfully!)

The other group I auditioned for (twice!) was The Limeliters. My first audition for the Limes was an amazing experience. The Limes and The Brothers Four had done a show in Seattle, and Lou Gottlieb had mentioned to me that Glenn Yarbrough was leaving the group and they were casting around for his replacement. He invited me to come and sing with him and Alex Hassilev at his satellite Morning Star commune in Seattle the next night.

I met Alex at the hotel and we drove out to a house in the west part of town which was the home of the Seattle contingent of Lou's Morning Star Ranch. About twenty hippies lived in this house and when we walked in, Lou was sitting cross-legged on the floor of the living room, holding forth to a circle of likewise cross-legged hippies. Alex and I took a similar pose and nestled into the circle.

Lou explained that they were sharing their spirituality in music that evening and each member of the group was being asked to lead a song. A guitar (and a bong) was being passed from person to person as the song leadership was going around the circle.

As the guitar was coming my direction I began to panic. I didn't have a clue what to sing that would fit into this format. This was well before my return to the church, and I was not particularly spiritual at the time. My musical tastes were running along the lines of Kinky Friedman, Dan Hicks and David Allen Coe. Yes, I was a sick puppy! And I knew that "Cum Stains On My Pillow" was not going to wash with this crowd.

I was two hippies and a bong hit away from the guitar and I still didn't have any idea what I was going to do when my turn came. I knew I couldn't just sit there like an idiot and go, "Uh, let's see - what do I know? Any requests?" Now it's just one more hippy away – I'll pass on the bong hit, thank you very much. Oh what to do – what to do?! (The soundtrack features rising diminished chords, building the suspense!)

Then, just as I'm putting the strap over my neck and adjusting the tuning, it hits me. "Get Together"! I couldn't believe that nobody had played it yet. And it was a song I knew because we were doing it in The Brothers Four show at the time. Well, it brought the house down and of course, everybody knew it, so it was a perfect sing-along. All the hippies, including Lou and Alex, joined me in glorious harmony (or so it seemed in our collective inebriated state). And yes, I'll take that bong hit now, thanks!

After the music, Lou did his guru thing for about 1/2 hour, lecturing on something profound in his professorial persona. Lou had a way with words and I always loved his introductions to songs during a Limeliters show. Somehow through his use of over-your-head language, he would say the funniest stuff.

Anyway, the session ended with cookies and tea and I drove Alex back to the hotel. I got a call from him a few days later informing me that they had selected Red Grammer to take Glenn's spot. As a life-long fan of the Limes (my dad had bought their first album in about 1960 and I was hooked immediately) I didn't think anybody could replace Glenn, but Red did a great job.

The other time I auditioned for The Limeliters was after my departure from The Kingston Trio in 2005. Alex was planning to retire after Bill Zorn and Rick Dougherty had left to become 2/3 of The Kingston Trio. He'd hired Andy Corwin to replace Bill (Andy recreated Lou's part incredibly well – he did a very believable rendition of "Have Some Madeira, M'Dear"), and after Rick left, Mack Bailey took that spot. Meri and I had taken a two-month vacation to Hawaii and Alex asked if I could route our return thru LA and come out to his house to audition to take his place in the group.

Alex emailed me the audition song-list and some charts and I put in some very minimal time on trying to learn my parts. But my heart wasn't really into it – hey we were in Hawaii! And I don't think I really wanted this gig anyway. I was sorta thinking – Brothers Four – Kingston Trio – Limeliters – nice resume. But I was also sorta thinking –retirement – solo career.

So, we got to LA, had a very nice evening with the boys and flew back to Denver the next day. I didn't think I'd get the gig, and sure enough, Alex called a few days later to inform me that they'd hired Gaylan Taylor. I was actually relieved.

Oh – I did offer my services to one other group. Noel (Paul)

Stookey was one of the artists who graced the stage at The Kingston Trio Tribute show at the Birchmere several years ago. Mary Travers had just been diagnosed with leukemia and wasn't planning on touring. So I told Noel that I'd be glad to take her spot if they needed me. He responded that "Peter, Paul and Bob" just didn't seem to have marquee appeal. I had to agree.

JOHN STEWART

John Stewart and me.

When Dave Guard left The Kingston Trio in 1961, Nick and Bob went on a hunt for someone to replace him. Among those considered for the spot were Chip Douglas (who later founded the Modern Folk Quartet and then went on to produce The Monkees), Roger McGuinn (a founding member of The Byrds), John Phillips (subsequently known as the head Papa of The Mamas and Papas) and songwriter, Rod McKuen. But it was a Dave Guard protégé named John Stewart who finally got the call.

John was already on the group's radar, having written two songs that the Trio had previously recorded, and he was as close to a Dave Guard clone as they could hope for. An avid Kingston Trio fan, he had immersed himself in Dave's guitar and banjo styles and shared a similar vocal range. A bonus was John's song-writing ability, which was destined to contribute substantially to the group's repertoire.

To be honest, I was never a huge John Stewart fan. For me, Dave was hard to replace. But John proved to be a great fit for the group and The Kingston Trio forged ahead for several more years cranking out hit records and selling out concerts world-wide. Then came a band from England called The Beatles and the music landscape evolved, leading to the Trio disbanding in 1967. John Stewart struck out on his own and continued writing songs, amassing a catalog of over 600 compositions. One of his biggest post-Trio hits was a song recorded by the Monkees, "Daydream Believer." And in 1969 his own recording of "Gold" made it to #5 on the charts.

Occasionally John would be booked to open shows for us, so I got to know him a bit. I remember one such occasion at a beautiful concert venue in Marin County. It was an afternoon concert and the promoter informed us that some organization had bought tickets for and bussed in about 100 teen-agers for our concert. That seemed a little odd to us, since our target demographic was the fifty-plus age-group. But we thought OK, here's an opportunity to give these kids a little cultural enlightenment.

So John went on and did about a half hour. He came back to the dressing room after his set and said, "Man, I've never played for such a dead-assed crowd. Maybe you guys can liven 'em up." So we went out and hit the stage with a forceful version of "Hard Ain't It Hard" only to be met with a mild smattering of applause. And that's the way it went for the whole forty-five-minute set. Back in the dressing room we were all scratching our heads, wondering what had just happened. The promoter came in to pay us and we asked him if we'd done a sub-standard show or something, because the audience seemed unimpressed. He said, "Oh, those kids they bussed in were all from a school for the deaf." Say what??? You take deaf kids to a music concert? Well, maybe they just couldn't read our lips, so that's why they didn't respond.

Oddly, there was another similar occasion when Stewart opened for us. It was a show at a college somewhere in the Midwest and this time we were fore-warned that some of the audience would be hearing-impaired. However, there would be a signer on stage who would translate our lyrics with sign language. At sound-check she came out and we talked with her about how this was going to work. She said she had researched our songs and had the lyrics printed out and had actually practiced with our recordings before-hand. So we ran through two or three songs with her and watched her signing to the music and we were actually kind of fascinated with her art.

So at showtime Stewart went on to do his opening set to a rousing response from the audience. When he came back to the dressing room he raved about the great job the signer had done and said that they had interacted a bit. So as we were getting ready to go out for our set, Shane says, "Hey – I have an idea. Let's mess with this chick. Just follow my lead." So we dived into "Hard Aint' It Hard" and when it came around to Shane's verse he just sang jibberish. And the poor signer gal was looking perplexed and flustered, trying to sign the words he was singing. Well, George and I caught on and we carried the bit into the next couple of songs. Finally this poor gal turned to us and said, "Those aren't the lyrics I heard on the recording." Well at that point we were busted and we had to admit to our game. I hope the audience thought it was as funny as we did.

I did have one somewhat frightening experience with John Stewart. The Kingston Trio was planning a recording project and we were working up a list of songs as potential repertoire for the project. We were all in agreement that there should be at least one Stewart song on the recording, and one we all particularly liked was "Heart Of A Kid." As we were working up an arrangement of the song we came up with a different order for the verses, because we wanted the last verse to be "We're still singin', singin' the songs we've always known..." and we wanted to make that a group verse. That meant we were one verse short if we wanted to have a verse for each of us to solo on.

So I took it upon myself to write another verse, which was very much in context with the rest of the song, we all thought:

I'M STILL DREAMIN' OF THE WAY THINGS OTTA BE
I'M STILL DREAMIN' OF PEACE & HARMONY
I'M STILL DREAMIN' AND IT'S EASIER SOMEHOW
KNOWING THE THINGS THAT I KNOW NOW
I'M STILL DREAMIN' LIKE I ALWAYS DID
DREAMIN' WITH THE HEART OF A KID
WITH THE HEART OF A KID

A few weeks later John was on a show with us back east somewhere and he cornered me after sound check and gave me a royal reaming for messing with his song. Somehow it had gotten back to him that I'd written an extra verse and that was off-limits! Now, I still sing the verse I wrote and so far I haven't yet been struck by lightning.

Another re-write that he never knew about, and so far has not responded to with a lightning bolt, was his song, "Comin' From The Mountains." I always thought the last verse of that song was a little lame:

THE BOYS WITH DAVY CROCKETT
WHO DIED AT THE ALAMO
I HEARD THEM SAY WHEN THEY ATTACKED,
"I KNEW THIS ROOM WOULD KILL THE ACT"

Instead, I sing:

WE LOVE THIS MOUNTAIN MUSIC,
WE HOPE YOU LIKE IT TOO
WE PLAY ALL DAY, WE PLAY ALL NIGHT
PRETTY SOON WE'LL GET IT RIGHT

ALLIGATORS

This event occurred prior to my joining The Brothers Four, but it's a hilarious story that I've always enjoyed telling. Early in the group's career they were booked to perform at a Columbia Records convention in Florida. Label executives, PR reps and sales personnel had gathered to get the latest scoop on new and long-time acts and The Brothers Four performed for the gathering on one evening.

After the event Dick Foley, Mike Kirkland and John Paine went club-hopping with one of the local reps, while Bob Flick joined some friends and went elsewhere. Returning to the hotel with the label rep, Dick, Mike and John stopped to check out a caged area in the front of the hotel that enclosed a small pond populated with several alligators. The label rep, somewhat inebriated, informed the guys that he was an expert at catching alligators and to prove it, he hopped the fence and returned with a small gator rapped in his sport coat. Wanting to show off his new pet, he offered to carry it up to their room.

The boys were sharing a two-bedroom suite and since Bob Flick was still out with friends, they decided to lay the alligator in his bed. He was fairly calm, despite his capture and kidnapping into the hotel. The plan was hatched to surprise Bob when he returned, so the Columbia rep pulled the covers over the critter and told the boys that as long as he was not disturbed he would remain calm and probably go to sleep.

So the trap was set and the conspirators waited for Bob's return. Pretending to be asleep in their beds, they let Bob prepare to hit the sack. When he pulled the covers back the gator awoke with a wide-mouthed hiss that sent Bob to the other side of the room. Erupting with laughter, the rest of the group came to life to enjoy the prank.

Well, that was fun, but now what do we do with this alligator? The Columbia rep had told the guys that when they removed him from the bed, they should wrap his snout and his tail with towels to keep him from causing any damage. So they retrieved a couple towels from the bathroom, carefully wrapped each end per the instructions, and carried him out to the hall. Deciding that it was best not to leave him in the hallway, they took him on down to the elevator and pushed the call button. When the door opened they tossed the gator in, pushed "Lobby" and sent him on his way. Returning to their suite, the boys laughed themselves to sleep wondering what happened when the elevator opened and the alligator strolled out into the lobby. We're left to imagine the rest of the story.

♪ ♪ ♪

I have another alligator story, and although I heard about this one years later, it bears retelling. Through a mutual friend, I had been introduced to a gentleman named Forrest Fenn. He was a fascinating personality with an amazing past. He had written a book, an autobiography basically, called *The Thrill Of The Chase*. The theme was that most often, the journey towards any goal in life has a more profound impact on us than the actual arrival at the destination. Forrest asked me to write a song to accompany his book, which I did. He invited me to sing it at his book release event in Santa Fe. So Meri and I took a road trip to New Mexico.

When we arrived we were treated in grand fashion to a deluxe room at the Inn at Loretto. Forrest and his lovely wife, Peggy, were gracious hosts and we were honored to be invited into their home while we were there. Following Forrest's discharge from the service after the Viet Nam war he started a business selling art pieces, including paintings and sculptures. He developed a clientele that attracted buyers like Jackie Onassis, Ted Turner, Suzanne Summers and other celebrities. He put together a huge art gallery complex that included a large outdoor area populated by an array of stone sculptures.

In the center of this virtual park was a large pond. At one point Forrest had purchased two alligators to inhabit this pond, and he actually considered them to be his pets. There was a large flat boulder at one end of the pond where he would stand to feed his pet gators. When they saw him on the rock they knew it was chow time and they would swim over and jump up out of the water to grab their meal in mid-air.

One day Forrest hosted a campaign fund-raiser for someone running for a political office in New Mexico. The event was held in the Fenn outdoor gallery. When it came time for the candidate to speak to his donors, he stepped up onto the feeding rock to address the crowd. The gators, spotting a human on the rock, assumed it was feeding time and made their way over. Expecting a meal, they began leaping toward the man on the rock, snapping their jaws in anticipation of their food. Well, the crowd reacted in horror before the candidate even realized what was nipping at his heels. Once alerted he hopped off the boulder as Forrest came to the rescue with a bucket of raw meat. And believe it or not, this was a candidate that Forrest supported!

Bob Haworth

WHY I BECAME A "FISHYTARIAN"

People occasionally ask me why I don't eat meat. I don't consider myself a vegan or a vegetarian because I do eat seafood. It's just that I exclude anything with legs (shrimp, crabs and lobsters excepted) from my diet. But when people do ask, I recount this story about what led me to adopt the "fishytarian" lifestyle – and it had nothing to do with health or dietary concerns.

I've owned pets all my life – cats, dogs, rabbits, salamanders. I have special memories of some of them, but one that stands out is a critter that came to our family in an interesting way. We were invited to a party at a rural home that had some livestock, including a few goats, chickens, a couple horses and some pigs. One of the sows had recently given birth to a litter and the party hosts decided to offer one of the piglets to the winner of their Greased Pig Contest. Well, my ex-wife decided to enter the contest and after a rambunctious romp around the pig pen, she emerged, mud-caked, with a greased-up little piggy in her arms.

We cleaned up the pig (and the ex) and headed home. On the way we stopped at a pet store and bought him a harness and a leash. We were the talk of every rest stop along the way, walking our little piglet on a leash!

I'm not sure how we settled on his name, "Rooter," but it proved to be prophetic. Within hours he had outgrown his harness, and he quickly ballooned to a hefty 300 pounds. I rigged up a pen for him, but he preferred to hang out with the neighborhood dogs that were allowed to run loose. Of

Graham "playing" with Rooter.

course, the dogs spent plenty of time on the beach, and Rooter became a regular beach-hog. But his free-roaming days ended when, living up to his name, he rooted up our neighbor's front yard.

Rooter had become very difficult to handle, having grown up as a free-range pig. Getting him into his pen was time-consuming and often unsuccessful. He'd outgrown his cuteness and we were forced to make a difficult decision. We called a local butcher and arranged to have Rooter transformed into ham and bacon. I didn't want to have anything to do with his demise, so we asked the butcher if he would come while we were out of town for a weekend gig up the peninsula.

Returning from our trip on Sunday, we were surprised to find Rooter still alive in his pen. I called the butcher the next day to find out what was up. He said that he had tried to get the pig out to the street where he could, uh…do what he had to do. But Rooter was just too unruly to handle, and he had to give it up. So, we rescheduled with the promise that I would lead Rooter out to the street for his dispatchment. Despite my effort to avoid that moment, there I was, forced to watch our pet's life come to a violent end.

We loaded him up into the butcher's truck and off he went to be transformed into ham and bacon. Many friends and neighbors raved about his great flavor, but no part of him ever crossed my lips. And from that day on I gave up all pork, beef, poultry and even my favorite chocolate-covered ants.

POLITICS

Unlike many of the folk artists of the 1960s, The Kingston Trio as a group has always eschewed spewing politics from the stage, preferring to simply "shut up and sing." I assume that was partly a result of the divergent political viewpoints within the group. I know Bob was very conservative, while Nick leaned more liberal. I don't know which side of the fence Dave Guard grazed on, but John Stewart was very much a Kennedy fan. When Robert Kennedy was running for President in 1968, John rode the campaign train with him and was even at the Ambassador Hotel when Bobby was killed. But this was all done on John's personal time and did not involve The Kingston Trio.

Another factor in the group's conscious avoidance of political rhetoric from the stage was a strong commitment to entertaining the audience. To that end, we loved to make fun of politics with some of our between-song commentary. For example: "The word 'politics' comes from two Greek root-words: 'poly,' meaning 'many' and 'tics' – 'blood-sucking insects.' Or, "The problem with political jokes is that they sometimes get elected."

The Trio's repertoire scratched the surface of politics with songs like "Where Have All The Flowers Gone" and Stewart's "New Frontier," but I personally consider those to be more social commentary than political. Surprisingly, however, the song, "Charlie On The MTA," is itself a product of politics. And if you think politics stinks today, here's a story that easily rivals any modern-day scandal.

In 1945, James Curley opted to vacate his congressional seat to run for the office of mayor of Boston. Curley was a professional politician and he had served as Boston's mayor three times previously. Despite the fact that he was then embroiled in two separate indictments for bribery and mail fraud, he remained popular with his Irish-American base and won the election with 45% of the vote. In 1947, he was found guilty of the mail fraud charge and sentenced to six to eighteen months in Federal prison. City Clerk John B. Hynes (I'd be changing my name if I had that one) served as mayor during Curley's incarceration. That only lasted five months, thanks to President Truman's commutation of his sentence. He returned to Boston and a hero's welcome, resuming the job of mayor.

In 1949, Curley ran for re-election and Hynes decided to run against him. Also on the ticket was Progressive candidate, Walter O'Brien. At that time, the fare for a ride on the MTA was ten cents. Candidate Hynes was proposing an increase in the form of a five-cent exit fee. A dime to board and a nickel to get off. O'Brien decided to make that his campaign issue and he enlisted Bess Hawes and Jacqueline Steiner to write him a campaign song. Bess was the sister of musicologist Alan Lomax and she had previously sung with The Almanac Singers. Steiner wrote the lyrics and they used the melody from an 1865 song called "The Ship That Never Returned" to create the story of "Charlie on The MTA." Then with their group, "The Boston Peoples Artists," they recorded the song and had it pressed to a 78 RPM record.

O'Brien couldn't afford newspaper or radio ads, so he outfitted a truck with loud speakers and drove around Boston broadcasting the "MTA" song and staging mobile rallies. He received a ten-dollar citation for disturbing the peace, and although he caused a stir with his unconventional campaign, he lost the election with only 1% of the vote. John B. Hynes won and Boston said goodbye to ten-cent subway rides. Walter O'Brien was branded as a communist and was forced out of politics. But the song had a life of its own.

Folk singer, Will Holt, heard the song from one of O'Brien's former staffers and released his recording of it on Coral Records in 1957. When it aired in Boston there was such an overwhelming public outcry against Walter O'Brien and his perceived communist leanings that the song was banned from the radio. But when The Kingston Trio heard Holt's recording, they perceived it as a playful story. And being sensitive to the recent blacklisting of groups like The Weavers for their communist affiliations, the Trio chose to omit some of the more progressive verses. They also changed Walter O'Brien's name to George to further distance the song from its origins. As a result, the song was divorced from its political roots and became a big and enduring hit for The Kingston Trio. And Charlie became the face of the Charlie Card fare system that the MBTA (formerly the MTA) initiated in 2004. So much for "many blood-sucking insects."

MORE POLITICS

In 2007, I happened to read an article on the internet that put a backward spin on the issue of illegal immigration at our southern border. What if I decided to sneak into Mexico bypassing the legal process of entry? What if when I got there, I demanded that the Mexican government provide me with free health care, public school education for my kids in English and the right to wave my American flag and celebrate the 4th of July while enjoying the hospitality of a foreign country? In Denver that year, Cinco de Mayo brought out a parade of illegals waving the Mexican flag and demanding those benefits from our government. I couldn't comprehend why someone would break into a foreign country and then demand these things while waving the flag of the country they had abandoned.

The article inspired me to write a song and poke a little fun at this issue. The title is "Can You Get Me In" and here are the lyrics:

WELL, I WROTE MY CONGRESSMAN TO LET HIM KNOW
THAT I'M THINKIN' 'BOUT HEADIN' DOWN TO MEXICO
AND I WAS HOPIN' HE COULD PULL SOME STRINGS TO GET ME IN
YA SEE, I DON'T WANNA BOTHER WITH LEGALITIES
NO PASSPORTS OR VISAS, IF YOU PLEASE
I'M JUST ASKIN' FOR THE SAME DEAL THERE THAT WE GIVE THEM

CHORUS:

AND I SAID, "CAN YOU GET ME IN? CAN YOU GET ME IN
I MIGHT STAY FOR AWHILE AND PRETEND I'M A CITIZEN

BUT I DON'T WANNA LEARN THEIR NATIVE TONGUE
AND I WON'T PAY TAXES – THAT'S NO FUN!
I JUST WANNA START A BRAND NEW LIFE IF YOU CAN GET ME IN"

NOW I PLAN TO TAKE THE WHOLE FAMILY
ALL MY COUSINS, MY SIBLINGS AND EVEN AUNT BEA
WE'D ALL LIKE JOBS AND A REAL NICE PLACE TO LIVE
I WANT MY KIDS IN AN ENGLISH SPEAKING SCHOOL
I WANT FOOD STAMPS AND HEALTH CARE – I'M NO FOOL
'CAUSE ALL THAT STUFF IS MY PREROGATIVE!

CHORUS:
SO, CAN YOU GET ME IN? ...etc.

BRIDGE:

WELL, LAW AND ORDER ACROSS THE BORDER
IT DON'T MEAN A THING TO ME
IT'S SO EASY WHEN THE WHEELS ARE GREASY
JUST OPEN UP THE GATE AND TOSS AWAY THE KEY

NOW ON THE 4TH OF JULY I PLAN TO MAKE SOME NOISE
MIGHT THROW A LITTLE PARTY FOR ME AND THE BOYS
WE'LL GO WAVIN' OUR AMERICAN FLAG ALL OVER TOWN
WE'LL DRINK BUD AND COORS AND HAVE BARBECUE
TALK BASEBALL, APPLE PIE AND MOTHERHOOD TOO
AND WE DON'T WANT THE LOCAL POPULATION
TRYIN' TO PUT US DOWN

CHORUS:

SO CAN YOU GET ME IN? CAN YOU GET ME IN?
I MIGHT STAY FOR AWHILE AND PRETEND I'M A CITIZEN
BUT I DON'T WANNA LEARN NO ESPANIOLE
PRESS "ONE" FOR ENGLISH, THAT'S ALL I KNOW
I JUST WANNA START A BRAND NEW LIFE IF YOU CAN GET ME IN
(TAG LINE): NOW PLEASE MR. CONGRESSMAN
CAN YOU GET ME IN?

Because this issue was a point of discussion on talk radio at the time, I recorded the song and sent it to The Peter Boyles show on KHOW Radio. Peter played it a lot and as a result I was getting requests for it at my live performances. I had a weekly Thursday night gig at The Atlanta Bread Company in Lakewood and one night, after receiving several requests from audience members to play the song, I found myself in trouble with the PC police.

"Illegal alien blues"
Washington Times Newspaper
October 25, 2007

By Valerie Richardson - LAKEWOOD, Colo.

Folk singer Bob Haworth lost a gig after a high school teacher accused him of racism for his song parodies about illegal aliens. Now Mr. Haworth says the teacher should lose his job, too.

Mr. Haworth, who sang with the Brothers Four and Kingston Trio revival groups, pleaded his case two weeks ago at a Jefferson County school board meeting, arguing the teacher should be fired for using class time to defame him in front of students.

"I asked for the appropriate discipline, and I indicated the appropriate discipline would be dismissal, which is what he asked for me," Mr. Haworth said. "I'm just hoping the school board will do the right thing."

It began Sept. 13 during one of Mr. Haworth's regular Thursday night performances here at the Atlanta Bread Company. The audience had requested several of his song parodies, including "Pizza for Pesos" and "Can You Get Me In?"

Both tunes, which he wrote for KHOW-AM radio in Denver, poke fun at federal and local immigration policy. "It was a very casual atmosphere, lots of people having a good time," Mr. Haworth said. "But there was one very touchy customer who apparently didn't like my songs and wrote a letter demanding I be fired." Included in the letter was a business card identifying the customer as a teacher with the Jefferson County public schools.

Rob Rudloff, the restaurant's owner, said he initially tried to suspend Mr. Haworth for a few performances. When Mr. Haworth balked, Mr. Rudloff took him off the schedule, but then said he wanted to work out a compromise.

"We're personally fairly conservative. But when we put on our Atlanta Bread Company shirts, we get really uncomfortable when politics come up," Mr. Rudloff said. "We want an environment that's comfortable for everyone's political beliefs."

Mr. Haworth said he would have been willing to take the immigration songs out of his repertoire. "I respect an owner's'right to have control over what goes on in his walls," he said. "It's not a free-speech issue. They're paying me, so it's their prerogative." It looked as if Mr. Haworth would get his job back, which is why he said he was startled to receive an e-mail from Mr. Rudloff a few days later bidding him adieu. "At this point, I don't see any way of reconciling this with you. Good luck going forward," said the Oct. 2 e-mail.

By this time, Mr. Haworth was telling his story on talk radio, finding a sympathetic audience on KHOW-AM's "The Peter Boyles Show." He was also trying to learn the name of his accuser when the show received a call from a woman he had never met named Jennifer Barbagiovanni. She had learned of Mr. Haworth's plight from a friend who listened to the Boyles show, and it all sounded familiar. Her son,

Joey, a 15-year-old sophomore at Arvada High School, had been complaining about an English teacher who was trying to have a singer named Bob Haworth fired for his "racist" and "offensive" songs. "He said how flat-out racist these songs were against Mexicans and Asians," Joey said. "He talked about it the whole class period. He said he wrote a letter and told them he didn't want Bob Haworth ever playing at this restaurant again."

Joey identified the English teacher as Scott Murphy. Jefferson County schools spokeswoman Lynn Setzer would not confirm the teacher's name, and a message left with her for Mr. Murphy was not returned by press time.

Ms. Setzer said the teacher had been scolded for including his business card with the letter of complaint. The restaurant does about $8,800 annually in catering business with the district, she said.

"The teacher did have a conversation with the superintendent of schools, who told him it was bad judgment to include his business card," Ms. Setzer said. "He's not representing the school district by any means. He agreed it was an error in judgment."

BANDANAS

As a seasoned traveler, I learned to travel light. And I've found over the years that carrying a few items in my pockets could serve me well in a number of situations. My left front pocket is for cash – a selection of bills in various denominations totaling about $50 and a coin pouch. My right pocket carries a small ball-point pen, a mini sharpie (for signing autographs) and a small Swiss Army knife with a knife blade, screwdriver, scissors, toothpick and tweezers. Of course, after 9/11, TSA no longer allowed me to carry the knife on the plane, although in reality, it's a much less dangerous weapon than my belt.

But my biggest pocket asset resides in my left hip pocket. It's a 20″x 20″ cotton bandana that serves multiple purposes. I have them in various colors and designs, and I'm confident that with my Swiss Army knife, my bandana and a little duct tape I can pretty much deal with any situation that might arise.

Of course, they work well as clean-up rags, either wet or dry, but it's straight to the laundry after that. And although I avoid this at all costs, there have been occasions to use my bandana as a snot rag. Again, straight into the laundry hamper (or maybe the trash). On a hot day I'll run a bandana under the faucet, wring it out and stick it in the freezer for a half hour. It's then ready to wrap around my neck, providing some soothing cool relief. And here are a few more ways to employ a bandana....

Cowboy stylin'...

Or wear it this way...

Cure for a bad hair day...

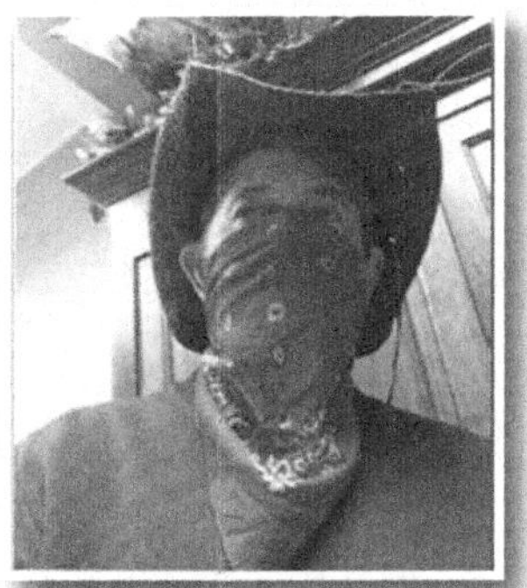

Does not work for Covid, but takes the edge off when cleaning the cat box...

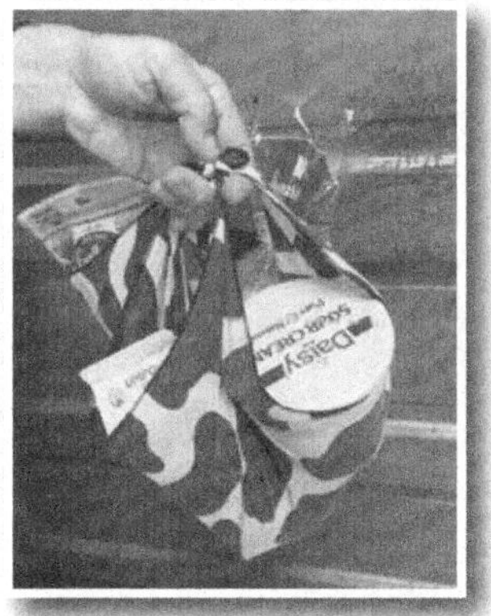

Emergency grocery bag...

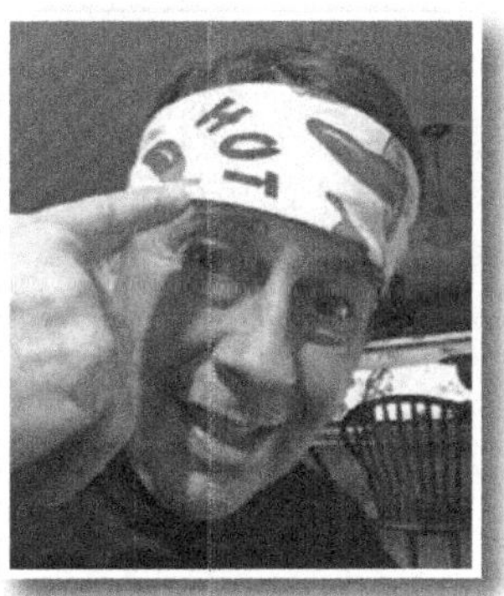

For a hot look...

Home-made bandage
or tourniquet...

A parachute...

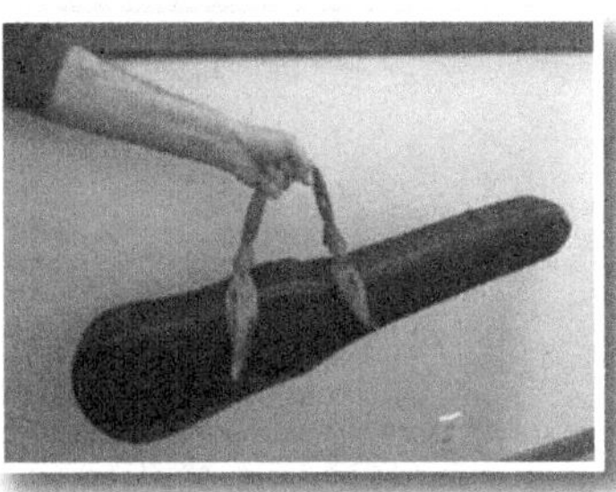

Need a handle for your
violin case?...

I surrender!...

Where's that
darned piñata?...

And my all-time favorite
use for a bandana.

MUSICAL INTERLUDE
BY JACK MULLEN

Jack Mullen was one of my classmates at Medford High School. He sent me the following chapter from his own autobiography and allowed me to reprint it here. This is Jack's account of his own early musical influences and a later encounter he and I had at the Fairmont Hotel in San Francisco.

♪ ♪ ♪

Music always plays in my head, and heaven knows, as my wife Jennifer can vouch, I have no musical talent whatsoever. Does music help define one's life? Maybe, maybe not, but music has always accompanied me along life's journey.

As the youngest of four, my musical exposure started with my older siblings, first with my sister Marilyn. I assume, exhausted from raising three children, my mother was all too willing to allow Marilyn, 12 years older than me, to take some of the heavy lifting to raise her fourth. My first musical exposure came through the pre rock-and-roll songs that appealed to teenage girls. Songs of the early and mid-1950s still bring me back to that era. I shared the joy of "Sh-Boom, Sh-Boom, ba-doh, ba-doo-ba-doodle – ay (sh-boom)" whenever Marilyn played that on our 45 record player. And I still maintain "Mr. Sandman, bring me a dream" is a most pleasant way to fall asleep.

If my parents ever gave me an allowance, I never felt flush enough to go downtown and buy records. Medford radio and my brother Jay's various 45 purchases kept me up with the times, and then, a 45 Kingston Trio song,

"Three Jolly Coachman" with "Scarlett Ribbons" on the reverse side, caught my fancy, even though I didn't know what the word "sober" meant. But I liked 'Here's to the girl who steals a kiss and stays to steal another'.

The Kingston Trio appealed to the college scene, and when Jay returned from the University of Oregon he purchased the first two Kingston Trio albums. When he returned to school he left them at home, where I played them day and night. Although favored by college students, the Trio's songs trickled down throughout kids at Hedrick Junior High. Mark Milne, like me, bought the *hungri i* album, played it until his mother heard the song "Zombie Jamboree" and the words "and I don't give a damn because I heard that already," and banned Mark from ever playing it again. Another friend, Bob Haworth, a Medford transplant from Spokane, Washington with a family history embracing a musical background, not only sang along with the albums, but learned to play the songs along with his banjo.

Bob and I became acquainted in the ninth grade when we performed in the school operetta, O Susana. My insignificant role was as a "river tough" while Bob plucked his banjo and sang, making clear musical inroads that left me jealous. The only solace I could muster on that May evening performance of O Susana was that earlier in the day I set the Hedrick Junior High school record in the 660 at 1:30.00. What I appreciated about Medford during my school years was, although lacking ethnic diversity, there was a huge diversity of talented and skilled individuals, and we had a school system that helped nurture those skills.

Years later, living in the Bay Area, I thumbed through the Arts Section of the *New York Times* and read an article on the Kingston Trio and then, WHAT? a Mr. Bob Haworth of the Trio was mentioned in the review. This happened the same day as, newspaper junkie that I am, I read in the *San Francisco Chronicle* that the Kingston Trio was performing at the Fairmont Hotel's Venetian Room that evening. I took a deep breath, gulped, called the Fairmont and asked for a Bob Haworth. Last seen, Bob and I graduated in 1965 and now it was twenty years later, would he even remember me?

"Hello, Bob, this is Jack Mullen."

"Jack, how's it goin'? Say, you want to be my guest tonight at our performance?"

"Are you kidding me, of course I would."

"Meet me in the lobby at 6:30."

Bob comes to the lobby, we hug, begin talking and then, all of a sudden, Tommy Smothers appears. Smothers has come down from his home in Sonoma to take in the show, and comes over to our table and sits down. Bob excuses himself to prepare for the show, leaving me with Tommy Smothers and Bob Cato, a friend of the Trio. I had a great time pinching myself while having an easy conversation with Tommy about Bob, how Haworth ran the 1320 in the ninth grade with me, and how Tommy was a pole vaulter at San Jose State.

Show time, the Trio's Bob Shane comes down, introduces himself, and tells the main usher to escort me and my date to the front row under the stage. "You'd better get a move on," Smothers sternly tells me. No sooner do we sit down, the curtain opens and the Kingston Trio, in their white shirts with broad purple stripes, sing "Three Jolly Coachman," the first song I ever heard them sing. By god, were they doing this just for me?

"Great show, Bob, thanks for a great evening."

"Hey, stick around, we have a second show coming up."

OK, why not? We catch the second show from the balcony, and the Trio sings some of my favorite, although probably lesser known, songs from their albums. Afterwards, Bob invites us to the after-show party in their room. Little did I realize this was to be an all-night affair. Bob Shane, the only original member of the Kingston Trio left, and a friendly sort, conversed with me for quite a while. After inquiring about my job and my telling him I worked for a newspaper, he put some little white powder beneath my nose and asked "Do you know what this is?" Smothers already hinted to me that Shane liked the white stuff. Bob Shane felt the real story about the Kingston Trio had never been written and I think he was trying to entice me into taking on the project. I acted interested but never considered following up.

I soon became a Kingston Trio groupie, as every time they appeared in the Bay Area I was there. Shortly after Bob Haworth left the Trio, we'd meet up at the occasional Medford High Class of '65 reunions. My musical circle rounded out when Jay and I performed on stage at one of those reunions with Bob Haworth providing the accompaniment. Jay and I sang "*Cuando Caliente el Sol*" in a somewhat Smothers Brothers style and then finished it off with a college fight song from Amherst that actually left much of the audience clapping in rhythm, including my big sister watching her two little brothers perform. So goes my life in music.

DOWN UNDER

The Kingston Trio had three weeks off in February of 2005, and Meri and I had planned to spend that time in New Zealand and Australia. Our friend Richard Kelley, owner of the Outrigger Hotel chain, had invited us to visit and stay at several of his properties in both countries. The finale of our trip was to participate in the grand opening of his new hotel just south of Kingscliff in the state of New South Wales.

A ROUGH START

After a show in Madison, Georgia, on January 28th, I arrived home late on the 29th. That gave us one day to get packed and organized for our departure to Auckland on the 31st. We got very little sleep the night before and headed out to the airport before dawn on Monday in a snowstorm. We boarded the plane on time and actually left the gate early, but the de-icing procedure took over an hour, seriously eating into our layover time in Salt Lake City. When we landed in SLC we dashed to the gate for our LA flight and got there just as the agent was walking up the ramp after closing the door to the plane. I won't print our response here – I'll let you imagine our remarks. The domino effect was now in motion, as there was no way for us to get to LA in time to make our international connection to Seoul and then on to Auckland on Korean Air.

Fortunately we were on Delta, having cashed in several thousand frequent flyer miles that I'd saved up over the years. Delta was our favorite airline, hands down, and I had a vague sense of confidence that things might work out. I left Meri with our carry-ons (including my Gold-Tone Baby Banjo and my new Martin LX1E) and headed down to the International ticket counter. Trent Overton, the agent on duty, worked for well over an hour to save our vacation. The end result was that Delta actually purchased Business Class seats for us on Qantas, which is not a Delta code share partner. They re-booked us on a later flight to LA and confirmed our Qantas flight from LA to Auckland (eliminating the Seoul leg). Whew! We were going to make it!

I headed back to the gate where I'd left Meri and she had used the hour in my absence to make a lot of friends. Kurt Pace, Delta's Service coordinator in Salt Lake City, had taken a special interest in our problem after finding out that a member of The Kingston Trio was involved. He'd been on the phone from the concourse working with the reservations office and Trent at the ticket counter to revamp our itinerary. In the meantime, Delta agent Walt Price, who was working Gate D-4, had been entertaining Meri with a song he'd learned during his two-year missionary service in New Zealand. It's called "*Puha* and *Pakiha*" and it was a novelty hit in the early 1960s. *Puha* is a local leafy vegetable used in soups and salads, while *pakiha* is the Māori word for "white man." The song tells of a British chap who is lost in the forest for days and comes upon a Māori camp. He tells the chief that he desperately needs a bath and the chief invites him to bathe in a large pot filled with water and puha. As the man is bathing he realizes that he's being cooked. We found out after seeking out a recording of the song in New Zealand that it's considered politically incorrect there, since it supposedly demeans the pakiha and talks of Māori cannibalism. Well, it's a funny song, just the same, and I coaxed Walt into a repeat performance for the video camera.

During our layover in LA we were walking through the airport and a voice called out my name. We were surprised to be approached by Tom Lamb, whom we had met the previous August at Fantasy Camp in Scottsdale. He and his wife were on their way to Maui, and we took a few minutes to sit and chat with them. We were a bit amazed to encounter Kingston Trio fans in the middle of a busy airport like that!

NEW ZEALAND

The rest of the trip went smoothly and we arrived in Auckland the next morning, which was actually two days later, having crossed the International Date Line. We had booked lodging at the Sky City Hotel, which is a landmark hotel and entertainment complex in the heart of the city. Arriving well before check-in time we decided to stroll down to the waterfront. The QE2 had just docked and passengers were milling around and embarking on day-trips around the city. We encountered an elderly gentleman who was walking slowly with a cane and Meri struck up a conversation. It turned out that he was on a four-month round-the-world cruise to escape the winter snows of his native Ithaca, New York. As he was nearly blind, we offered to walk with him and guide him around a bit. Actually, he pretty much guided us, as it was not his first time in Auckland. We helped him find a duty-free shop to buy champagne for his cabin, and then we treated him to lunch at a harbor-side restaurant. After guiding him back to the ship, we headed for the hotel to check in. We got to our room and jet lag hit us. Zzzzzz!

The next day we headed to the zoo in search of a kiwi bird. It's a nocturnal bird, and although they keep the habitat pretty dark, none were out. We explored the rest of the zoo, met a nice family who showed us the crocodiles that we'd missed and then returned to the kiwi house. This time he was out. I was totally fascinated with this odd flightless bird, having spent many hours shining shoes as a youngster (Kiwi shoe polish?). We spent several minutes watching him foraging for bugs and then we caught the bus back to the hotel. That night we had a very special dinner in the revolving restaurant atop the Sky City Tower and watched a beautiful sunset as we revolved twice around the city.

The rest of our New Zealand stay (ten days total) included a visit to the glow-worm caves (wow – pretty cool!), an aborted swim with the dolphins in the Bay of Plenty (the weather just didn't co-operate), a visit to the hot springs in Tauranga, a scenic drive down to Wellington (it took awhile to learn to drive on the wrong side of the road, but I only got pulled over once), a lovely ferry ride from Wellington on the North Island across to Picton on the South Island and a fabulous five-hour train ride down the east coast to Christchurch.

But one of the highlights of the trip happened totally by accident. When we were planning our trip months earlier, Bob Shane had asked me to try to locate a gentleman named Sir Howard Morrison. He's an entertainer of Māori descent whose group, The Howard Morrison Quartet, had opened for The Kingston Trio when they toured New Zealand in 1961. Sir Howard's group was quite well known there and Bob had very much enjoyed meeting him and the rest of his quartet. We had asked about Sir Howard through several sources, including my best hope, a Māori cultural center in his hometown of Rotorua. But I hadn't had much success in finding out how to contact him.

On the day that we were supposed to be swimming with the dolphins we had walked into the town of Tauranga, where we were staying, and stopped into a CD store. We were chatting with the clerks, who said that they normally carried at least one Kingston Trio CD but were currently out of stock. I asked about Sir Howard Morrison and they showed me several of his CD's. He was still quite well known there, although his style of music was hardly contemporary – he was more of a Tony Bennett style entertainer. Glancing through his CDs I noticed several covers of Kingston Trio songs, including "Tom Dooley" and "Where Have All The Flowers Gone?" I asked the clerks if they had any idea how to contact Sir Howard and one of them went to the office and made a few phone calls. He came back out and gave me a name and phone number for a lady in Rotorua. It turned out that Sir Howard was doing a concert that night (he was only performing once every four years at the time), and the woman whose phone number I now had was part of the promotional staff for the concert. I called, told her who I was, and she invited us to come up and enjoy comp tickets to the show. I asked her about meeting Sir Howard and she said she'd pass the message on to him.

We made a pleasant one-hour drive up to Rotorua, a pretty little lakeside town, and found the concert site. I asked a security guard if we could meet with Sir Howard and he took us back to his "caravan" (that's what they call trailers there.)

We realized what a rare honor it was to be meeting Sir Howard, as he was still a huge star in New Zealand. He was very gracious and invited us in for a glass of wine and a visit. He said that the pairing of his quartet with The Kingston Trio had actually been a little awkward. It seems that their version of "Where Have All The Flowers Gone?" was a national hit in New Zealand at virtually the same time that The Trio had the hit on it in the rest of the world. It apparently caused a bit of confusion among the local fans, who perhaps thought that The Trio had "borrowed it" from The Howard Morrison Quartet. He asked about Bob, Nick and John, and then it was time for him to dress for the show.

We really enjoyed the concert, which opened with a traditional Māori greeting ceremony, complete with spears, war paint and tongues out to here. Sir Howard followed with a few numbers and then acted as MC, introducing a variety of musical guests who were all nationally known artists in New Zealand. It was fascinating to watch the audience and see the reaction to each of the different performers, ranging from Sir Howard's Vegas style show to a '60's-era rock star to an Abba parody group to three of the latest contemporary pop artists with current hits. The crowd was all about families, which was something we noticed in general there – lots of family activities. But it was interesting to see all ages singing along with all styles of music. The kids knew the old songs and the grandparents knew the latest pop songs. It was a curious thing to observe and the evening became one of the highlights of the New Zealand leg of our trip.

Our overall impression of New Zealand was that it's a very laid-back country. In fact, the Australians have a saying: Q: "What time is it in New Zealand?" A: "1950." And that's the way it felt – very retro. The only freeways we encountered were within the immediate vicinity of major cities. The rest of the highways are all two-lane roads. We saw virtually no litter or graffiti anywhere, as respect for the land is a high priority. The two cultures, Māori and European, have integrated comfortably (although some tensions still exist at a political level), and the Māori culture is still very vital. English is spoken by everyone, but I got the impression that Māori children are taught to speak in their native tongue and traditional ceremonies feature the beautiful sound of Māori language and song.

AUSTRALIA

We flew from Christchurch to Sydney on February 10th, arriving around 8:00 in the morning. As we were coming out of customs we once again heard someone calling out our names. Lo and behold, John Hilvert, a long-time KT fan from Down Under, had come to meet us! He didn't even know what flight we were on, but he knew about what time we were supposed to arrive and he took a chance on catching us. Amazingly, out of hundreds of people coming through those doors he spotted us! We sat down and chatted for a while and then he offered to drive us to our hotel. Off we went, checking into the Grace Hotel in downtown Sydney. We told John that we had plans for the day but said we'd meet him again around 6:00 for drinks and conversation.

Our goal for the day was a visit to the Koala Sanctuary Park where it was advertised that you could get up close and pet the cute little critters. We got directions to the train and rode for about forty minutes out into the north end of Sydney. We then took a bus to the park and arrived just at koala feeding time. The caretaker gave a little talk about koalas and then invited one of them down from his perch in a tree, offering him some special leaves. Everybody in the crowd had an opportunity to come up and pet him and get a picture taken. We fell in love with the little fellow and his buddies in the trees nearby. They're just too cute!

After the feeding session we wandered into an area where they had kangaroos running loose. We were allowed to interact with them and it was a real thrill to get up close and personal with these unusual animals. One of the mamas had a little Joey in her pouch and she allowed Meri to pet him as she stood up tall and proud. We continued to explore the other habitats, which included several cassowaries, which are large flightless birds similar to an emu. There were all sorts of other native birds, including cockatoos, colorful lorikeets and laughing kookaburras. We also saw wallabies, wombats and other animals unique to Australia.

We said one last goodbye to our favorite little koala bear and caught the bus back to the train station for the ride into Sydney. When we arrived back at the hotel, John Hilvert was there to meet us. He guided us down to the harbor for a view of the famous Sydney Opera House and then we sat at an outdoor pub for an hour or so drinking Australian beer and talking Kingston Trio. It was a very pleasant time and a good way to start our stay in Oz.

The next day we flew to Coolangatta on the Gold Coast in the state of Queensland. We rented a car and drove just a few kilometers south into the state of New South Wales to

Kingscliff. Our destination lay just to the south of this charming town in an area called Salt. This was the site of a brand new development that was to be completed later that year, including a new Outrigger Hotel. We would spend the next six days there as guests of Richard and Linda Kelley.

Our friendship with the Kelley's began with an introduction by Bob Shane at a show in Denver a few years ago. Bob and Richard were classmates at Punahou in Honolulu, and Richard's father owned the land on Waikiki where the first Outrigger Hotel was later built. During Bob and Richard's youth, Art Shoen, Bob's father, rented space on the property for his sporting goods store. Richard and Linda had lived in Colorado for several years and we got to know them quite well, often joining them at their ranch near Granby where I entertained for their parties.

We had already been their guests at the Outrigger in Tauranga in New Zealand and then at the Outrigger Clearwater Resort in Christchurch. But the Outrigger Resort at Salt was the crown jewel of the chain, occupying a beautiful stretch of secluded beach. The grand opening of this hotel had originally been scheduled for the day we arrived there. The Kelley's had invited me to perform at the ceremonies, to be attended by the Prime Minister, but as it turned out, construction delays pushed the grand opening back to April. But we'd already made our travel plans and since The Trio was booked for most of April, we couldn't rearrange our schedule. The hotel was already open for business (although a couple wings were still under construction) and we were escorted to the fabulous owner's suite on the top floor overlooking the ocean. Our suite featured a master bedroom with a Jacuzzi tub in the bathroom, a second large bedroom with its own deck overlooking the ocean (plus its own private bathroom), a third guest bathroom, a dining room, living room, kitchen and a huge main deck with a panoramic view of the Pacific Ocean. What a jaw-dropper!

One of the highlights of this part of our trip was a visit with Kingston Trio fan Ken Bradshaw and his lovely wife, Jane. They lived near Brisbane, about an hour to the north, and we had invited them to stay overnight with us in the master bedroom (we'd chosen the other one because of the private lanai.) Meri fixed a nice dinner and made a lei out of some orchids that Ken and Jane brought, cleverly stringing them onto a broken banjo string. We then went down to the lobby where I entertained some of the hotel guests for about an hour. Later we returned to our suite and Ken regaled us with stories of Dave Guard's time in Australia, a subject on which Ken was quite an authority. He had brought along some video clips from *Dave's Place*, the TV show that Dave produced out of Sydney in 1965. We had a great evening watching some vintage television and talking Kingston Trio.

On Valentine's Day the hotel offered a special event for married couples. It was a ceremony to renew our wedding vows, and we couldn't have picked a more beautiful location to do this. We gathered in the lobby with three other couples and waited to be escorted out to the poolside by a free-spirited aging hippie woman who presided over the ceremony. As we had done fourteen years previously, we once again vowed to love, honor and cherish each other for the rest of our lives. I'm sure I saw Cupid fly by sending arrows through all our hearts.

We enjoyed our stay in Salt, doing little other than relaxing on the beach and exploring the vicinity. We really fell in love with the area, with its many beaches and laid-back atmosphere. One day we met a local fisherman on the beach who showed us how to dig clams with our feet. We collected enough for a nice meal. Although we never saw any wild kangaroos, the warning signs were posted here and there along the roads, so we were always on the lookout.

We hated to leave, but our schedule called for us to pack up and head north on February 17th. We flew into the town of Cairns (pronounce "Cans") where we spent the balance of our vacation. Actually, we stayed about fifteen miles north of Cairns in an area called Palm Cove. Once again, we were treated to special accommodations at the Outrigger Resort there. This was a fabulous property with a huge swimming pool that even had a sand beach sloping down into the pool. Here we enjoyed a penthouse suite with our own private rooftop terrace complete with a spa and barbecue facility.

There's plenty to do in this area and we were especially looking forward to a trip to the Great Barrier Reef for some spectacular snorkeling. We booked a tour on a boat called *Calypso* out of Port Douglas, and I took my guitar along to regale the group with some calypso music during the one-hour cruise out to the Reef. Once there we enjoyed some of the most amazing underwater scenery you can imagine, including fish and coral of all shapes, sizes and colors. We had purchased some cheap disposable waterproof cameras and got some amazing pictures of Neptune's world.

Back on dry land, we went into Cairns one evening and strolled around the waterfront. We stopped into a shop that sold didgeridoos and got a free concert/demonstration from the proprietor, an aborigine gentleman who made these instruments. They are actually tree branches that have been hollowed out by termites. He painted them in bright colors, applied a "mouth-piece" of bees wax and turned out a work of art. The sound is somewhat akin to a jaw harp and it's used primarily as a rhythm instrument.

Walking further we happened to notice a sign that boasted, "Home of the World Famous Toad Races." This piqued our curiosity and we stopped in to see what it was all about. As a lead-in to the races, a fellow named Terry Doyle was performing with an acoustic guitar, doing a music/comedy act. He had his son with him playing electric guitar and melodica, and they did a kind of sing-along show featuring mostly Australian music. I was playing harmonica along with them from my seat and before long they invited me up on stage to sit in. We did a few numbers and then it was time for the toad races.

Terry made a costume change, coming out in a jungle safari outfit. The toads were numbered on the back and the audience was invited to purchase a particular toad for each of three races. I bought #5 in the first race. Each "owner" was then required to handle his toad, placing him into a can with no bottom at the center of the ring. Once all the toads were in their cans, the cans were lifted up and the toads are off as Terry narrated the race like a sports announcer. First one to touch the edge of the ring was the winner. #5 hopped once and then just sat there. "Loser!"

On February 21st it was time to head home. We really hated to leave, as we were having a great time and could have easily spent another month over there. But with a

Kingston Trio concert tour starting on the 25th we had to get back. We were standing in line waiting to board our flight from Cairns to Sydney when a voice called out, “Bob – are you enjoying your vacation?” *What*?! We’re in Cairns, Australia, for crying out loud! *Who knows me here*? Well, it turned out to be Dave and Irene Hanley from Calgary, B.C., whom we had met on our Alaska cruise in 2001. It was quite a coincidence to see them again half-way around the world. But we did find out later, much to our surprise, that fans had been tracking our itinerary somehow and posting it on one of the Kingston Trio message boards. So that explained all those unexpected encounters we’d had with people on this trip.

Once in Sydney we transferred over to the international terminal and said goodbye to Australia. Our return trip took us through Seoul on Korean Air Lines, and as fate would have it, we flew into a snowstorm there. Our connecting flight to LA was delayed due to the de-icing procedure (where have we heard this story before?), so we missed our flight out of LA to Salt Lake City. Amazingly, the airline had already taken care of rebooking us on another flight (thanks again to Delta Airlines and their KAL partner!) and we made it home later that day.

We were exhausted from nearly two days of travel, and yet we were exhilarated from our trip and still riding the wave of excitement from all that we’d seen and done. But there was little time for reflection, as I had to unpack my bags and reorganize for a one-month concert tour. Time to start accumulating those frequent flyer miles again!

Sir Howard.

The Kingston Trio in Aukland.

Meri meets a cute koala bear.

Bob gives a kangaroo bunny ears.

John Hilvert and me at Sydney Harbor.

Bob Haworth

LOST AT SEA

In the early summer of 2015, I got a call from our accountant, Rick McGee. Rick had been Bob Shane's CPA for years and he took us on as clients at Bob's urging. The purpose of his call was to invite me to crew on his forty-six-foot sailboat, *Glory*. Meri and I had actually spent an afternoon aboard *Glory* when she was moored in San Diego a few years earlier. But now she was moored in Honolulu and Rick wanted to bring her back to the West Coast. I told Rick that I had very little sailing experience, except for some lake sailing as a Sea Scout in high school and a few nautical excursions on Puget Sound. He assured me that my duties would be minimal and would include entertaining the crew as we made our way across the Pacific.

To flesh out the crew, Rick had enlisted the services of an experienced sailor named Leszek Kotzian, a Polish citizen working in the Bay Area on an H-1 visa. He had years of experience sailing with his father on the North Sea and he really knew the ropes. Knowing that I was in the company of two well-seasoned sailors, I was looking forward to a once-in-a-lifetime experience. I packed my travel guitar and a backpack full of essentials and hopped a plane to Honolulu, arriving on August 11th.

Glory was still undergoing some repairs and outfitting for the trip and it was several days before she was ready to sail. I was glad to have that time to spend with my brother, Sam and his partner, Dick, and I got in a bit of beach time as well.

Glory's fuel capacity was 150 gallons, but in anticipation of the possibility of hitting areas with little wind, Capt. Rick had purchased two seventy-five-gallon fuel bladders which were strapped to the deck, one on the bow and one aft. In addition, we had ten five-gallon jerry cans of fuel, so if the wind didn't blow, we could still motor along.

We finally left Ala Wai Harbor on August 17. Capt. Rick assigned us each six-hour watches, but despite my Dramamine and sea sickness wrist bands, I spent the first three days going between my bunk and the head. Once I finally got my sea legs, I joined the crew on deck and started to contribute to the duties required to navigate the 3000 miles to our destination. As Rick had expected there was very little wind for the first few days. When the on-board fuel tanks went dry, we filled them with the fuel from the deck-bound bladders, which were then folded and stowed.

On our seventh day out, we finally got enough wind to turn the engine off and put up the sails. And that's what we came for. *Glory* heeled over on a nice starboard tack and away we went. The next day the electrical system went wacky. In order to charge the batteries, Rick had to run the engine, despite the fact that we had a steady breeze. But now we had no running lights and no refrigerator, and we couldn't use the microwave. We also discovered that the toilet in the aft head wouldn't flush. Luckily we still had the forward head, until the next day when that one failed as well. No big deal for me, since I was constipated and we were all pissing over the rail. Meal time now involved eating directly from a can or soaking ramen noodles in cold water until they were soft enough to eat.

On the tenth day at sea, the batteries were charged and

the wind was strong, so once again we were under full sail. Dawn of day eleven came with a spectacular sunrise and continued strong winds. Later in the day the winds began to shift, and in order to maintain our course we had to tack several times to find the wind. As the boom was crossing the deck on a port tack we heard a loud crack and watched in shock as the main mast broke and fell into the ocean. Seeing no way to save the sail and hearing the broken end of the mast smashing into the hull, Rick made the hasty decision to cut the shrouds and send the mast and sail down to Davy Jones's locker.

At this point we were about 1,300 miles from Los Angeles with 150 gallons of fuel. Rick did some math and estimated that if we were lucky we might get 1,200 miles out of the fuel we had left. Rick called the Coast Guard on his satellite phone and alerted them to our situation. They said they could track us, but we were too far out for any kind of rescue.

On day fifteen the engine died. Rick cleaned the filters and made some other adjustments, but it still wouldn't start. As I was assisting him by handing him tools, I began to pray to God asking that He start the engine. My prayer was answered in less than a heart beat as the engine roared to life. But Rick found that the engine was running rich and burning more fuel than it was supposed to. As a result, our fuel supply was not going to last as long as we had hoped.

In his next call to the Coast Guard, Rick informed them that we were going to be short on fuel. Amazingly, the Coast Guard called back and let us know that a Chinese freighter was headed our way and they had offered to give us some fuel. A few hours later we watched the *Fortune Wing* come over the horizon and head our way. She was a huge freighter, 623 feet long with a 105-foot beam, bound for Kobe, Japan.

We retrieved the fuel bladders from below deck and lashed them down, ready to be filled. The captain of the *Fortune Wing* instructed Rick to pull around to their stern, where they would be able to drop a hose down to us. As we attempted to get into position for this fuel transfer, the sea was choppy and I nearly fell overboard a couple times. In addition, we ended up colliding with this huge freighter several times, and we later discovered that one of those collisions had resulted in a fairly large hole in *Glory's* bow.

After what seemed like hours, and maybe it was, the crew on the freighter finally lowered a hose down and we managed to fill both fuel bladders. During the process the hose had somehow shifted around toward our stern and had become entangled in *Glory's* propeller. We tried to communicate to the Chinese crew six stories above us that we had a problem and, since they were not able to understand us, they just disconnected the hose and dropped it into the water. We needed to get away from the freighter in order to deal with this hose issue, and Rick was finally able to get the captain to resume his trip to Kobe, leaving us with plenty of fuel but no way to start the engine.

I had brought along some swim goggles and a snorkel and I volunteered to dive down and cut the hose from the propeller with a steak knife. When I get under the boat, I was able to cut the hose loose, but I found that we had also accumulated a wad of fish net and rope that was now wrapped around the prop. I came up and asked for a hacksaw to cut the netting lose, but as I was waiting for Rick to retrieve it, the chill of the water hit me and I started to shiver uncontrollably. I had no choice but to abandon my effort and turn the job over to Leszek.

Once the prop was cleared, Rick tried to start the engine, but it wouldn't go. Again I began to pray to God to please start our engine, and...voila! It started! But now there was an issue with the shifting device. More prayers and finally we began to move ahead. But *Glory* just wasn't running normally and Rick feared that the propeller had probably been damaged when it picked up that fish netting and rope.

Over the next couple of days we fought engine troubles constantly. And every time I prayed to God for help, He started our engine. Until day nineteen, when we sputtered to a stop after burning our last drop of fuel. Now we were 250 miles from Los Angeles and contemplating rowing to shore. Rick apprised the Coast Guard of our situation and they offered to send a helicopter to pull us off the boat. They told us we could only carry minimum essential items with us and that Rick would have to scuttle his beloved *Glory*. "Not an option," said Capt. Rick.

After some discussion up the chain of command, the Coast Guard called and said they were sending a Coast Guard cutter out to tow us in. Once again, I felt the hand of God on us. We were going to be saved after all. The next day, the cutter *Blacktip* arrived and after a couple passes to assess our situation, they told Rick that because of the large hole in our bow from the collision with the freighter, they were reluctant to attach a tow line for fear of pulling *Glory* apart. Rick responded that he would take responsibility for any mishap, and so they threw us a line. Leszek masterfully attached the line to the bow cleats and with a gentle tug to test it, everything held in place. The *Blacktip* picked up speed and we were on our way home. The Coast Guard had sent a radio over to us so we could communicate with them and as we proceeded through the night we checked in with them hourly to report that all was well. I was on watch for part of the night and on one of those statis calls I responded, "All is well on the *Good Ship Lollipop*", which prompted a laugh from the crew. I then decided to regale them with a rendition of the Coast Guard anthem.

We're always ready for the call – We place our trust in thee
Thru howling gale and shot and shell to win our victory
Semper Paratus *is our guide – Our pledge, our motto too*
We're always ready –Do or die Aye!
Coast Guard, we fight for you

They radioed back some applause and we proceeded to sail on through the night. At dawn we reached a point that was approximately 100 miles from our destination. Rick had arranged for a company called Boat US to meet us there and tow us on into port. Boat US is akin to AAA for sailors, but they have a 100-mile from shore rescue limit. So we disconnected from the *Blacktip* and bid farewell and mega thanks to her great crew.

We then fell in behind the Boat US tow boat for the twelve-hour trip into Los Angeles. As we sailed along I told Rick and Leszek that this adventure had reminded me of a song. However I had vowed to myself that I wouldn't sing it to them unless we were confident of our rescue. At this point we were virtually assured of making land, barring any unforeseen tidal wave or something. The song was the precursor to the Kingston Trio's hit recording of "Charlie on The MTA." Bess Hawes and Jacqueline Steiner had written that lyric to the tune of an 1865 folk song about a ship that had set sail from her home port never to be seen again.

'Twas a summer's day when the waves were rippled
By a soft and gentle breeze
When a ship set sail with a cargo laden
For a port beyond the seas

There were fond farewells, loving remonstrations
By the ones who were most concerned
Tho They knew it not, 'twas the fatal voyage
Of the ship that never returned

CHORUS:
Did she ever return? No she never returned
And her fate is yet unlearned
Tho for years and years there were fond ones watching
For the ship that never returned

Well, thank God that wasn't our fate. When we arrived at the marina where Rick was planning to moor *Glory*, his whole family was waiting for us on the dock. We were a motley looking crew as we stepped off the boat and kissed the dry land that we had feared we might never see again. Rick's cousin offered to drive me to his aunt's house where I was invited to spend the night. When we got into the car, she asked me if there was anything I wanted to stop for on the way and I said, "I'm craving a chocolate malt." So she took me to a Baskin & Robbins where I tasted real food for the first time in weeks. The next day I caught a flight back home to Medford, and at our next Yard Concert I sang a couple of songs that I had written during this harrowing adventure. The first is one I wrote and sang continually as we limped home. It's called "The Sailor's Prayer."

Give me strength, Lord, strength, Lord, to get thru this day
Give me strength, Lord, strength, so I don't lose my way

Give me hope, Lord, hope, Lord, that the future is bright
Give me hope, Lord, hope, that I will bathe in your light

Give me grace, Lord, grace, Lord, and forgive me my sins
Give me grace, Lord, grace, when I stumble again

Give me faith, Lord, faith, Lord, please hear my prayer
Give me faith, Lord, faith, to know you'll always be there

Give me peace, Lord, peace, Lord, as I rest in your arms
Give me peace, Lord, peace, Lord, and keep me from harm

The other song pretty much describes how I felt at the end of this ordeal:

Please don't send me off to sea no more
There's nothin' for me on that distant shore
I'm happy just sittin' by my own back door
I don't wanna go to sea no more

The porpoise and the mermaids laughed with glee
As I was tossin' up my cookies on the open sea
A sailor's life is not for me
I don't wanna go to sea no more

The ship it rocks and the waves do roll
I bang my head and I lose control
I'd rather be dancin' at some waterin' hole
I don't wanna go to sea no more

The diesel and the head and my body stink
The water won't drain from the galley sink
What I wouldn't give for an ice cold drink
I don't wanna go to sea no more

And if I ever get back home
I'll nail my shoes to the floor and I'll never more roam
I've had about enuff of the briny foam
I don't wanna go to sea no more

I miss my kitty and I miss my wife
I'm just not suited to the seaman's life
Too much worry and too much strife
I don't wanna go to sea no more

When I hit land and I leave these decks
I hope my woman will not object
If I trade my sexton for a ton of sex
I don't wanna go to sea no more
No, I don't wanna go to sea no more

Captain Rick spent a couple years repairing *Glory*, patching the hole in her bow and replacing her mast with the mast from the *Virginia Jean*, the boat that Robert Redford sailed in the motion picture, *All Is Lost*. Apparently it was a perfect fit and restored *Glory* to her former glory. But *Glory* has since been sold and Captain Rick has traded his sexton for (hopefully) a ton of sex!

Bob on watch aboard *Glory*.

Coast Guard to the rescue!

Glory before...

Glory after.

Freighter *Fortune Wind* bringing us fuel.

JAZZ BANJO MAGAZINE

The fall 2007 issue of *Jazz Banjo Magazine* featured me on the cover along with the following interview:

JBM: How did you get started playing the banjo?

BH: I actually had to endure a few years of piano lessons thanks to Mom and Dad. Mom said you should learn how to play the piano because it is a basic instrument. She played the violin so she had some knowledge of music theory.

My first piano teacher was just horrible and we couldn't get along so I was able to convince my mom to pay for banjo lessons. This came about because both of my grandfather's brothers played banjo. Uncle Wayne played tenor banjo and Uncle Carl played plectrum banjo. Both of them had interesting backgrounds. In the 1920s Uncle Wayne played banjo in the orchestra of the ships that sailed out of Seattle to China. Uncle Carl lived in the Spokane, Washington area and played with Bing Crosby.

Whenever we would have a family gathering Uncle Wayne and Carl would play the banjo. My great grandfather also played the piano so it would be quite an event. Uncle Carl played all over town and he knew most of the musicians. One of his friends was "Dutch" Groshoff who played banjo and guitar. He was my banjo teacher for about three years. Dutch had a small banjo band with all of his students and when you were good enough to play "Bye, Bye Blues" you became part of the band.

JBM: What year was this?

BH: This would have been somewhere between 1956 and 1958 when I was 10 to 12 years old. In the band there were between 4 to 6 students including Dutch's son Larry. It seems as though life goes in circles. When I joined The Brothers Four I replaced a person by the name of Mark Pearson. Coincidentally Mark also took lessons from Dutch and was in the banjo band at that time. We kind of knew each other, although not well, because the band would only get together a few times a year for special events. But my parents were well aware of Mark's father, who was a prominent doctor in town.

JBM: What happened next in your banjo career?

BH: My family moved to Oregon in 1959 so I had to give up my banjo. It belonged to my uncle and he didn't want it to leave town. We moved to Medford, OR and by now I had picked up the guitar. I still wanted a banjo and my dad kept looking in the newspaper and one day he found an ad that said: "Vega banjo for sale - $150.00." We went over to look at it and the lady had it in the attic where it had been for who knows how long. It belonged to her brother and she wanted to get rid of it. I wiped out my paper route account and bought the banjo. This banjo has been my work horse ever since and I can't even image the value of it today. The new instrument got me back into playing the banjo and then folk music hit the scene. The Kingston Trio came out with "Tom Dooley" in 1958. One day I sat by the radio and listened to the song. I said, "Two chords, what are they? Hey I can play that song." From that point on folk music became part of my life. Throughout junior high and high school, I sang with a friend of mine from Medford, Oregon, John Eads. We were known as the Kinsmen, and with Medford being a small community we were known quite well around town. We were always getting out of school to play for various service clubs such as the Lions, Rotary and Elks clubs. We learned all of the folk music we could from groups like The Kingston Trio, The Limeliters, The Chad Mitchell Trio and Peter, Paul and Mary.

JBM: That sounds like the equivalent of a garage band back in the '50s.

BH: Yes I guess it was. I graduated from Medford High School in 1965 and then went on to U.C.L.A. (University of California at Los Angeles) where I decided I was going to major in music. However, that was when my academic career started to go down hill. I took a job playing at Shakey's Pizza Parlor on the weekends to make some money to put myself through school. I had this little Honda motor scooter that I would ride all over town with my banjo strapped to my back. I played with several piano players but the one notable player I worked with was Ben Sands. His son was the actor/singer Tommy Sands. For a few years Ben and I played at pizza parlors all over Southern California.

I was also involved in a few recordings projects which gave me a taste of the music business and that really excited me. Eventually I decided to transfer back to the University of Oregon. It was in Oregon that I received a call from a person that I had known from my high school days in Medford. He was in the radio business and at that time he was managing a group called The New Yorkers that later became known as the Hudson Brothers. They had a Saturday morning variety show back in the 1970s. I joined their group as a rhythm guitar/keyboard player and I was also an occasional banjo player on novelty songs. We used to do "The Sheik of Araby" or something Arabic sounding and Bill Hudson would roll his stomach. The crowd would go nuts.

JBM: He was imitating a belly dancer! It's amazing what entertains people.

BH: I worked with that group for a few years before I realized that I wasn't going in the direction I wanted to go. The three brothers were on the road to success but I was like the fourth wheel on a tricycle. I decided to leave the group and let them do their Saturday morning TV show and I went back to the Northwest playing the nightclub circuit.

JBM: Did you know the McKinley's?

BH: Yes I knew who they were. It was John McKinley and his son. We were invited to one of their annual picnic gatherings in Salem. It was at a state park and we were a little late getting there. We were in the park looking at a map to find them, because it was a nice day we had the windows down and all of a sudden I could hear this plunk-a-plunk-a-plunk-a. As we drove up to the location we could see a hill side with what seemed like about 400 banjo players playing "Chinatown, My Chinatown." I had never been to an event before with so many banjo players.

During this time I also did some occasional studio work for Jerry Dennon, who owned Jerden Records, the label that The New Yorkers had recorded for. He called me one day and said, "I have some partners on a radio station down in Seaside and you may know them as The Brothers Four. I said, "I certainly do!" and Jerry told me that they were looking for a tenor vocalist to replace Mark Pearson. I went to audition and the next week I was in Bermuda on stage with The Brothers Four. I performed with them from 1970 to 1985 and that was when The Kingston Trio called me. Initially The Trio wanted me to fill in for their tenor vocalist, Roger Gambill, who was ill in the hospital. Sadly, two weeks later Roger passed away and Bob Shane asked me if I wanted to stay on. It really was a difficult decision because during the two weeks this took place I was singing with both groups. I finally decided to go with the The Kingston Trio because I thought that working with them would be a lot of fun. The group had once asked me earlier to join them but since they were on the road all the time I wasn't ready then to travel that much. In 1985 I was now ready to make the commitment and off I went for the next 20 years.

JBM: Before you joined The Kingston Trio didn't you make a record album called *The Banjo King Plays Ragtime*?

BH: Yes. That was during The Brothers Four era and it was really a separate project. That was presented to me by Jerry Dennon from Jerden Records. He came to me with this concept of "The Banjo King" hoping to capitalize on the banjo "Dueling Banjos" craze that had hit the country at that time. He had a feeling that the banjo sound, be it 5-string, tenor or plectrum, was a hot marketable commodity.

JBM: Was this in the early '70s before the banjo club scene died?

BH: No, this was in the late '70s and Jerry had some marketing arrangements to sell the album overseas. After the LPs release Jerry told me that the album was a big hit in

Turkey. I never did receive a copy of the Turkish edition so I don't know if it was any different from the US version. It was a fun project and I was actually paid for it.

JBM: Were you playing any of the songs on the album before you recorded it?

BH: A lot of the songs I put together just for the album. I did a lot of research on the ragtime songs because I wanted to play them in their original form. The "Maple Leaf Rag" is a song of which you usually hear only the first part and you rarely hear the entire song. I wanted this recording to recreate these songs with all the various sections and repeats. It was fun doing the project because I perceived it as a historical resurrection. One of the songs I really enjoyed working out was "Nola." I had always toyed with the song and wanted to learn it so this was my opportunity. Some of the songs on the album like "Alley Cat," "The Third Man Theme" and "Tiger Rag" were already in my repertoire. It was two years later that Jerry came back to me and said, "We did really well on that album. Do you want to do another one?" He had a concept that he was going to do a whole series of Banjo King albums. The first one was Ragtime and for the second one he came up with the title *The Banjo King Plays Favorites*. It covered a broader category and I included songs like "Classical Gas."

JBM: I have never heard anyone attempt that on the banjo before.

BH: Actually, when I told Mason Williams that I had arranged his composition for banjo he informed me that he'd originally written it on the banjo. That song goes over really well in my shows and now I do it on the 5-string banjo.

When the second album came out it was only on a cassette tape. I don't know why it wasn't produced as an LP but it never went anywhere. The interesting thing about those recordings is that someone licensed some of the songs from the Ragtime album and put them on a compilation album with artists like Pete Seeger, Earl Scruggs, Mason Williams and...who's this Bob Haworth? There I am among all of these 5-string players. It's a huge three-record collection and I have 8 cuts on the project. Oddly, I wouldn't have even known about it except for a friend mentioning it to me.

JBM: Did you continue to play the banjo when you joined The Kingston Trio?

BH: George Grove was with group when I joined them. He has studied the 5-string where l have just toyed with it. My training has been mostly with the plectrum banjo. I always viewed the 5-string as some kind of hybrid that I didn't want to know about. I think that was an attitude I got from my teacher Dutch who favored the plectrum style banjo. When I started playing folk I was using my plectrum, since that's all that I owned. Then I started hearing things that didn't sound like the plectrum and I realized it was a 5-string banjo. It was a friend of mine in high school who bought the first 5-string long neck Vega that I had ever seen. I used to go over to his house and fool around with it but it wasn't until I joined The Brother's Four that I owned my first 5-string banjo. I bought a 1928 Vega "Griffin" model.

Since I am self-taught as a 5-string player I have made up different picking patterns than most bluegrass players use. With The Kingston Trio I only played 5-string on a song called "To Morrow," written by Bob Gibson (who also wrote

"Super Skier," among other things.) It's a song about a guy trying to take a train ride to the town of Morrow, Ohio. It's kind of a tongue twister and a funny song leaving today to go to Morrow. Dave Guard originally worked out an arrangement of it in "G" tuning, but being a plectrum player I learned it in "C" tuning, and the song's in "C" anyway, so my version is a little different than the original. I also played plectrum banjo on "Worried Man Blues" just like Bob Shane did on the original recording. Dave Guard played 5-string on that song. Most people didn't know that Bob Shane played banjo and he had given it up by the time I joined the group.

When Dave Guard started playing banjo with the group he would do a lot of "frailing" – also known as clawhammer style. He didn't have a good grasp of the best way to play the instrument with the group so he took lessons from Pete Seeger and that's how he developed a completely different style. On the original material you hear a lot of strumming and single picking. Bob Shane probably played plectrum on four or five of the original recordings with "Worried Man Blues" being the most notable. Anything that Bob Shane played banjo on I would play on the plectrum banjo if I had one with me.

JBM: How many years were you with "The Kingston Trio?"

BH: I joined them in 1985, but Nick Reynolds came out of retirement in 1988. I took a leave of absence, but I always kept a suitcase packed to fill in when Nick was unable to tour. During the 1990s when he was touring I probably filled in a dozen times. In 1999 Nick decided to retire again and so I came back into the group full time.

JBM: What were some of the bigger shows you played?

BH: The one that really sticks out in my mind was with

The Brothers Four. It was the first time we went to Japan and when the curtain went up I saw 4,000 people in front of me and it was the biggest crowd I had ever played for. I was about 22 at the time and I said to myself, "They all came out to hear us?" There was also a similar size crowd that I remember when we went to South Korea. The guys had warned me about it and said that this is garlic country. When the curtain went up all you could smell was garlic coming from the breath of 4,000 people. It was pretty amazing. The biggest crowd that I ever played for was with The Kingston Trio. We used to do a lot of summer festivals. One time we played a festival in Kansas City and we were on a street. We were told there were 12,000 people there. You couldn't even see the end of the crowd.

JBM: Did you ever deviate from the standard repertoire of The Kingston Trio?

BH: Bob Shane was not one to experiment. He found a formula that worked for him and liked to stick to it, even down to repeating the same joke from night to night. Bob would give George and me solo slots in the show and that was the only opportunity that we had to do new things. Initially I would do my own original material but then Bob decided that he wanted everything to be The Kingston Trio material that was recorded between 1957 and 1967. Bob felt that the audiences wanted to hear the old Kingston Trio material and he kept pretty close to that format.

JBM: How did Bob O'Luney come about?

BH: Dick Van Dyke had a one-man band in the movie *Mary Poppins*. It was very simple with a bass drum on his back and he played banjo and harmonica on a rack. That was my basic inspiration for Bob O'Luney. I thought *Wow, that's really cool!* I started with the bass drum, harmonica and banjo but then I began to think about all the different things I could do. I added a washboard and a lot of other percussion instruments. On my harmonica rack I added a kazoo, jug, slide whistle and siren whistle. Bit-by-bit, as it grew, I found places on my body that I could add more instruments. After I had been out in the public for awhile the costume started to evolve. Once it developed into the red, white and blue costume I have today my biggest day of the year became the Fourth of July.

A couple of years ago, my wife Meri and I became involved with the Parkinson Foundation. We did a couple of concerts in Colorado and we brought in The Brothers Four to be the headliners promoting the events as "Concerts for a Cure." As part of the promotion for these concerts I was going around as Bob O'Luney with a can attached to the side of the bass drum. On the can it said "Donations for Parkinson Research." People would stuff that can with money and I would come away from the promotional events with $50 to $100. Realizing the potential of this gimick, I dreamed up a campaign called "Bob O'Luney Marches Across America for Parkinson Research." The concept originally was to start at the west coast and go all the way across the country on foot.

JBM: How many months will that take?

BH: About 3 or 4 months, but then I started calculating the cost of shoes for the journey and we've scaled back. We will take our RV for most of the trip but I will walk into the cities where I am going to be featured at and we'll show up for their Walk-A-Thon. By walking into town we will be able to get press coverage.

JBM: Bob, you mentioned that you had a 7-string banjo?

BH: I worked with Greg Deering on that project and my concept was to have it built like a 6-string banjo but have the 7th string like the drone string on a 5-string banjo. But instead of having the 7th string attached to a tuning peg on the side of the neck, I wanted the string to run all the way up to the head stock. I also wanted to have a 7th string capo that would run from the head stock all the way to the 12th fret. I asked Rick Shubb to make the capo for me and he made two of them since he had to go through all the work of re-tooling to make the special capo. I then told Rick that I wanted to have the capability to mute out the 5th, 6th and 7th strings at various times so I can play it like a five or four string banjo. He said, "I have just the thing for you." He came up with this brass clip that attaches to the head and the string can be lowered below the other strings and attached to the clip. I have three of them now on the head. By muting the different strings I can now play the different banjo styles of the 4, 5 and 6 string banjos on one instrument. I also have one of these mutes on the 5th string of my 5-string banjo so it can double as a plectrum. I recently saw a video of Doug Mattocks playing a 5-string as a plectrum with one of Rick Shubb's string mutes attached to the head.

JBM: Bob, now that you have retired from traveling with The Kingston Trio what projects are you working on now and planned for the future?

BH: Recently I have written a few songs as satires about political issues that have been in the news recently. Two of the songs are: "Can You Get Me In?" and "Pizzas for Pesos." The first song makes fun of how easy it is to get into the United States without documentation and talks about wanting the same treatment for traveling to Mexico. The second one makes fun of the fact that a pizza store in the United States now accepts pesos as currency.

JBM: I bet this has raised a few eyebrows?

BH: This is also raising awareness about these issues and the songs are getting air play on radio stations all around the country. You can hear sample clips on my website: *bobhaworth.com*.

BANJO NEWSLETTER

(Reprinted from Banjo Newsletter, December, 2017
https://banjonews.com/2017-12/bob_haworth.html)

Bob Haworth
By James K. Koshmider

Multi-instrumentalist Bob Haworth has had a distinguished career in folk music, working first with the Brothers Four, and then with the Kingston Trio. One of Bob's major achievements during his time with the Trio was writing and recording the song MTA Revisited that answered the question of what happened to Charley on the MTA.

Bob was born in Spokane, Washington, and grew up in a musical family. His great-uncle Carl played plectrum and sang in a band with Bing Crosby in the 1920s. His uncle Wayne played tenor banjo and played on cruise ships in the 1920s. While in high school, Bob co-founded a band called The Kinsman that basically "aped" The Kingston Trio, The Limeliters, Peter, Paul and Mary and other folk artists of the day.

Bob first heard the 5-string as a teenager, when his father brought home the Limeliters' *Tonight: In Person* album. "My family pretty much wore out that LP," Bob remembered, "we became huge fans. But I'd lived around plectrum and tenor banjos all my life, and the 5-string was a whole different animal that I didn't have any association with. I was quite enamored with The Kingston Trio the first time I heard Tom Dooley, but then, that was a plectrum, too."

The first time Bob saw an actual 5-string was when his

high school friend got a Pete Seeger longneck. By then Bob and his friends were all into folk music of one sort or another (his friend was a New Lost City Ramblers fan, while Bob and his singing partner, John Eads, preferred the commercial music). And even though Bob knew that folk groups were using 5-strings at that time, he pretty much stuck with his plectrum.

Bob says he was "kind of forced into playing 5-string" when he joined The Brothers Four. In fact, he used the banjo that belonged to the group for many years, being too cheap to buy his own. Bob was hired to take over for Mark Pearson, who had replaced original member Mike Kirtland the previous year. As the designated banjo player, Bob had to take a crash course in three-finger style and figure out what to do with the 5th string. He got Pete Seeger's book and then Earl's book and basically taught himself. Luckily, the parts he had to learn for The Brothers Four repertoire weren't too complex, so he managed, being a graduate of "The School of Fake-ology." Bob never had any official lessons on 5-string—"I'm totally self-taught," he says, "as anyone who hears me play 5-string can tell."

Bob was a member of the Brothers Four from 1970 through 1985, recording over a dozen albums with them and touring internationally. Bob then joined The Kingston Trio that same year, and was a full-time member until 1988, after which he'd fill in whenever Nick Reynolds couldn't perform (and he later had a second full-time stint with the Trio from 1999 to 2005). As Bob admits, he was never the Trio's main banjo player—his main instrument was tenor guitar (a la Nick Reynolds), but he also played 5-string, plectrum banjo, guitar, and sang. As Bob said in a 2003 interview, "I'm nowhere near the 5-string banjo player that George Grove [whom James Koshmider interviewed for *BNL* in March 2001—Ed.] is. And, in my opinion, George is the best banjo player The Kingston Trio ever had. Granted, Dave Guard was innovative and set the style, John Stewart did his best, too, but George has a real flair for the material. I got a chance to play a couple things that Shane used to do on plectrum, mainly 'New York Girls.' I used George's 5-string and flat-picked it, keeping it in G tuning (well, actually A tuning, since it was capoed up and we played the song in D). I normally didn't carry a banjo on the road because we traveled primarily by air and they limited the amount of luggage we could check. But occasionally if we were performing around Denver or if I'm within driving distance of a gig, then I'd take my plectrum for the show. In that case, I'd play 'Worried Man' and we'd use both banjos as the original Trio did when Shane played plectrum and Guard played 5-string. The other song on which I regularly played 5-string was the Bob Gibson song, 'To Morrow.'"

In 2005 Bob left the group to concentrate on his solo career. That includes his Bob O'Luney's AMAZING One-Man Band, which began as an act for the Vashon Island Strawberry Festival Parade. Bob originally had a bass drum on his back with a beater attached to a strap that ran to his right foot, a tambourine on his left foot, banjo and a rack with kazoo, harmonica and siren whistle. The band now includes his 7-string banjo, clapping hands (his own invention attached to the top of the bass drum), cymbals between his knees, accordion, bicycle horn, and ship's bell, along with slide whistle, train whistle, jug, washboard, bicycle bell, virba-harp, cowbell, jingle bells, wood block, desk bell, bosun's whistle, samba whistle, parade whistle, jaw harp, maracas, Pan flute, and penny whistle. It all weighs just under 100 pounds. He's looking for a way to add a pocket trumpet.

Bob's other recent project is Akoostikats, an acoustic

music duo with singer and multi-instrumentalist John Hollis. Presenting a show called "Tales & Tunes from the Folk Music Era," Akoostikats recreate the hit songs of The Kingston Trio, The Brothers Four, Peter Paul & Mary, The Weavers, Woody Guthrie and other heros of the "Folk Scare" of the 1950s and '60s. Bob ties the music together with tales about the tunes and the artists.

Bob's main 5-string these days is a Deering Vega #5, but he also plays his Deering custom 7-string. Bob explains: "At one point I decided I had to have a 7-string banjo that I could play as a 6-string, 5-string or 4-string. So I had my friend, Jack Hansen in Seattle, build me one. He took an old 11-inch rim from some junk pile and carved me a really nice neck—short scale. Since it was small, I could pack it around easily and use it to practice both guitar or banjo. It was stolen from my van in Seattle one night and I was heartbroken. I finally talked Jack into building me another one, which I still own. When I met Greg Deering I showed him the thing and asked if he would consider building me one with a full-length neck. He pretty much laughed me out of the place and it took me a few years and some more coaxing to finally get him to do it.

"Greg started with one of his 12-string necks and worked out the string spacing to accommodate the seven strings. It's a beauty and I really love it. I use it mostly for my one-man band act, as it lends itself to just that application. The 7th (drone) string runs all the way up to the peg head and I had Rick Shubb (this took a little coercing, too) make me a custom 7th-string capo that runs from the nut to the 15th fret.

"He also came up with these cool little mutes that are like little brass fingers with a piece of rubber attached. I can hook the string under the finger and that brings the string in contact with the rubber, thus muting it. I have these for the 7th, 6th, and 5th strings, giving me the option of muting any combination of those strings to give me a 6-string, 5-string, or 4-string configuration.

"The original installation method for these mutes was to super-glue them onto the head just beyond the end of the fingerboard. The super-glue would eventually pop loose, though, so one day I dared (don't try this at home folks!!!) to drill a tiny hole through the head and bolt the mute on with a teeny-tiny nut and bolt [through a backing plate on the underside of the head]. I thought sure I'd split the head—but no! It's still intact after many years and it didn't affect the tone at all!"

The story has a strange ending. After performing with The Kingston Trio for a few years, Bob began writing his column "The Colorado Trail" for Alan Shaw's *Kingston Korner* newsletter. Its focus was to interview folk artists living in Colorado. He interviewed John Denver and Jimmy Ibbotson (of The Nitty Gritty Dirt Band), and also Dick Weissman, founding member of The Journeymen. After the interview, just as Dick was about to leave, Bob brought out his Jack Hansen 7-string and said, "Have you ever seen anything like this?" Dick glanced at it and replied, "Oh, I've got one just like that." After Bob's initial shock, they discussed how he had acquired it and Dick related that he had bought it at a pawnshop in Seattle during a visit. It was the same one that had been stolen from Bob years earlier and it, like the #2 (as well as Bob himself), had finally ended up all together in Colorado. Since Bob had already received an insurance settlement for it, Bob let Dick keep it.

Discography: Bob has 3 self-produced CDs on his website, *www.bobhaworth.com*, along with 15+ recordings with the Brothers Four and The Kingston Trio that are out of print, except as rare items on Ebay. Bob is available for teaching on Skype—visit his website for additional info.

POPULAR FOLK MUSIC TODAY

Long-time Kingston Trio fan, Allan Shaw, published a periodical newsletter called *Kingston Korner*. The magazine followed The Kingston Trio, of course, but also supported other artists in the folk music genre. In the 1990s, this evolved into a larger publication called *Popular Folk Music Today*. Allan invited me to contribute to the newsletter with a regular column called "The Colorado Trail." The title was borrowed from a Kingston Trio song written by Carl Sandburg and Lee Hayes and reflected the fact that I was residing in Colorado at the time.

The title also emphasized the fact that the subjects of my articles were folk music artists based in Colorado. Some were nationally and internationally known performers, but all were well-known and respected within the Colorado music community.

On the following pages are interviews I did with these Colorado musicians:

Dick Weissman
John Denver
The Motherfolkers
Jimmy Ibbotson

POPULAR FOLK MUSIC TODAY — FALL 1991 PAGE 1

The Colorado Trail

By: Bob Haworth

Like so many Coloradoans, Dick Weissman came from points beyond to discover the many-faceted beauty of Colorado. A Boulder resident for the past decade, Dick is well-known in the music community not only here, but around the country. As a member of the often underrated "Journeymen" of Capitol Records fame, Dick Weissman played an important role in the popular folk movement of the early 1960's, and his influence is still being felt today through his capacities as record producer, performer, writer and educator. Dick stopped by my office in Golden recently and we had a very enjoyable conversation about his past, present and future.

How did you get started in the music business?

I was a graduate student in sociology at Columbia in the late '50s and I used to hang out at the Folklore Center in Greenwich Village. I always had two different musical styles—the straight folk life and the commercial life. Most people either go one way or the other, but I sort of always went both ways at the same time. I was also doing recording dates around New York during that time, and one of the dates I did in 1960 was for a group called "The Smoothies," whose line-up included John Phillips and Scott MacKenzie. They were doing kind of a "Four Freshmen" think, but it wasn't really happening, so they thought, "Well, maybe we should do some folk stuff." So they did this date for Decca which Eric Weissberg and I played on, and it was considered the first pop-folk session in New York. It was a mixture of folk players and regular studio guys, who had never seen a 12-string guitar before. Anyway, John Phillips and I sort of hit it off, and we decided that we'd get together in a few weeks after our scheduled commitments. We initially concentrated on putting an album together and we spent seven or eight weeks rehearsing six days a week, eight hours a day.

How'd you get hooked up with the Frank Werber organization?

We signed with ITA, who were booking The Kingston Trio, and the Werber group became interested in us as insurance against the impending break-up of the Trio. They thought they could use us to fill dates for the Trio—That was one plan. Later they developed a plan to have John Phillips replace Dave, put me in as a back-up player and send Scott out as a single. Of course, none of that ever happened. Anyway, they took us to Capitol for whom we did three albums. I also recorded a solo album of protest songs for them. I was like their answer to Bob Dylan, I guess.

So what happened after the Journeymen split up?

I went back to New York. I had a song-writing deal with The Richmond Organization and I subsequently got into producing records. My first record was a Jean Ritchie record for Warner Brothers. I did some rock 'n' roll for Capitol and I did some of the first Moog synthesizer music. Then in '68 and '69 I was a staff producer for ABC and I produced everything from R&B to electronic music to The Glenn Miller Band. Also during that time I did a lot of session playing for all kinds of people: The Brothers Four, The new Christy Minstrels, Connie Francis, Steve and Edie and lots of national jingles.

What brought you to Colorado?

I realized at some point that if I wanted to stay with records I'd need to move to L.A., which I didn't want to do. So I decided to come out here and study theory, harmony and arranging, which I'd never really done. So I came here in '73 and enrolled in the University of Colorado at Denver, where I now teach. I also put out a banjo book, which, fortunately, came out at the same time as Deliverance. I made a ton of money off of that, which was really kind of funny, because I actually learned to play bluegrass banjo to play on jingles. I got my degree from UCD and decided to stay in the area, performing occasionally, producing some local artists, doing film scores as well as teaching and writing.

What kind of things excite you these days?

More and more I've gotten into writing instrumental music more than anything else. I still write songs—there are two songs on my new album—but I'm really much more focused on writing instrumental music. I feel that's were my real talent lies at this point in my life. I like experimenting with different instrumental combinations, like banjo and saxophone. And I like exploring various cultural influences. For example, I have one piece on this new album

Dick Weissman

which is based on Tunisian music, so I'r playing on the banjo with a slide in a altered tuning and I'm playing the drur with fingerpicks. For want of a bette term I call what I do "folk jazz."

As a banjo player, I'm reall fascinated by this album. How long ha it been in the works?

I started working on it about fo years ago. It's all been recorded here i Denver at FTM Studios, produced b Harry Tufts and myself with Stev Avedis engineering. Like I said, I'v done a lot of unusual things with th banjo and with the form of th compositions. The extended pieces hav several different instrumental section and then a vocal section, which is kind c backwards from the way you normall think of structuring. Most people stick a instrumental section in to break up th vocals, but because of my orientatio toward instrument music, I'v approached the structure from a differe angle. The album's entitled Ne Traditions and it'll be out on Folk E hopefully sometime in December.

***

Dick Weissman rarely performs i person, but his new album, Ne Traditions, will really give you th Weissman fix you've been craving. B it! It's hot! Until next time...

In August of 1987, Robert A. Jones printed the first issue of the Veterans' Voice, a newspaper for all veterans from all armed services, reguardless of what years they served. This was expanded to cover all active duty military as well as national guard and reserve forces. The Veterans' Voice has been with our troops in Operation Desert Shield since August of 1990 and will continue until our troops return home.

The Veterans' Voice is dedicated to: Independence, Freedom, Peace through education.

The Veterans' Voice emphasizes veterans activities and governmental entitlements, plus articles on health, Social Security, financial investing, youth, environment, entertainment, book reviews and special events.

Robert A. Jones served on active duty from 1952 - 1959. first with the U.S. Army, 2nd Div. 9th Regt. Korea, (pre-Vietnam) U.S. Air Force with the Strategic Air Command.

The Veterans' Voice is distributed in all 50 states plus 18 other countries. Help us to continue our free distribution to Operation Desert Shield and our VA Hospitals throughout the U.S.

Subscription Form

Name

Address

City ______ State ZIP

Phone (____) ______

• 1 YEAR - $15.00 • 2 YEARS - $28.00 • 3 YEARS - $42.00

Mail to: The Veterans' Voice of America
354 West Windsor Ave.
Lombard, Illinois 60148 U.S.A.

Or Call: (708) 629-8189 Charge to VISA or Master Card
* Add $10.00 for postage outside U.S.

Dick Weissman.

Page 22 POPULAR FOLK MUSIC TODAY Fall, 1992

THE COLORADO TRAIL

By: Bob Haworth

What comes to mind when you think of Colorado? Most people answer: "mountains, snow, skiing, pennies (the Denver Mint), roaming buffalo and John Denver." Indeed, John has been one of Colorado's hottest commodities since the late '60s when Peter, Paul and Mary scored a number one hit with his composition, *Leaving On A Jet Plane*. John's solo career took off shortly thereafter with big hits like *Take Me Home, Country Roads, Rocky Mountain High, Sunshine On My Shoulders, Annie's Song* and many more. As one of the top five recording artists in the sales history of the music industry, John Denver is without a doubt one of the most successful "folk singers" of all time. John called me recently from LA International Airport en route with his band to China for a concert tour and we had a chance to chat about his career—past, present and future. Here's how the conversation went:

John, I've always been grateful to you for a rather selfish reason. You see, I got the gig that you turned down. Back in 1968, The Brothers Four asked you to join their group replacing Mike Kirkland. You opted to pursue your solo career at that time and I ended up performing with The Brothers Four for fifteen years. So I just want to say "thanks!"

Well, I'm glad that worked out for you.

When you joined The Mitchell Trio in 1965, did the musical direction of the group change or did you basically pick up the existing repertoire as Chad's replacement?

I don't know that it changed a great deal. I brought in a few songs for the first album we did together, which was called THAT'S THE WAY IT'S GONNA BE which is an old Bob Gibson song. I contributed that song and *Mr. Tambourine Man* and a couple of others, and it came to a large degree out of the stronger things that I was doing myself at the time and the fact that I played guitar on those songs.

What about the stage show?

There was no change at all. We still used accompanists except periodically in the program I'd step up with my guitar and we'd do the kind of songs that I mentioned. But we maintained the satirical material—there were a lot of new songs that we learned. The first

John Denver…

engagement we had was at the Cellar Door in Washington, DC, and we were makin' a pretty big deal out of that. We introduced quite a few new songs at that show—I think *Lucy Baines* was one and *I Was Not A Nazi Polka*.

When was Chad's first name dropped from the group name?

It had dropped some time before I joined, basically out of personality and ego differences within the group.

Over the years "Folk Music" has been a rather nebulous musical category. How do you define "folk music?"

To me, folk songs are old songs that have survived; songs that came from people who were pretty close to the land, ya know. I don't think anything in rock will ever be considered like folk music, although I think some of the rock songs will last a long, long time. Over here where I sit, I think that most of what I've been doing is folk music, although I would call it modern folk music because the songs are too young, even at this point, to be considered folk songs. Things like *Leaving On A Jet Plane* and *Rocky Mountain High* and *Calypso* will be considered folk songs one day. To me, a folk song is something that one person with an instrument can play and make the song work—and communicate the song. I don't think that's what happens with rap music; I don't think that's what happens with rock 'n' roll; I don't think that's what happens with Michael Jackson.

Who were some of your early musical influences?

Oh, I think all the people you'd expect: Tom Paxton, Judy Collins, Joan Baez, Phil Ochs, people like that. And Elvis. Before that I guess it was country music. My father was a big country music fan, and back in those days it was called country and western. Ya know, people like Hank Williams, Hank Snow, all those old Hanks.

In the '70s when country music began crossing over into

John Denver, cont….

Page 24 POPULAR FOLK MUSIC TODAY Fall, 1992

pop, and vice versa, you played a major role in breaking down those boundaries. In fact, weren't you honored as Entertainer Of The Year by the Country Music Association in 1975?

That's correct. But it was interesting at that time, having a broader success sort of turned Nashville against you. And I feel to some degree that's still in effect. But now, ya know, it's that broad appeal and it's gained by the wide variety of the kinds of songs that people are doing. So, ya know, it all changes. Wait long enough and it'll change again.

Has there every been a tally made of your total album sales worldwide?

Oh, quite a few years ago RCA said it was over 100 million, but that's not counting the black market.

John, how long have you lived in Colorado?

Since 1970.

Do you feel there are any qualities about living in Colorado that stimulate or enhance your creativity?

Oh, absolutely. I think, first of all, it's been a real blessing for me not to live in New York or LA or Nashville. When I was growing up I was an Air Force brat and my best friends were my guitar and the out of doors. Consequently when I began to try and express myself through song writing I used a lot of images from nature, and that's continued. So all of my music is full of pictures from nature; and it's being able to stay out close to that environment, as opposed to being in the city, that allows me to write like that.

As a song writer I'm always interested in other people's writing techniques. Do you have a system that you use for writing?

No, I don't sit down every day and try to write a song. Quite often it's when I'm driving or walking that something starts to come into my head. It usually begins with a phrase, like "leaving on a jet plane" or "follow me" or Rocky Mountain high." I play with that in my head while I'm walking or driving until I have a chance to get home and sit down with a guitar and take it from there.

Do you write best by yourself or in collaboration with other people?

I very rarely write in collaboration —I do think I write best by myself.

What do you think is the best song you've ever written?

I would have no idea. I think my most popular song around the world is *Annie's Song*, followed closely by *Sunshine On My Shoulders* and *Country Roads*.

I've been listening to your most recent album, DIFFERENT DIRECTIONS and I'm enjoying it immensely. I was delighted to see some friend of mine credited on a couple of cuts: Jim Salestrom from Breckenridge, who was Dolly Parton's banjo player for years, and Gordon Burt, a Denver boy, on fiddle. But there were a couple of other names that jumped out at me. I see you've got James Burton from Elvis Presley's band on guitar.

Yeah, in fact James and Glen D. Hardin (keyboards—also on the album) and Jerry Scheff (bass) are all part of my band. We're all sittin'

John Denver, cont....

Fall, 1992 POPULAR FOLK MUSIC TODAY Page 25

here in the JAL lounge on our way to China.

The King's own band? Who could ask for more? Now, there's one other name on DIFFERENT DIRECTIONS—a fiddle player named George Colorado. Tell me who that really is.

(Laughs) I can't. It's a product of his contractual obligations to his recording company. The name was his idea.

What kind of advice do you give to young people aspiring to a career in the music business?

Well, I usually say, find out the truest expression of yourself. Don't try to copy anybody. You know, people can have success imitating somebody else, but I think if you're gonna have really great success it's gotta come out of your own creativity, rather than trying to copy someone else.

I imagine, like most of us, you started out covering other people's music and styles. When did you finally become comfortable with being yourself as a performer?

My first hero in music was Elvis Presley. And the thing about Elvis, not all of his songs, but he was an original. No one else before had sounded anything at all like him. The thing that I've always been able to maintain regarding my own music and my career is that this is what I want to do—and I don't think anybody else writes songs like *Rocky Mountain High* or *Calypso* or *Eagles And Horses* off the last album or *Foxfire Suite* on this album.

A couple of questions off the subject of music. You've made a secondary career of your quest to save the planet, and your activities in that regard have received attention world-wide. What are some of the things you do in your own home to help preserve the environment?

Solar power has always been the major way that I've heated my house, with a passive solar system, and it works very, very well. The one thing that I've done in the last few years is change to the very low wattage neon light bulbs. We've cut the expense of electricity for lighting by sixty percent. I really recommend trying it.

John, who's got your vote for president?

I don't know yet. Not George Bush.

When are you going to run for president?

Not a chance!

****

With that we said our good-byes and I wished John well on his month-long tour of mainland China. Having never met John Denver previously, I found him to be quite warm and down to earth—no big star pretenses. This actually surprised me and I was quite impressed with his natural candor. Also, I really did enjoy John's latest album, DIFFERENT DIRECTIONS, on his own Windstar label. It has a good variety of music and some great production. I recommend it—that and neon light bulbs!

Until next time…

John Denver.

POPULAR FOLK MUSIC TODAY — WINTER 1992 PAGE 9

The Mother Folkers

The Colorado Trail

By: Bob Haworth

First, a quick addendum to my article on Dick Weissman in the last issue: Several years ago when I was living in the Seattle area I commissioned my friend, Jack Hansen, to build me a prototype 7-string banjo. A year later it was stolen from my van, so I had Jack build me a second one. Subsequently, I had Greg Deering put together a real slicked-up version. I keep the second prototype in my office and when Dick was here for the interview I proudly showed it off to him, asserting that it was my own concoction and one of a kind. Completely unimpressed, Dick responded, "Oh, I've got one of those." After further incredulous inquiry on my part I found out that he had purchased his 7-stringer in a pawn shop in Seattle last summer, and, as it turns out, it's the same one which was stolen from me. Strange coincidence that after all this time it would show up again—and clear out here in Colorado! So now Dick and I are talking about working as a duo with both of us on 7-string banjos. (Sounds like something out of a Gary Larson nightmare!)

And now for something completely different. I recently had an opportunity to chat with Mary Stribling and Kathi DeFrancis, both of whom are members of one of Colorado's most elusive folk groups. Their name, as the promo material reads, is "the most carefully pronounced name in show business." Allow me to introduce you to **The Mother Folkers.**

I know The Mother Folkers is almost as big as The Mormon Tabernacle Choir, but could you give me a rundown on the personnel?

Oh-oh, memory time. Well let's see, there's Mary-Mary: that's Mary Stribling (bass, vocals, M.C.) and Mary Flower (guitar, dobro, vocals); then there's Bonnie-Bonnie: Bonnie Phipps (autoharp, percussion, vocals) and Bonnie Carol (hammered and mountain dulcimers, congas, vocals); and Ellen-Ellen: Ellen Klaver (guitar, banjo, percussion, vocals) and Ellen Audley (mandolin, guitar, vocals); and now it gets tough. Let's see, Sumi Seacat (vocals—she's got such a great voice she doesn't need any other instrument); Carla Sciaky (concertina, guitar, accordian, violin, psaltery, keyboards, vocals); Eileen Niehouse (vocals, mandolin, mandola, guitar - and her specialty is dadgad tuning, which is an Irish open tuning); Kathi DeFrancis (keyboards, guitar, vocals); and who else? Oh, yeah—Vicki Taylor (keyboards, guitar, fiddle, vocals.) Did we forget anybody? Our current line-up is these eleven ladies, although we have had a few changes over the years. We even have some alumni who have gone on to do quite well. Like Katie Moffatt and Lynn Morris, who is an incredible banjo player!

From whose twisted mind did the group's name come?

Eileen Niehouse—it's her fault! Back in 1973. And when we first started performing the newspapers refused to print our name. So they'd publish these articles that sounded like something out of some journal or something real boring. They'd say, "Women Musicians Perform," ya know. Now they print the name in bold, but most radio announcers still have a fit with it.

What was the impetus for putting this group together?

We were all connected to the Denver Folklore Center in one way or another. And you know how it is when you say, "We should get together some time and play." So finally Mary Flower said, "Well, let's book a concert and then we'll have to play." So we did that, and it was so successful both on a personal level as well as on the audience response level that we decided to do it again. And then it became this annual event that people kind of wait for each year. This year we've got three venues booked: The Lincoln Center in Ft. Collins on April 4th, The Boulder Theatre on April 5th and the theater at Teikyo Loretto Heights College in Denver on April 10th and 11th. The hardest thing is scheduling time when all of us are free, but over the years we've found that April seems to be a slow time for bookings. So now we all have gigs in April. It's wonderful!

Each year you do a completely different show. Do you have a format for planning your concerts?

Well, the only format, really, is that each person is responsible for two songs. And you can do any style of music you want and assemble any kind of instrumentation. It's not like when you're in a band with a set group of people and you have to figure out how to make your stuff work within those limitations. For example, with **The Mother Folkers**, you can do one song with bluegrass instrumentation and the other selection can have keyboards and percussion and be completely different. There are people in the group who play old-timey music and blues and Irish music; and one year Carla did a Bulgarian tune; Bonnie Carol and Ellen Klaver have a real connection with Central and South American music and Tex-Mex—it's an opportunity for each of us to experiment with musical combinations and styles that we never get a chance to work with otherwise. This is really a musician's fantasy!

For those who can't make it to one of your concerts this April, are there recordings available?

As a matter of fact, **The Mother Folkers** just released a new CD. It's called CONFLUENCE and it's on Resounding Records. Our first album was called **THE MOTHER FOLKERS LIVE AT THE ARVADA CENTER**. We decided to record this new one in the studio, but we did it mostly live. It has a lot of energy and it feels like a live performance. A good portion of the material is selections from last year's show—mostly original music—and we think there's some really terrific stuff on here. There are twelve cuts, so each member is represented with one song, and then we did our encore tune, *Honey In The Rock*, which features the whole group. And you know, it's kind of funny, but we're all working musicians with not a lot of money; and when the CD came out we realized that none of us owns a CD player. So we had to go down to the record store to listen to our album!

Does The Mother Folkers have any goals or aspirations as a group?

Well, it's difficult with each of us pursuing our own individual goals and careers. It'd be pretty hard to think about touring—we'd need a really big bus for one thing! But it's kind of like the swallows of Capistrano, ya know. Each year we get together and do this thing. And our 20th anniversary is coming up in 1993—or is it 1994? (We've lost track!) Anyway, that's sort of like a goal. We're looking forward to the party!

* * * * * * * * * *

The Mother Folkers is definitely a unique Colorado phenomenon. If you're a traveler it's well worth the trip in April to catch these swallows of Colorado in their annual migration to the stage. If you can't make it (or even if you can), add one of their albums to your collection. It's a fun group! Until next time...

The Motherfolkers, Winter 1992.

THE COLORADO TRAIL

By: Bob Haworth

First of all, I want to say that I had a great time filling in for Nick Reynolds while he took a forced leave of absence from **The Kingston Trio** in November and December. It was fun to see a lot of the Trio fans and find out that many of you actually read this column. I took my family up to Boulder when the group played there at the end of January, and it was great to see Nick back to his old self again. He thanked me for the Christmas card I sent him, which read: "Nick—thanks for getting sick—I needed the work." Luckily, he took it in the humorous vein in which it was intended!

And now to the business at hand. One of my all-time favorite bands has a name which I've always thought was really strange. **The Nitty Gritty Dirt Band**. The first time I saw this group was back in the 60's when they were playing the coffee houses and clubs around the L.A. area. I was just a wide-eyed web-foot from Oregon attending U.C.L.A. as a freshman, but I knew these guys were happenin' from the very first note I heard. The cool thing about **The Nitty Gritty Dirt Band** was that you really couldn't put your finger on their stylistic orientation. There were elements of folk, bluegrass, jug-band, blues, country and rock that all blended together to create a wonderfully tasty musical goulash. At one point the entire band made their homes here in Colorado. Presently, singer/songwriter/guitarist/drummer Jimmy Ibbotson is the one remaining Coloradoan in the group, residing in Aspen. I met up with Jimmy recently at the Denver airport as he was en route to a tropical get-away.

So, where are you off to this time?

I'm headed for the Caribbean. A lot of times the songs come out of trips to the beach. In fact, the first song that I wrote for WILD JIMBOS II is a song called *It's Morning*. It's about one morning in the Yucatan. It's funny—I've been writing off a certain percentage of my Caribbean vacations for the last ten years, although my accountant won't let me write off my wardrobe.

Well, this is a good time of the year to head for warmer climes. How long have you lived in Colorado?

We first got here in 1970, I believe. We were touring promoting *Mr. Bojangles*, and we played at Marvelous Marv's in Denver. Then we played the Aspen Inn in Aspen, and from that time on various members started moving to Colorado. I think it was in 1971 that the whole band moved en masse to Evergreen. Jeff Hanna, who is the lead guitar player and lead singer for **The Dirt Band**, is really scared of earthquakes—he grew up in California. And I guess Edgar Cayce said that the safest place to be would be Boulder, Colorado. The rest of the Dirt Boys have since moved on—Bobby Carpenter our piano player, is in L.A.; old John McEuen, who's not in the band anymore, is in Utah; and then Jeff Hanna and Jimmie Fadden are in Nashville.

Now, you joined the group in, what—about 1970?

Actually, it was 1969. The first album I made with them was UNCLE CHARLIE AND HIS DOG TEDDY, which contained *Mr. Bojangles*.

And what were you doing before that?

Well, in the summertime I had what we thought was a folk trio, 'cause it was two guys and a girl. We were called **The Wharf Rats**, and we played mostly on the Jersey shore at a place called Beach Haven. I'm from the western suburbs of Philadelphia and we always spent our summers down on the shore. Then during the winter I played rock 'n' roll at college fraternity parties with any number of different people, and I actually graduated from college! I graduated from DePauw University the same day Dan Quayle did.

Can you spell "potato?"

I hope so—I was forty points ahead of him in graduation. Anyway, on graduation day this woman came by and gave me this single of Jerry Jeff Walker's *Mr.*

Jimmy Ibbotson, Winter 1993…

Winter, 1993 POPULAR FOLK MUSIC TODAY Page 15

Bojangles and I said, "Oh, that's great—I've heard that song and that's just the kind of stuff I like." But she looked deep into my soul and said, "No, you're really gonna like this record." and I said, "Well, it's my only record, so, yeah, it's really cool." Anyway, I threw the record in the trunk of my car and headed for L.A.

I spent some time playing drums for whoever would have me—I worked with the Hager Twins and a bunch of people. When **The Dirt Band** showed up on my door step a few months later, they had just made the movie "Paint Your Wagon" and they were makin' like $3,000.00 a week. They had sort of broken up at that point, thinking they had enough money to last the rest of their lives. A couple of the guys had gone to The Troubadour one night to see Richard Furay's band **Poco**, which was actually called **Pogo** at that time, until the cartoon sued them. I guess Jeff was upstairs and said to somebody, "Man, we could have a band like that if we just had a drummer who could sing." One of the people who was in the room was a roommate of my bass player, and he said, "Hey, I know just the guy." So they came and knocked on my door that night and signed me up.

After rehearsal one day we were driving through a Jack In The Box and we were talking about material for the next album. And Jeff says, "Ya know, I heard this song on the radio last night about an old guy and a dog and jail and I was cryin'—the hair was standing' up on my neck." And I said, "Wait a minute." So we're sittin' there in line waitin' for our order and I turned off the car, jumped out and opened up the trunk, went under the spare tire into this pool of rusty water where my record collection was, and I pulled it out and said, "You mean this?" So we went back to Johnny McEuen's house and put it on his record player which didn't have an amplifier—we just listened to it off the needle—and we learned *Mr. Bojangles*. We got a couple of chords wrong and twisted some of the words around. I think the line is, "and he spoke right out" and we sang, "as the smoke ran out." Since then Jerry Jeff has told me, "Yeah, I like they smoked their last cigarette, so this smoke ran out." But that was a good record for us.

That was a great record! Now, you left the group for a while, didn't you?

Yeah, I left in 1976—I was real excited about the bicentennial. Then I came back into the band in 1981. That's when **The Dirt Band** went to Nashville and cut our first country record. The producer, Norbert Putnam, said, "There's no way in the world you guys are gonna get played on country radio," so when we got down there he tried to make an album that would have like *American Dream* and *Make A Little Magic*, the last pop hits that had happened for the band. But there was one song, second side, last cut *Dance Little Jean*, that I'd written and I kind of threw a fit when they weren't gonna record it, ya know. So they did it and Norbert produced it real sparsely, with just the acoustic guitars, and of course that became our first top ten country single.

What precipitated your involvement with The Wild Jimbos?

I've always written too many songs for just **The Dirt Band**, and the deeper we got into country hits, the fewer of my songs we recorded. Ya know, we're competing with acts that are using really calculating song writers, so we've had to do that too. Now I'm stuck with ten or fifteen songs a year that have no home. But I don't

Jimmy Ibbotson, cont....

Page 16 POPULAR FOLK MUSIC TODAY Winter, 1993

WILD JIMBOS

think any song is worthy of the junk heap if it's a decent song. Finally, Chuck Morris, **The Dirt Band's** manager said, "Listen, why don't you do your own album, but I don't think it should be a solo record. Why don't you put a band together?" And I said, "Well, you know I'm playin' with Jim Ratts and Jim Salestrom," so he came up to Vail and heard us one time and after the show he said, "I can get you guys a deal." So he took us to Nashville and MCA signed us. Our idea was that we were going to make country hits, and there's a song Jimmy Ratts wrote on the first album called *Howlin' At The Moon* that just fit the format—it would've been perfect. But we fell prey to video and we put out a video of John Prine's *Let's Talk Dirty In Hawaiian* and that just about killed us for country radio. (laughs)

The WILD JIMBOS II album grew out of my frustration with Nashville, knowing that we were just too wild for Nashville. I'd go down to Jim Ratts' studio and lay down as many songs as I could in a day—I had about ten songs I really wanted to hear—and I thought that maybe Jimmy would like two or three of them enough to record them with Salestrom and start the project without me. I just felt that we had started something, and, ya know, a lot of people really like that music.

So Ratts took it upon himself to start bringing in people to overdub on these tunes, and when he sent me up some rough mixes, it was obvious that this sounded better than the Nashville record. We'd kind of rushed through that first album, because we just had a bare-bones budget. But with the work that Ratts put in on this, and of course Salestrom's high harmonies and high country guitar, we're really proud of this record.

So I take it you really enjoy this departure from the country star thing.

Well, you know, when I first joined **The Dirt Band** Jeff and I were always singing Everly Brothers and Buddy Holly—we were just attracted to that sound. So our job was always being a pop band in L.A. forcing country and acoustic and wooden music down the throats of the people. Then suddenly we're in Nashville soundin' too much like rock 'n' roll. We've always been sort of on the edge, and I kinda think we're on the edge now. But you know, country music has become such a big business, and there's so many lawyers telling so many producers just how the record's gotta sound. The drums've gotta be this sampled sound—and they know it—it's a number somewhere on file. And they've gotta have this kind of echo, and there's only about four people who are writin' all the songs now, and we don't fit. We're too—rough! So, yeah, it's nice to have an escape. **The Wild Jimbos** provide that for me.

I know you've got a plane to catch, but I'd like to hear a little bit about your involvement with the new Chieftains album, ANOTHER COUNTRY.

Well **The Chieftains** have always been fans of especially WILL THE CIRCLE BE UNBROKEN, #1, and we'd often read our name in their interviews. So when they decided to come to Nashville and do their Circle record they asked us how to do it. We turned them on to Jerry Douglas and Mark O'Connor and a bunch of people we knew in Nashville. And then I said, "Ya know, I've got this song called *Killybegs* that I wrote while I was in Ireland and maybe you'd be interested in it." So he says, "Well,

Jimmy Ibbotson, cont....

Winter, 1993 POPULAR FOLK MUSIC TODAY Page 17

send it over to us and we'll see what we can do with it." So we talked to each other across the ocean and he says (imitates Irish brogue) "Well, I've got an idea, Jimmy. How 'bout if I put a little half-reel and a slip-jig in the middle of it." And he sang it for me—and oh, it's this magical thing. The word "collaboration" finally came to me. Ya know, it's one thing if we all know how to do the same thing—like if Charlie Daniels or Ricky Skaggs comes together with **The Dirt Band**—we all know what to do. But when you're sittin' down in a room full of leprechauns and one guy's squeezin' bagpipes and this other guy's playin' a hammered dulcimer and they're all playin' by what sounds to us like magical rules—we were just amazed that we were able to collaborate and blend those two styles together.

****

So there you have it! A peek into the wildly diverse world of Jimmy Ibbotson. He's really a fun guy to talk with, and in my opinion, one of Colorado's most talented musicians. The new WILD JIMBOS II album is available on Resounding Records—if you can't find it write to me c/o this publication and I'll put you in touch. **The Nitty Gritty Dirt Band** has a new album out called NOT FADE AWAY for the country fans. That's on the Liberty label. And for everybody, you have to get **The Chieftains'** ANOTHER COUNTRY on RCA-Victor. The album's up for several Grammies and it's a wonderful blend of Ireland and Nashville, if you can imagine such a thing.

Until next time...

[ANOTHER COUNTRY is available through the REDISCOVER MUSIC CATALOGUE, and is also featured in the catalogue supplement of this current publication.—Ed.]

MORE GORDON LIGHTFOOT CDs COMING FROM BEAR FAMILY

REST OF UNITED ARTISTS MATERIAL COMING SOON

By: Allan Shaw

During the last half of the 1960's, Gordon Lightfoot recorded five albums for United Artists containing many of his best known and, some would say, his best songs. Regardless of whether you agree with the latter part of that assessment, many of those early songs, such as *Early Morning Rain, For Lovin' Me* and *Did She Mention My Name* are not only the songs that brought him prominence, but are also the songs included in the repertoires and on the albums of artists performing and recording today.

About a year ago Bear Family Records brought out a CD, called LIGHTFOOT!/THE WAY I FEEL, of some of this UA (United Artists) material. Given the care that Bear Family gives to all of their releases, LIGHTFOOT!/THE WAY I FEEL is a well produced CD, much better in many respects than some of the domestically produced releases of some of this early Lightfoot material. It left many of us thirsting for more.

Our thirst is soon to be quenched. Just after Christmas we got the word that Bear Family has obtained the rights to re-release the rest of the UA material on CD, including some songs not released on LP record, but only on 45s, songs such as *Tom Thumb's Blues*. In most cases, we understand (but unfortunately not with *Tom Thumb's Blues*.) that the original masters had been found and are being used, thus promising some real sound treats.

In the Winter 1988 issue of FOLK ERA TODAY (a predecessor publication to POPULAR FOLK MUSIC TODAY), Steve LaCrosse wrote of the Gordon Lightfoot UA material then available on CD that, "Unfortunately, the unsophisticated analog equipment used at that time.....does not transfer well to laser technology. It is doubtful that EMI used the original master recordings for each of these songs. It is more likely that the secondary compilation master tape was utilized...." Well, Steve, not this time, and if my knowledge of what can be done today, as opposed to as little as five years ago, with digital (laser) technology means anything, taken with the painstaking care that Bear Family gives to their CDs, we've got another great CD coming.

Citing Steve LaCrosse's article further, he closed it by saying, "It might be worthwhile for his fans to send a short note to....EMI-Manhattan Records (the then owners of the UA masters) urging them to release Gordon Lightfoot's entire catalogue on this new (CD) format. ...those of us who appreciate his work should strive to have assurances that the music will survive the longevity of the artist. I can think of no better legacy for one of North America's finest troubadors than to preserve his work for generations to enjoy on compact disc."

Steve sure called that one, didn't he? Now all we have to do is to be a little patient. Although we weren't given an absolute, firm release date, we were given to understand that it could be as early as April or May. We hope to know more, and hopefully be able to offer this new release with the next issue of POPULAR FOLK MUSIC TODAY. Be watching for it.

Jimmy Ibbotson.

DISCOGRAPHY

THIS SECTION IS, ADMITTEDLY, FOR readers with way too much time on their hands. Over the years I've spent hundreds of hours in recording studios, both as a solo artist and with the various groups that I've performed with. Here is a complete discography documenting all the recordings that have been commercially released that include my vocal and instrumental contributions. I've separated this list into four sections:

Bob Haworth Projects
The New Yorkers
The Brothers Four
The Kingston Trio

I dare anyone to bother to read this, but I guess it has some historical relevance vis-a-vis my contributions to the world's audio library. A few of these recordings are still available directly from my personal stash.

DISCOGRAPHY - BOB HAWORTH PROJECTS

This is a list of recordings I've either done solo or with other musical collaborators. The two Banjo King recordings were done under contract for Jerry Dennon.

Home Made – A Baker's Dozen
13 original songs by Bob Haworth
Self-released cassette – 1989
CCA-1001

Side 1:
If It Takes All Night
Before I'm Gone
Ridin' Into Town
After All These Years
Allergic To Work
Who Really Knows
Finger Lingus

Side 2:
Just Say Goodbye
Livin' In The Country
Fair And Tender Ladies
In The Middle Of The Night
Hair Today, Gone Tomorrow
Songs That Never Die

The Fabulous Bo Mooney Show/Featuring the Luna Chicks
Self-released cassette – 1991
CCA-1003

Side 1:
Party On A Saturday Night
Rawhide
Motown Medley
Tiger Rag
White Collar Holler

Straighten Up And Fly Right
Livin' In The Country
Mariah

Side 2:
In The Mood
Jump In De Line
Here To Stay In Colorado
Ghost Rasta
The Ultimate Recycler
Happy Trails
Railroad Medley
Bo Mooney Theme

After All These Years
13 original songs by Bob Haworth
Self-released CD – 2003

What's So Bad About Feelin' So Good?
Here To Stay In Colorado
Right Smack Dab In The Middle of Love
Scorpion's Lullaby
The Good Old Days
Songs That Never Die
Don't Ever Give Up
Ridin' Into Town
Snoqualmie Rag
Grazin' In The Catbox
Who Really Knows
MTA Revisited
After All These Years

Christmas All Over The World
Self-released CD – 2004

Christmas Is Coming (Haworth)
Christmas All Over The World (Haworth)
It's Christmas The Way It Used To Be (Haworth)
Colorado Christmas
I Want A Hippopotamus For Christmas
Mele Kalikimaka
White Christmas
"Saw"lent Night

Christmastime Is Here (Haworth)
Sleigh Ride
Santa Claus Got Stuck In Our Chimney (Haworth)
The Christmas Song

The Banjo King Plays Ragtime
LP - 1977
Picadilly Records Pic 3302

Side 1:
12th Street Rag
The Entertainer
Up The Lazy River
Temptaion Rag
Third Man Theme
Music, Music, Music

Side 2:
Maple Leaf Rag
Alley Cat
Under The Double Eagle
Nola
Tiger Rag
Basin Street
Brazil

The Banjo King Plays Favorites
Cassette only – 1979

Side 1:
St. Louis Blues
Mr. Sandman
Marie
Classical Gas
Up The Lazy River
Theme from "Zorba The Greek"
Side 2:Brazil
Lullaby of Broadway
Moonglow
Caravan
Vashon Island Moon
Medley:
 -Down Yonder

-Waitin' For The Robert E. Lee
-Alabamy Bound
-Camptown Races
-Dixie

The Banjo – A Collector's TreasuryTriple LP set
Murray Hill Records S-5395X/3 (Year uknown)

Record 1, Side 1:
Foggy Mountain Breakdown (Flatt & Scruggs)
Feuding Banjos (Weissberg & Brickman)
Greenback Dollar (Dick Rossini & Jim Helms)
12th Street Rag (Bob Haworth)
My Bluebell Gal (Denny Wright)
Toot Toot Tootsie (Denny Wright)
Banjo Hello (Mason Williams)

Record 1, Side 2:
Goin' Down There (Mike Seeger)
Saturday Night Banjo (Mason Williams)
Banjo Cantata (Jim McGuinn)
The Entertainer (Bob Haworth)
Alley Cat (Bob Haworth)
Just Ramblin' Along (Denny Wright)
In The Evening When The Sun Goes Down (Pete Seeger)

Record 2, Side 1:
Cripple Creek (Mike Seeger)
Flop Eared Mule (Joe Maphis)
Be My Honey Do (Denny Wright)
Carolina In The Morning (Denny Wright)
Mad Mountain Medley (David Lindley)
Joe's Breakdown (Joe Maphis)

Record 2, Side 2:
Third Man Theme (Bob Haworth)
Tiger Rag (Bob Haworth)
Banjo Workout (Joe Maphis)
The Johnston Boys (David Lindley)
Down In Mobile (Denny Wright)
Swannee (Denny Wright)

Record 3, Side 1:
Bonapart's Retreat (Erik Darling)
Holston Valley Breakdown (Mike Seeger)
Movin' Down The Line (Jim Helms)
Waiting For the Robt. E. Lee (Denny Wright)
Alabammy Bound (Denny Wright)
Up The Lazy River (Bob Haworth)

Record 3, Side 2:
Temptation Rag (Bob Haworth
Rumblin' On (Jim McGuinn)
Hundreds Of Miles (Billy Cheatwood)
Music, Music, Music (Bob Haworth
Basin Street Blues (Bob Haworth
Is It True What they Say About Dixie (Denny Wright)

From Rags To Rhythms
Self-released CD – 2007

12th Street Rag
The Entertainer
Up The Lazy River
Temptation Rag
Third Man Theme
Caravan
Music, Music, Music
St. Louis Blues
Maple Leaf Rag
Alley Cat
Under The Double Eagle
Classical Gas
Nola
Moonglow
Tiger Rag
Basin Street Blues
Brazil
Marie
Theme from Zorba The Greek
Medley: Down Yonder,Waitin' For The Robert E. Lee,
Alabamy Bound, Camptown Races, Dixie
Vashon Island Moon
Bucks...and More
Bo Mooney & Cheeks

EP – 1980
Cheryl Records CH-101-EP

Side 1:
Bucks (Haworth)
Lonely Heart

Side 2:
What A Difference A Day Made
The Sheik of Araby

SMUT
Mooney & Starz
Self-released cassette – 1984
Recorded live at Lake Quinault Lodge

Side 1:
I Feel Like Singin'
Stacey Brown
Wasn't That A Party
Dolly Parton's Tits
Dueling Banjo
I Know Pubic Hair
Teddy Bear's Orgy
It Ain't The Meat It's The Motion
Railroad Medley

Side 2:
Too Much Fun
Dancin' In The Nude
Waitrett Oh Waitrett
Vee Zoo Vee Doo
Why Don't We Get Drunk And Screw
Hava Tequila
Asshole From El Paso
Street Walkers In The Night
Allergic To Work (Haworth)
The Rodeo Song

DISCOGRAPHY - THE NEW YORKERS

This is a list of recordings I did with the New Yorkers. I believe there were others, but I have lost some over time.

45 Single
Jerden Records 45-JD-272-273

Side 1:
Adrianne

Side 2:
Ice Cream World

45 Single
Jerden Records 45-JD-278 / 277

Side 1:
Land of Ur

Side 2:
Michael Clover

45 Single
Scepter Records SCE-12199

Side 1:
Mr. Kirby

Side 2:
Seeds Of Spring

45 Single
Decca Records 32569

Side 1:
I Guess The Lord Must Be In New York City

Side 2:
Do Wah Diddy

DISCOGRAPHY – THE BROTHERS FOUR

This is a list of albums I either recorded with the Brothers Four, or in a couple of cases, were mistakenly credited.

The Brothers Four Golden DiscSingle LP **(Year unknown)**
Fantasy VIP 10009 (I'm not on this, but my picture is...)

Side 1:
Greenfields
If There's A Chance
November Snow
Going Back To Big Sur
Theme From Love Story
As Long As We Live
Affair On Eighth Avenue

Side 2:
Four Strong Winds
Reason To Believe
El Condor Pasa
Song Of Hope
Here I Go Again
Hey, That's No Way To Say Goodbye
Seven Daffodils

The Brothers Four
CBS-Sony SOPM-61– 1971

Side 1:
People Got To Be Free
She (Foley)
Before I'm Gone (Haworth)
Someone Who Cares
Keep The Customer Satisfied
Medley Schmedley: Without You, Without Her

Side 2:
Love The One You're With
Sadder But Wiser Man (Paine)
Girl My One And Only

Country Road
I Believe In Music

The Brothers Four Golden Disc
Double LP - 1972
Fantasy LFP-95045 BDics Labeled: LFP-95045 A & B
LFP 95046 A & B (I'm not on this, but my picture is...)

Side 1:
Greenfields
El Condor Pasa
Proud Mary
Song of Hope
Color of Love
Toys
Reason To Believe

Side 2:
Seven Daffodils
Goin' Back To Big Sur
Put Your Hand In The Hand
Here I Go Again
Affair On Eighth Avenue
10-Minute Hour
Who'll Stop The Rain

Side 3:
Love
November Snow
If You Could Read My Mind
The Hippotamus
Kaze
The Love Of The Common People
Darlin' Be Home Soon

Side 4:
Theme From Love Story
Four Strong Winds
As Long As We Live
Holy River
Have You Ever Seen The Rain
If There's A Chance
Hey, That's No Way To Say Goodbye

The Brothers Four Live In Japan
CBS-Sony – 1973
SOPJ- 56 & SOPJ- 57

Record 1, Side A:
Try To Remember
Mr. Bojangles
500 Miles
Last Thing On My Mind
Where Have All The Flowers Gone
Sloth

Record 1, Side B:
Yesterday
Early Morning Rain
San Francisco Bay Blues
The Green Leaves of Summer
Shenandoah
Try To Remember

Record 2, Side A:
City of New Orleans
Leaving On A Jet Plane
Teach Your Children
Dueling Banjos
Suite: Judy Blue Eyes

Record 2, Side B:
Someone Who Cares
Take It Easy
One Toke Over The Line
Where I'm Bound To Go
The Cover of The "Rolling Stone"
Bridge Over Troubled Water

Somewhere Sometime
East Word EMI (Year unknown)
EWS-81326

Side 1:
Don't Say Good-bye
The Immigrant
Don't Cry Mary

Lovin'As Time Goes By
Side 2:
Song Of Love
Silence In The Morning
I'm Coming Home
Sincerely Lovely Song
Somewhere Sometime

Where the Eagles Fly
CBS-Sony – 1976
25AP-144

Side 1:
Where The Eagles Fly
Anohi-ni KaeritaiIchigohakusho-o Moichido
Like The Wind
Takeda-no KomoriutaOretachi-no Tabi

Side 2:
Shikuramen-no KahoriTonari-no Machi-no Ojosan
Pictures
Roses In The Rain
Ano Subarashi Ai O MoichidoToku-e Ikitai

The Brothers Four Now
First American 7705 – 1977

Side 1:
Yesterday Once More
Have You Ever Been Mellow
Killing Me Softly With His Song
You're The Sunshine Of My Life
We May Never Pass This Way Again
Sunshine On My Shoulders

Side 2:
Mandy
Sundown
I'll Have To Say I Love You In A Song
Seasons In The Sun
Tie A Yellow Ribbon 'Round The Old Oak Tree
The Most Beautiful Girl

Greenfields & Other Gold
First American
FA-LP-7722 - 1977

Side 1:
Greenfields
The John B. Sails
Scarlet Ribbons
Lemon Tree
Try To Remember
If I Had A Hammer

Side 2:
Michael Row The Boat Ashore
Shenandoah (The Wide Missouri)
Blowin' In The Wind
Tom Dooley
Marianne

Side 3:
The Green Leaves of Summer
This Land Is Your Land
Yellow Bird
Both Sides Now
Scotch and Soda
Green Green

Side 4:
San Francisco Bay Blues
Don't Think Twice
Where Have All The Flowers Gone
Lady Green Sleeves
Walk Right In

Some Nice Songs
CBS-Sony – 1978
25AP-1113

Side 1:
Stay With Me
How Deep Is Your Love?
We're All Alone
Don't It Make Your Brown Eyes?

Blue
Goodbye-Girl
You Light Up My Life (strings by Haworth)

Side 2:
Sands Of Time
Just The Way Your Are
Can't Smile Without You
Lyin' Eyes

The Brothers Four Gold Disc
CBS-Sony – 1978
26AP-1315

Side A:
Greenfields
Where Have All The Flowers Gone?
This Land Is Your Land
If I Had A Hammer
Puff (The Magic Dragon)
Toku-e Ikitai
San Francisco Bay Blues

Side B:
Seven Daffodils
The Green Leaves of Summer
500 Miles
Michael Row The Boat Ashore
Four Strong Winds
Try To Remember
Ano Subarashii Ai-o Moichido

New Gold
First American – 1979
FA-7728

Side 1:
Stay With Me
How Deep Is Your Love?
We're All Alone
Don't It Maker Your Brown Eyes Blue?
Can't Smile Without You
You Light Up My Life (strings by Haworth)

Side 2:
Sands of Time
Goodbye Girl
Blue Bayou
Just The Way You Are
Lyin' Eyes

As Time Goes By – Great Folk Hits
East World – 1979
EMI EWS 40191-9

Side 1:
As Time Goes By
Mr. Lonely Man
The John B. Sails
Scarlet Ribbons
Lemon Tree
Try To Remember

Side 2:
Greenfields
Michael Row The Boat Ashore
Shenandoah (The Wide Missouri)
Blowin' In The Wind
Tom Dooley
Marianne

Side 3:
The Green Leaves of Summer
This Land Is Your Land
Yellow Bird
Both Sides Now
Scotch and Soda
Green Green

Side 4:
San Francisco Bay Blues
Don't Think Twice
Where Have All The Flowers Gone?
Lady Green Sleeves
Walk Right In
If I Had A Hammer

Silver Anniversary Concert
Live recording, April 2, 1983
American Licensing Company
Collector's Edition

CD:
Midnight Special
Early Morning Rain
The Hammer Song
Shenandoah
Medley: City of New Orleans, Wabash Cannonball,
Orange Blossom Special
Greenleaves of Summer
The Sloth
All My Life's A Circle
Medley: Man of La Mancha, Dulcinea, Impossible Dream
This Land Is Your Land

The Brothers Four – Greenfields
American Licensing Company – 1985
Collector's Edition

Side 1:
Greenfields
Where Have All The Flowers Gone
San Francisco Bay Blues
Don't Think Twice
Michael Row The Boat Ashore
Blowin' In The Wind
Yellow Bird

Side 2:
Try To Remember
The John B. Sails
Scarlet Ribbons
Walk Right In
Both Sides Now
Marianne
Lady Greensleeves

DISCOGRAPHY - THE KINGSTON TRIO

This is a list of albums I recorded with The Kingston Trio. Two of these CDs include other artists that were on the program.

Kingston Trio – Best of The Best
Recorded live at The Crazy Horse Saloon
CD – 1986
Intersound CDP 702

Hard Travelin'
Greenback Dollar
Merry Minuet
Zombie Jamboree
Medley: M.T.A., Tom Dooley
Tijuana Jail
Raspberries, Strawberries
Where Have All The Flowers Gone?
Hard, Ain't It Hard
Sloop John B.
Scotch and Soda
Worried Man
Reverend Mr. Black
California

Kingston Trio – Tom Dooley & Other Hits
Recorded live at The Crazy Horse Saloon
CD – 1993'
First Choice FC4507

Hard Travelin'
Greenback Dollar
M.T.A.
Tom Tooley
Tijuana Jail
Raspberries, Strawberries
Where Have All The Flowers Gone?
Worried Man
Reverend Mr. Black
California

By Special Request
Self-released CD – 2000

Hard Ain't It Hard
Greenback Dollar
Chilly Winds
Three Jolly Coachmen
Tom Dooley
Bimini
Early Morning Rain
To Morrow
Home On The Range (musical saw)
Reuben James
Raspberries, Strawberries
M.T.A.
Scotch and Soda
The Reverend Mr. Black
With Her Head Tucked Underneath Her Arm
A Worried Man
Five Hundred Miles
The Tijuana Jail
Where Have All The Flowers Gone?
San Miguel
I'm Going Home
Scotch and Soda (reprise)

This Land Is Your Land
CD from the PBS Television Show – 2002
Rhino Records R2 73776

Tom Dooley (The Kingston Trio)
Try To Remember (The Brothers Four)
Mr. Tambourine Man (Roger McGuinn)
Green, Green (Randy Sparks & The Minstrels)
Michael (The Highwaymen)
Baby the Rain Must Fall (Glenn Yarbrough)
There's A Meetin' Here Tonight (The Limeliters)
Where Have All The Flowers Gone? (The KT)
Turn! Turn! Turn! (Roger McGuinn)
Greenfields (The Brothers Four)
This Land Is Your Land (Sparks & Minstrels)
Generic Up-Tempo Folk Song (The Limeliters)

Eve Of Destruction (Barry McGuire)
Greenback Dollar (The Kingston Trio)
A Worried Man (The Kingston Trio)

45th Anniversary Tribute
Recorded Live at The Birchmere – 2002
World Folk Music Assoc. WFMA 6202

Introductions
The Shaw Brothers:
  I'm The Man Who Built The Bridges
  Follow Me
The Limeliters:
  Medley:
    Hard Travelin'
    Wayfaring Stranger
    Lonesome Traveler
    Generic Up-Tempo Folk Song
Ronnie Schell – MC
The Brothers Four:
  Whiskey In the Jar
  Green Leaves of Summer
The Recombinants:
  I Know You Rider
The Kingston Trio:
  Hard Ain't It Hard
  Three Jolly Coachmen
  M.T.A.
  Band member introductions
  Mission of San Miguel
  Stage patter
  Coast of California
  Tom Dooley
  Scotch and Soda
  I'm Going Home
Ensemble:
  Where Have All The Flowers Gone?
  This Land Is Your Land

Still Goin' Places
Recorded Live at Del Webb Sun City – 2004
Self-released CD

Corey, Corey
Oh Miss Mary
Intro: Our latest hit
Greenback Dollar
Intro: Oakland
Bimini
Everglades
Hard Days Are Gone
Bad Man's Blunder
Intro: Sister ships
Sloop John B.
El Matador
Looking For the Sunshine
Intro: Paul Gabrielson
M.T.A.
Intro: North Carolina
Tom Dooley
Long Black Veil
Intro: Three banjos
Worried Man
Where Have All The Flowers Gone?
I'm Goin' Home
Intro: Bob Shane
Scotch and Soda

The First 50 Years
Selections from each KT configuration
Self-released CD – 2007

You're Gonna Miss Me (aka Frankie & Johnny)
Blue Skies & Teardrops
Three Jolly Coachmen
Lion In The Winter
Looking For the Sunshine
Gypsy Rose and I Don't Give a Curse
Grandma's Feather Bed
Bimini
The Seine
Reuben's Train
Hawaiian Nights
To Morrow
Zombie Jamboree
Band Man's Blunder

Bob Haworth

I'm Going Home (California)
Genny Glenn
Like Old Friends Do
Road To Freedom

Tales from the Road

About the Author

Bob Haworth grew up in a musical family that encouraged his pursuit of a career in the entertainment industry. From his first professional performance at the age of ten, he followed a trajectory that kept him on the road for nearly half a century. As a second-generation member of The Brothers Four, and later, The Kingston Trio, Bob travelled the world and accumulated enough great stories to fill a book. Turning his songwriting skills to prose, he shares his *Tales From The Road* with music fans who have been clamoring for a peak behind the curtain.

Returning to his home in Southern Oregon with his wife, Meri, Bob continues to perform, teach and write. Although he eschews social media, he invites visitors to his website:

www.bobhaworth.com. There you can keep tabs on his performance schedule and join in spirited conversation on his message board.

Bob Haworth

www.hellgatepress.com

Made in the USA
Middletown, DE
23 April 2023